SELFISH WOMEN

This book proceeds from a single and very simple observation: throughout history, and up to the present, women have received a clear message that *we are not supposed to prioritize ourselves.* Indeed, the whole question of "self" is a problem for women – and a problem that issues from a wide range of locations, including, in some cases, feminism itself. When women espouse discourses of self-interest, self-regard, and selfishness, they become illegible. This is complicated by the commodification of the self in the recent Western mode of economic and political organization known as "neoliberalism," which encourages a focus on self-fashioning that may not be identical with self-regard or self-interest.

Drawing on figures from French, US, and UK contexts, including Rachilde, Ayn Rand, Margaret Thatcher, and Lionel Shriver, and examining discourses from psychiatry, media, and feminism with the aim of reading against the grain of multiple orthodoxies, this book asks how revisiting the words and works of selfish women of modernity can assist us in understanding our fraught individual and collective identities as women in contemporary culture. And can women with politics that are contrary to the interests of the collective teach us anything about the value of rethinking the role of the individual?

This book is an essential read for those with interests in cultural theory, feminist theory, and gender politics.

Lisa Downing is Professor of French Discourses of Sexuality at the University of Birmingham, UK. A cultural critic of repute, she was the recipient of a Philip Leverhulme Prize in 2009. Downing is a specialist in interdisciplinary sexuality and gender studies, critical theory, and the history of cultural concepts, with an enduring interest in questions of exceptionality, difficulty, and (ab)normality. She is author or co-author of numerous books, journal articles, and book chapters, and is editor or co-editor of a number of book-length works. Recent titles include *The Cambridge Introduction to Michel Foucault* (2008); *Film and Ethics: Foreclosed Encounters* (co-authored with Libby Saxton, 2009); *The Subject of Murder: Gender, Exceptionality, and the Modern Killer* (2013); *Fuckology: Critical Essays on John Money's Diagnostic Concepts* (co-authored with Iain Morland and Nikki Sullivan, 2015); and *After Foucault* (as editor, 2018). Her next book project is a short manifesto entitled *Against Affect*.

"This is a startling, trenchant, and original book. It is written with clarity and passion. It shakes up feminism today in productive and sometimes disturbing ways. Downing's critical brilliance, command of the material, and uncompromising approach are dazzling."

Emma Wilson, University of Cambridge

"This is a book that will challenge conventional views of feminism, and of various women who have made a significant impact on modern culture and politics. It fills a significant gap in the scholarly literature and is written in a crisp, accessible style that will invite readers from all ends of the ideological spectrum to re-evaluate their own perspectives."

Chris Matthew Sciabarra, New York University

"[this book] is going to be a 'game-changer' in feminist thinking ... It dialogues with and deconstructs brilliantly French philosophy and ideas on feminism from the previous 'waves' to argue that 'we might adopt the term "self-ful" to describe an ethically aware strategy of self-regard.' The author's critical readings of images and discourses and well-known critics are razor-sharp and full of insight on how Western societies construct a toxic mix of praise and misogyny towards 'exceptional' 'selfish' women."

Katharine Mitchell, University of Strathclyde

SELFISH WOMEN

Lisa Downing

Routledge
Taylor & Francis Group

LONDON AND NEW YORK

First published 2019
by Routledge
2 Park Square, Milton Park, Abingdon, Oxon OX14 4RN

and by Routledge
52 Vanderbilt Avenue, New York, NY 10017

Routledge is an imprint of the Taylor & Francis Group, an informa business

British Library Cataloguing-in-Publication Data
A catalogue record for this book is available from the British Library

Library of Congress Cataloging-in-Publication Data
Names: Downing, Lisa, author.
Title: Selfish women / Lisa Downing.
Description: Abingdon, Oxon; New York, NY: Routledge, 2019. |
Includes bibliographical references and index.
Identifiers: LCCN 2019009499 (print) | LCCN 2019011466 (ebook) |
ISBN 9780429285349 (ebook) | ISBN 9780367249878 (hardback: alk. paper) |
ISBN 9780367249892 (pbk.: alk. paper)
Subjects: LCSH: Women—Identity. | Selfishness. | Feminism.
Classification: LCC HQ1206 (ebook) | LCC HQ1206 .D74 2019 (print) |
DDC 179—dc23
LC record available at https://lccn.loc.gov/2019009499

ISBN: 978-0-367-24987-8 (hbk)
ISBN: 978-0-367-24989-2 (pbk)
ISBN: 978-0-429-28534-9 (ebk)

Typeset in Bembo
by codeMantra

CONTENTS

FIGURES

ACKNOWLEDGEMENTS

This book began life as my inaugural professorial lecture, delivered at the University of Birmingham in November 2014. For according me two semesters of leave to begin writing this book, I am grateful to the College of Arts and Law at the University of Birmingham. For their individual and collective support in encouraging me to complete the project (including participating in a lunchtime workshop on "overcoming writer's block"), I thank my colleagues in the Department of Modern Languages, with especial thanks to Mónica Jato for her exceptional kindness.

For inviting me to present my material at their conferences, seminar series, or exhibitions, and for giving their time, intellect, and energy to reacting to my ideas, I thank Jennifer Barnes, Sam Bean, Larry Duffy, Jana Funke, Fiona Handyside, Navine G. Khan-Dossos, David Sorfa, Michael Syrotinski, and Edward Welch. A huge "thank you" in particular goes to Bob Brecher and his colleagues at the University of Brighton – Abby Barras, Jacopo Condo, Hannah Frith, Pam Laidman, Toby Lovat, Victoria Margree, Chrystie Myketiak, Carlos Peralta, Liliana Rodriguez, Ian Sinclair, Matt Smith, and Laetitia Zeeman – who workshopped my book prior to publication, commenting in detail on a whole draft of it.

For sharing a pre-published draft of her book *Mean Girl: Ayn Rand and The Culture of Greed* with me, I thank Lisa Duggan. For helping me to hunt down references or source images and permissions – and going beyond the call of duty in doing so in some cases – I thank Deborah Cameron, Erna Cooper, Martin Farr, Julie Lokis, Rachel Mesch, and Julie Rodgers. For their encouraging comments about, and helpful suggestions on, the manuscript of the book, I thank the expert readers approached by Routledge: Emma Wilson, Chris Matthew Sciabarra, and Katharine Mitchell. All read with tremendous care, insight, and generosity and I am so grateful to them for "getting it." I also owe a debt of gratitude to my commissioning editor at Routledge, Alex McGregor, who has been a model of patience and efficiency throughout, and to my trusty expert indexer, Ralph Kimber.

For discussing selfishness and the process of writing about it with me (selflessly and at length), I thank Lucy Bolton, Lara Cox, Tim Dean, Alex Dymock, Robert Gillett, Miranda Gill, Libby Saxton, Nicki Smith, Ingrid Wassenaar, Andrew Watts, and Hannah Yelin. Your friendship and solidarity made the writing process a lot more bearable. And lastly, but very much not least, I need to thank – as always – that incomparable individualist M.B.D., without whom everything in life would be different and lesser.

An earlier and shorter version of my critique of contemporary iterations of intersectional feminism, which appears in Chapter 5 of this book, was published in a section of Lisa Downing, "Antisocial Feminism? Shulamith Firestone, Monique Wittig, and Proto-Queer Theory," *Paragraph*, 41:3, 2018, 364–379. Adapted and extended material from it appears here with the permission of the editors and Edinburgh University Press.

INTRODUCTION

Selfish – a judgment readily passed by those who have never tested their own power of sacrifice.

(George Eliot, *Silas Marner*, 1861)

Selfishness: nothing, perhaps, resembles it more closely than self-respect.

(George Sand, *Indiana*, 1832)

Selfishness is a profoundly philosophical, *conceptual* achievement.

(Ayn Rand, "Selfishness Without A Self," 1973)

"Selfishness" is an exceptionally timely concept for critical consideration; indeed, it is sometimes said to characterize the very cultural epoch in which we live. As a personal attribute, "selfish" is almost always a label levelled against another, and both negatively connoted and morally weighted. Yet it is also a heavily gendered concept, with female selfishness being understood very differently from, and as more reprehensible than, its male counterpart for reasons that are deeply embedded in cultural understandings of the nature and function of women and that work in the interests of a patriarchal status quo. Given that men are supposed to be "full of self" (assertive, confident, self-assured, driven), male selfishness is a minor infraction. For women, who are supposed, in this binary logic that casts them as the mere complement of men, to be life-giving, to be nurturing, to be *for the other*, and therefore literally *self-less*, it is a far more serious transgression to be selfish while a woman – indeed it is a category violation of identity. Elsewhere, in a critique of contemporary identity politics, I have developed the concept of "identity category violation" to describe those individuals whose political affiliations or personal actions are at odds with the perceived normative characteristics of the group to which they are ascribed. A "selfish woman" is, in this sense, an example of identity category violation.[1] We might also think back to the fact that, in 1792, Mary Wollstonecraft had identified the so-called "feminine virtues" as perversions of true virtues, that is as a way of flattering women while trapping them in a series of unsatisfying roles.[2] There are few "feminine virtues" of which this is a more accurate description than "selflessness." A contention of this book, then, will be that female selfishness, as a radical and deviant departure from the expected qualities of "woman," may indeed be properly considered to be a strategic, political, and personal *achievement*.

Hence, it is not coincidental that the first two quotations of my epigraph above, about what selfishness is and how it may be misrepresented, were produced by nineteenth-century female authors (who also happen to be two of my favourite female Georges). Women artists in eras unconducive to female autonomy were positioned vis-à-vis power in such a way as to have an acute sense of which kinds of people, exhibiting what kinds of behaviours, and threatening what sorts of hierarchies, are likely to attract to themselves the label of "selfish." According to the third quotation by Ayn Rand, the Russian-American writer who has been dubbed the "prophetess of capitalism," selfishness should properly be understood as an achievement at a philosophical level in the context of a Christian worldview that promotes self-sacrifice as the highest human virtue. Rand was no straightforward feminist and her statement here deliberately does not ascribe a sex to that selfishness that is an achievement. While not proposing that "Rand was right" in any blanket way, for her pursuit of a project historically denied to women she deserves serious re-reading on her own terms. The fact that, for the most part, she is either vilified or ignored within feminism and the academic humanities, with a few key exceptions, bespeaks a strange sort of ideological purism that passes as ethical but that presses pause on critical thought and intellectual curiosity.

The association made in the twentieth and twenty-first centuries between positions that are explicitly in the interests of the individual and the often ill-understood, yet much critiqued, economic and political philosophy of neoliberalism has had the effect of tainting both the concept of *individualism* (perhaps understandably) and also that of *individuality* for those broadly on the left. The classical liberal concept of individualism holds that individual freedom is a more important social principle than shared responsibility, but considers harm to (the freedom of) the other as its ethical limit, while individuality can simply be understood as the notion that human beings need to be acknowledged as different from each other, with valid needs, wants, and equal rights. The pervasive spread of neoliberalism and the perceived severity of its social effects have resulted in the reinforcement of a simplistic moral binary that holds that a focus on the individual self is both selfish and "bad," while a focus on the other, or the collective, is concomitantly necessarily altruistic and "good." "Neoliberalism" is too often used interchangeably with "selfishness," or "individualism," without reference to the economic component of the system it describes, or the specific history of the concept. That said, the concepts overlap in a number of ways in our present moment, and the effects of this overlap are key to how we may think "self" currently and in recent history. Crucially for this project, one of the architects of the neoliberal economic and social project, and a vocal exponent of viewing the individual, rather than collective society, as the basic political unit, was a woman: Margaret Thatcher. Like Rand, Thatcher is a figure disavowed by feminism. She is often described as an "exceptional woman," a female individual who attained a position of power for herself but left intact the systems that prevent other women from progressing. The representation and self-representation of this exceptional woman are crucial indices of how selfish women are perceived.

Yet, the label of female selfishness is valid not only when considering exceptional and extreme women such as Rand and Thatcher. It is a means by which women are routinely policed and encouraged to self-police, whatever personal and political choices they might make. The decisions that women in the West[3] are charged with making – considering ambition, career, children, family, sexuality, and feminism – are shot through with value-judgment-laden discourses of selfishness, as recognized in the titles of recent books such as *Selfish, Shallow, and Self-Absorbed: Sixteen Writers on the Decision Not to Have Kids.*[4] Yet, while childfree women are routinely demonized for rejecting the role that has traditionally been seen as woman's "proper" one, women who do become mothers are not exempt from similar charges and also face gruelling amounts of cultural surveillance regarding their level of commitment to motherhood, measured by the various associations that accrue to staying at home or working outside of the home in popular cultural and media contexts and, in psychiatric and psychological ones, by suspicions of narcissistic mothering and "helicopter parenting."

By reading selfishness in terms of historical and contemporary expectations of gendered subjects, this book proposes to problematize the values commonly ascribed to the selfish/altruistic and individualistic/collectivist binaries. It also sets out to demonstrate the strategic value of a concept of selfishness for specific feminist or pro-woman aims. That is, the book proposes a way of exploring how selfishness and its close neighbours from varied disciplines and contexts – "self-interest," "self-regard," "self-actualization" – may be, not only tangentially expedient for a feminist political project in the twenty-first century, but programmatically necessary to it. In order to avoid both the conflation of these terms and the semantic slippage that is inevitable with such overused and freighted words, I will coin a term to exemplify the specific kind of strategic female selfishness that I am going to be considering. To do this job, I propose the term "self-fulness," as both the direct antonym of what women are traditionally exhorted to be – "selfless" – and as a value-judgment-free alternative to selfishness. The linguistically jarring nature of the neologism "self-ful" is intended to reflect the epistemologically and ontologically jarring nature of the very concept it is designed to describe, as it conjures up something rare, occluded, forbidden, nascent, or not yet fully brought into being.

The rise of the selfish woman = the fall of Western society

In August 2017 the Australian political and literary publication, *Quadrant Online*, featured an article by Michael Copeman entitled "The Rise of the Selfish Woman."[5] As an example of the discourses commonly used to coerce women into fitting the stereotypes expected of them, and the logic used to condemn those who refuse, this otherwise pedestrian article is virtually a textbook – and I will use it here to demonstrate exactly what it is that women are up against when they wish to be seen as "selves." The article begins by describing the cultural changes that have occurred in recent years with regard to the roles allocated to women:

> For millennia, almost all women had giving, unselfish roles thrust upon them. And they took these up with alacrity, despite great personal tolls [...] In the meantime, [Western] women have become "liberated" – allowed to work outside the home, to own property, to vote, to pursue secondary and then higher education, and to choose with whom and how often they have children.[6]

For any feminist scholar used to scrutinizing discourse for sexist assumptions, alarm bells ring from the off. These bells announce more than a mere quibble; indeed they sound the need to object vigorously to the redefinition of political history engineered by Copeman in insouciantly slipping in the suggestion that women have been "allowed" to work outside the home, to own property, vote, and so on, as if these "allowances" are acts of generosity that it was up to men to grant in the first place. Rather, women campaigned, fought, and in some cases died to claim these *rights* as human beings.

The author then goes on: "the result, quite understandably, is that Western women have become more selfish – selfish in the way that men have always been"[7] and "[t]here are some skilled and devoted male nurses. But perhaps it is most men's innate selfishness that stops most from ever contemplating a nursing career."[8] There is a significant contradiction here in the status that Copeman seems to believe "male selfishness" to have. On the one hand, he seemingly understands in the first quotation that what he is calling "selfishness" is the result or by-product of socialization. That men have historically been encouraged to live a life that they can shape according to their individual desires, talents, and tastes means that ("most" – note his qualifier) men are especially comfortable with "selfishness." On the other hand, however, in the second quotation (and despite the repetition of "most men"), he seems to suggest that selfishness is *properly* – indeed – "innately" male.

The argument that emerges about the rise of a generation of inconveniently selfish women in Copeman's article focuses on losses to the healthcare profession and social care system heralded by the shortage of women willing to do caring work. He argues that, as a combined result of women becoming more educated, the professionalization of nursing as a high-level career, and more women choosing to train as doctors rather than as nurses, we are left with a "crisis" caused entirely by women's pesky selfishness in seeking self-fulfilment and financial rewards, rather than being committed to caring for the other. "The worrying result," he writes, "is that our ageing society, with many more of us living with some sort of disability that requires skilled nursing help, is running out of its most vital resource – devoted young nurses."[9] Note: young women are not people with interests of their own here, but a *resource* to be deployed in the interests of the state. By referring emotively to "our" impending old age and vulnerability, Copeman makes a manipulative appeal to all right-minded readers to understand that instrumentalizing young women as carers – regardless of their wishes – is somehow morally right.

He goes on:

> As young Western women's options and aspirations have changed, so has the brave new (and more selfish) society they are creating. Today's average woman does better at high school, is more likely to go to and to graduate from uni, is more able to gain stable employment, is more likely to gain early promotion, and in some areas (e.g. medicine) is coming to dominate professions that 150 years ago were off limits to the "fairer" sex.[10]

That boys doing better at school than girls is commonly seen as natural and desirable, and the opposite state of affairs as some sort of apocalyptic crisis, is a phenomenon oft-commented-upon by feminists. It is a trope routinely produced by Men's Rights Activists (MRAs) and others who decry a "feminization" of education, allegedly correlated to, in Christina Hoff-Sommers's words, "feelings-centered, risk averse, competition-free and sedentary" schooling styles,[11] as well as to the low number of men teaching in primary schools. That little to no substantive research supports these claims does nothing to calm the frothing anti-feminist zeal with which they are regularly produced.[12]

Copeman continues:

> The flip side of this fast female advancement is that more men drop out of high school, fail to gain tertiary qualifications, have poor or unstable employment records – and are much more likely to be involved in risky behaviours (speeding, alcohol and drug abuse, gangs, criminal activities and suicide). Of course, those failures are not primarily women's fault (although there is an argument that today's mothers can/do devote less time to bringing up their boys to succeed, and thus more boys end up in low and risky avenues of life). Yet, today's women pay a price if they are unable to find a partner who can equal or complement them, or even stay the course.[13]

These three sentences contain a plethora of strands and varieties of woman-blaming. First, an equivalence is made between "female advancement" and the sad plight of men, implying a relationship of correlation or even causation and suggesting that success is a zero-sum game of gender warfare. To this is added a swipe at women for not being sufficiently solicitous mothers of boys, for increasingly working outside of the home and/or beginning to view themselves as multifaceted human beings *as well as parents*. When it comes, the back-handed assurance that he is not *blaming* women for daring *to want to be selves* rings hollowly – and is, in any case, immediately undone with that fatal word "although." Finally, the explicit heteronormative conservatism of this statement and of the article as a whole is made clear in the presumption that what women want most is inevitably and invariably to "settle down with a man." Also obvious is the barely disguised epicaricacy of telling women who do want this outcome that their bloody-minded and emasculating independence is precisely what will deprive them of it.

This is an author who clearly considers the prospect of selfish women as something deeply unnatural. Consider the following: "But the sad truth may be – as women increasingly adopt a *selfish male disregard* for the less-well-off – that governments can't keep up with the goals they have foolishly and deceptively set."[14] Here, selfishness is understood again as properly male, and male self-interest is understood as appropriate, whatever its deleterious effects on the poor, old, and sick – as responsibility for them lies squarely with women. The continued survival and thriving of this "male selfishness," regardless of societal consequences, is hoped for by the author; it is clearly the women inconveniently attending to their own self-interest who are the problem here. Had they stuck to their proper place, caring for the children, the sick, and the old, the men could continue being as selfish as they always had been – and "the government" would be exculpated for failing to meet its targets. Finally, Copeman comes clean: "In short," he writes, "the rise of the selfish woman may be sowing the seeds of destruction of our so-called compassionate society." A less compassionate society is, in fact, *all women's fault*, despite his earlier, mealy-mouthed caveats to the contrary.

The lazy biological essentialism underpinning the argument is made explicit in the next statement:

> No, there is nothing wrong in our society with anyone doing a job that requires unabashed service to others, and is rewarded more with satisfaction than oodles of cash. In fact, our society has always depended on most workers taking this approach. Yes, men should be enabled and encouraged to assist with all the formerly "female" tasks (except actually bearing children and breastfeeding) – but, no, their roles in these areas will never be equal to those of *the more genetically-adapted and usually better-suited women*.[15]

While pointing out that male-bodied people cannot give birth and breast-feed should be uncontroversial, the notion that women are somehow "*more genetically-adapted*" to the work of wiping bottoms and cleaning up mess that constitutes a large part of "caring" is an outrageous example of opportunistic false logic. In an article from 2003, concerning the legal ramifications of gender stereotyping assumptions, Caroline Rogus writes: "caregiving and childrearing are not necessarily instinctual, but are learned cultural experiences separate from the experience of pregnancy and birth."[16] Yet, the deeply ingrained cultural belief that these are innate characteristics of women, of the *same order* as the biological capacity to give birth, leads not only to cultural stereotyping and prejudice, but to legal judgments that impact women. Rogus uses the example of the Nguyen v. Ins judgment in the USA, in which the son of a non-citizen mother and a citizen father, who had been found guilty on criminal charges, was treated in violation of citizenships laws, on the grounds that it was presumed that the child would have bonded more with the non-citizen mother because, using logic based "not in biological differences, but instead in a stereotype, [...] mothers are significantly more likely than fathers to develop caring relationships with their children."[17] In this case, the statute governing the naturalized citizenship of children born to a citizen father and non-citizen mother was seen to violate the guarantees of the Equal Protection Clause. Rogus claims: "the Court's decision could have a lasting impact on preconceived ideas of gender roles"[18] and that "sex-based generalizations both reflect and reinforce fixed notions concerning the roles and abilities of males and females."[19] These fixed notions are not just the idle views of one journalist, then, but deeply pervasive cultural beliefs and fantasies that may shape the way that justice works, as well as the way that we understand culture and each other.

Returning to Copeman's article, having repeated the well-worn canard about women's biologically programmed propensity to care, he strikes the ultimate hyperbolic rhetorical blow: "The unmitigated rise of the selfish woman may [...] help hasten the fall of Western society – as we cease to provide the care that our weakest and oldest need."[20] The fallaciousness of Copeman's outrageous statement here is easily revealed. We are constantly warned that automation is in danger of taking away human jobs – in the light of this, why does he not suggest prioritizing the development of artificial intelligence applied to caring tasks? Such a suggestion may, in fact, be an extension of the logic of Xenofeminism, a recent branch of pro-technology feminism that has emerged as a response to impasses in feminist theorizations of care.[21] Yet the male journalist would much prefer that women return to their proper role – as he sees it – rather than fulfilling their individual ambitions (and, of course, the women most likely to be deployed in this way are working-class women, women of colour, and immigrant women – all of whom are the subjects most disenfranchised from lives built on considerations of choice and taste).

The journalist's insistence that women have a duty to sacrifice their individual self-interest for the greater good may well lead the feminist-minded reader to consider the unpopular idea that a strategic dogged insistence on *female individuality* rather than *social collectivity* may lead to better outcomes for women. One major reason *why* such an idea is currently unpopular among some feminists can be laid at the door of discourses that circulate around the idea of "neoliberalism."

On critiques of the neoliberal subject

Many critiques of the perceived selfishness of our age in the highly developed industrial nations of the West are linked to the pervasiveness of the effects of "neoliberalism" and the ways in which its logic has insinuated itself into all facets of life – including into feminism.[22] In the introduction to a Special Issue of *New Formations* on "Righting Feminism," Sara Farris and Catherine Rottenberg write that neoliberal capitalism has "incorporated feminist language in order to further intensify capital accumulation – and that this incorporation was facilitated by feminists' abandonment of a materialist critique."[23] They go on:

> Using key liberal terms, such as equality, opportunity, and free choice, while displacing and replacing their content, neoliberal feminism forges a feminist subject who is not only individualised but entrepreneurial in the sense that she is oriented towards optimising her resources through incessant calculation, personal initiative and innovation.[24]

Allowing the taint of "neoliberalism" to provoke suspicion of all iterations of the liberal values set out here – especially choice and individualization – runs the danger of sacrificing them in the interests of ideological purity. This would be a strategic error for feminist thinking, if that feminism wishes to work in women's interests. What is partly at stake in such critiques of both liberal and neoliberal concepts is the fact that too much focus on the individual is itself felt to be deeply unfeminist by many. In part, obviously, this is because of the collective origins of feminism as a social movement and its association with the left. But also, I contend, this is because the phantasy of woman as *innately* caring, collective, and compassionate, as discussed in the context of Copeman's article above, is the ghost that haunts feminism every bit as much as it haunts patriarchy.

Accordingly, it is possible, though seldom attempted, to make a feminist argument that living in a "neoliberal" world may have some compensations for women. One such compensation may be the fact that, at the very least, it provides some frameworks through which women might think themselves as independent individuals for perhaps the first time in a long history that has seen women as the possessions of fathers and husbands. The results of a combination of feminist struggles for rights of personhood (liberal struggles) and the current focus on the production of economic subjects mean that the much-critiqued "atomization" of society has – at least – created the possibility for those women who want to live outside of a milieu restricted to, and entirely predicated on, family and community to articulate and imagine these desires. However, the flip side of this potential is the hard cold fact that neoliberal policies, such as the deregulation of the banks in the USA and UK, in combination with wage stagnation, has led to a housing bubble putting affordable homes out of the reach of many women who would love to live as the "individuals" that neoliberalism promises they can be – i.e. alone – as well as out of the reach of families. Indeed, the negative financial effects of neoliberal policies may justify critiques of the system, but unfortunately this too often leads to a conflation of these negative economic effects, that have been argued to disproportionately affect women,[25] with the very *idea* of individuality which the figure of the neoliberal subject has helped to shape and describe. The result is that the valid female desire for individuality is demonized along with the current system in which the desiring is taking place. While not defending neoliberalism as an optimal mode of social organization, then, I would nevertheless like to make room to consider that some of the premises of neoliberalism may – at the very least – be a mixed bag for women and I would also counsel taking care to separate an ideal of individuality from a particular mode of governance.

It is worth noting that critics of neoliberalism are often unclear or in disagreement about their definition of the term, despite its pervasiveness as a generic term for our various contemporary ills. In *A Research Agenda for Neoliberalism*, Kean Birch argues that "[n]eoliberalism is [...] a word predominantly, if not exclusively, used in left-wing or centre-left circles."[26] And:

> It is primarily used as a derogatory or pejorative term to refer to someone who holds certain beliefs. Namely, that markets with no or very limited government intervention in restricting competition are the best – or "natural" – way to organize our economies and also our societies. This is based on the claim that markets are efficient, in that they lead to the lowest cost and resource use, and also moral, in that they support individuality, autonomy and choice.[27]

In a review of Birch's book, Christopher May concurs that

> students from undergraduate to PhD level, as well as academics and other commentators, use the term as if we all knew what it meant, and as a catch-all prejudicial accusation levelled at any aspect of the contemporary political economy they find unacceptable or malign.[28]

The term itself is often thought to have originated at the *Colloque Walter Lippmann*, organized in Paris in 1938 by French philosopher Louis Rougier, but even this point of origin is disputed. Its development is associated with several separate, but contemporaneously emergent, economic schools, including the Austrian school of economy, represented by Friedrich Hayek and Ludwig von Mises; the Chicago School of Milton Friedman and Gary Becker; and the German Freiberg or "Ordoliberal" School associated with Wilhelm Röpke and Alexander Rüstow. Following the Second World War, a number of Centre-Right think tanks were set up to theorize the deployment of free market economics for recovering Western economies, including, in the UK, the Institute of Economic Affairs (established in 1955) and the Adam Smith Institute (1977), and, in the USA, the Heritage Foundation (1973) and Cato Institute (1974) which emerged as reactions against the interventionist governmental policies associated with the "New Deal." These institutes promoted free-market ideology up to the governance of Reagan and Thatcher who implemented it on a large scale in their countries' respective economic policies.[29] Until the 1980s, so-called "neoliberals" had often used the term to describe themselves and their political position. It became a pejorative term in the 1980s, following the effects of Thatcherism and Reaganism. Increasing globalization and the domination of large corporations with influence over governments have been theorized as responsible for recent electoral decisions such as the vote to leave the European Union in the UK and the election of protectionist, nationalist presidential candidate Donald Trump in the USA. Writers such as Naomi Klein and George Monbiot lay such phenomena at the door of "neoliberal" policies.

Those propounding a left-wing condemnation of neoliberalism *tout court* tend to assume that it contains no elements intended to improve life for citizens and that, as a model, it is in some way inherently dehumanizing in comparison to more collectivist or socialist models. In an article for *The Week* entitled "What Neoliberals Get Right," Damon Linker writes:

> A libertarian or far-right Republican treats the market as sacrosanct and the government as a parasite that contributes little of value. A socialist begins with the state and the substantial list of social goods it should provide and views with suspicion the economic activity that takes place in the private sector. A neoliberal differs from both in regarding the market and the government as potential and rightful collaborators in generating opportunity and providing protections that will elevate standards of living and improve overall quality of life for the greatest possible number of citizens.[30]

While many would argue that the aim of "elevating standards" and "improving quality of life" has failed for the majority, the philosophy that underpinned what has become known as "neoliberalism" itself deserves more scrutiny for the potential it contained. In fact, it was a philosophy that fascinated Michel Foucault, a theorist and critic of systems of power as well as an exponent of new ways of imagining freedom, in his last years. Foucault's 1978–1979 lectures at the Collège de France, translated into English under the title *The Birth of Biopolitics*, focus, despite their title, not on biopower, but on the form of governance that is now known as neoliberalism.[31] The lectures were delivered at the very moment that Thatcherism and Reaganism took hold in the Anglosphere, and they were published in English at the height of the global financial crisis in 2008.[32]

Foucault's lectures build up a history – or better genealogy – of forms of governance, from a "classical" liberal economic model to the emergent "neoliberalism" of the late-twentieth century. Building on the model of panoptical power introduced in *Discipline and Punish* (1975), Foucault expands the metaphor from that of a literal panopticon, as per Bentham's prison architecture as a structure in which self-surveillance and self-policing are encouraged, to a way of understanding liberal economic philosophy. He describes how an early liberal form of governance can be understood as connecting state and market by promoting disciplinary techniques of surveillance that enable economic freedom. So, the state creates conditions of market freedom and then surveys the behaviour of the market, with intervention as a last resort.[33] Neoliberalism, by contrast, is understood by Foucault as a departure from classical economic liberalism with the free market placed at the very heart of governance. Focusing particularly on the German Ordoliberal group's revisionist model, Foucault notes the move towards adopting "the free market as an organizing and regulating principle of the state [...] In other words a state under the supervision of the market rather than a market supervised by the state."[34] In tandem with this change of organization, there is a shift in focus from the market understood in terms of free exchange, as for a classical liberal such as Adam Smith, towards the market understood as a mechanism of both exchange and competition.

Turning from the German model to the American one, Foucault notes that in the US context, in contradistinction to the European one, liberalism has been "the recurrent element of all the political discussions and choices of the United States."[35] Focusing on the work of Gary Becker, Foucault highlights the kind of subject produced by US neoliberalism: an individual who makes *choices,* called *homo economicus.* Economics thus becomes the business of "the internal rationality of [...] human behavior,"[36] such that "*homo economicus* is an entrepreneur, an entrepreneur of himself."[37] In an overview of Foucault's history of neoliberalism, Nicholas Gane describes this as "the birth of a subject that can be reduced to a form of capital and individualized according to its choices and behaviours."[38] Gane summarizes that the trends Foucault charts mark a shift towards more and more aspects of life being viewed through an "economic grid," including even "relationships between mother and child, which can 'be analyzed in terms of investment, capital costs, and profit – both economic and psychological profit – on the capital invested'."[39]

Scholars of Foucault and neoliberalism differ on the question of whether the French thinker offered merely a descriptive and analytical genealogy of the emergence of an idea in his lectures or whether he was attracted to the philosophy of neoliberalism and the subject positions it potentiated.[40] Some believe that, owing to the partiality of the history, the ways in which neoliberal politics expanded after Foucault's death (with the extent of the influence that multinational corporations would go on to have, in particular, being unimaginable at the time of his writing), and the suspicion hovering over Foucault's approval of the concept, his lectures are of limited use as critical insights into the emergence of neoliberalism.[41] Others argue that they provide a useful basis for consideration of the implications of neoliberal spread beyond the end of the 1970s.[42] Michael Behrant points out some of the ways that the broader precepts of Foucault's system of thought share features with neoliberal reason. Primarily, the model of power Foucault developed, that is understood as normative and reactive, rather than top-down or juridical, resembles a neoliberal form of power more closely than a Marxist dialectical one. Further, Foucault was suspicious of the powers of the state and of small statism and critical (to the horror of many of Foucault's followers) of social security, viewing it as "the culmination" of biopolitical control.[43] Gane writes of what he sees as the most valuable aspects of Foucault's lectures: first that he "refuses to treat neoliberalism as a single discursive entity" and second that he recognizes "neoliberalism as a form of political *reason*," that is "as a serious political and epistemological project rather than [...] as mere ideology."[44] To conclude, Gane suggests that we consider the ways that Foucault's lectures pose the key question: "what can truth and the self be outside of their current capture by the market?"[45]

Foucault's methods and theories have undoubtedly been relevant for many feminist critiques of the neoliberal female self, such as Rosalind Gill's notion of "sexual subjectification" and her critique, with Shani Orgad, of "confidence culture" (the glut of recent confidence-building techniques and technologies, including self-help, confidence coaching, and assertiveness training, especially aimed at women).[46] While nominally sharing Foucault's open and speculative analytical energies – they claim to be thinking "about the relation between culture and subjectivity in a way that is not reductive, deterministic, or conspiratorial"[47] – the logic of Gill and Orgad's formulations, like many other left-oriented analyses, presuppose that the forms of subjectivity produced under conditions of neoliberalism are inevitably and only negative, and that the antidote to "individualism" must be collectivism, rather than, for example, a restoration of the values of earlier modes of liberalism. For example, they state that truth can never be found in seeking "individual solutions to structural problems."[48] While this is, of course, true, equally looking only to collectivism as a catch-all "cure" ignores the crucial importance of nourishing individuality.

Similarly, in an article on the expectations placed upon twenty-first-century women to aspire to perfection, Angela McRobbie argues that "an ethos of competitive individualism"[49] predominates in culture, with some horrific consequences, such as the example of teenage girls who commit suicide as a result of being bullied "for some breech of teenage female etiquette."[50] Like Gill, McRobbie underpins her reading with a Foucauldian model of subjectification, as seen when she defines perfection as "a heightened form of self-regulation based on an aspiration to some idea of the 'good life'."[51] McRobbie writes of the way in which neoliberal iterations of feminism equate "female success with the illusion of control, with the idea of 'the perfect'."[52] Like Gill and Orgad, she blames this turn to "individualistic striving" on the discarding of the "older, welfarist, and collectivist feminism of the past."[53] One possible objection that could be made here is that the *character* of the technologies of "individualized perfection" critiqued by McRobbie is that of *conformism*; it is not a matter of *individuality* at all. To the problem of the "atomization" of "neoliberal" culture, the "welfarist and collectivist" imperative is posed as the properly female, feminist solution. However, the path to *self-fulness*, I would argue, can lie in neither direction (unthinking compliance with neoliberal norms or an idealization of collectivism), but must be found in a third way.

Both articles also agree that techniques such as those promoted by "confidence culture" and the culture of perfection are totalizing insofar as they encourage "turning inwards and working on the self through self-monitoring, *constant* calculation and the inculcation of an entrepreneurial spirit."[54] Although these features of contemporary culture are immediately recognizable, I wonder about the insistence on the term "constant" and the suggestion that there is *no way* of countering the trend described. What is absent in the analysis of confidence culture here is the understanding that these are strategies and technologies that individuals can partially use, accept fully or, indeed, resist. (The key Foucauldian notion of *resistance* is, in fact, greatly downplayed in these works.) The phenomena that Gill and Orgad and McRobbie discuss may be culturally widespread, but they are *not* totalitarian. Neoliberalism's modus operandi is, I would contend, pervasive, not coercive. Its power consists in its ability to insinuate itself into all corners of life, like the "lines of penetration" Foucault evokes to describe the workings of modern power, at the point of convergence of which are our bodies and selves, and against which there is "no single locus of great Refusal," rather "a plurality of resistances, each of them a special case."[55] And, in line with the Foucauldian conception of power and resistance, I would argue that in each case described by these writers, it is incumbent upon women to question whether a given cultural current or trend works in or against their own self-interest; whether a strategy is worth adopting, using against the grain, or resisting. To deny this possibility (ethical exigency?) is to assume that living "under neoliberalism" renders the individual entirely incapable of evaluating critically the materials encountered in daily life or of engaging in strategic deployment/rejection of the technologies with which one comes into contact.

The current book does not attempt to provide a wholesale defence of neoliberal subjectivity (indeed, the analysis in Chapter 5 will offer a critique of some discourses and phenomena within postfeminism and certain recent iterations of intersectionality that seem to use a logic that may be termed "neoliberal" on the grounds that they are not conducive for imagining a more productive female self-fulness). However, throughout, I will attempt also to consider the possibility that the individualization of culture in the twentieth and twenty-first centuries, often assumed to be the outcome of neoliberalism, might in some ways have offered and continue to offer women a better deal than a purely collectivist social alternative. This experiment in thinking should not, in turn, preclude our imagining more creative and productive forms of individuality after, beyond, or in excess of neoliberalism.

Female "self-fulness," feminist selves

The counterintuitive, because counter-discursive, phrase "the virtue of selfishness" is heavily associated with Ayn Rand, who gave this title to her 1964 collection of essays. In *The Virtue of Selfishness* (1964), Rand provides the following, simple definition of selfishness: "selfishness is concern with one's own interests."[56]

She goes on to state that being "the beneficiary" of one's own "moral actions" is "the essence of a moral existence."[57] The *Oxford English Dictionary*'s definition of selfishness, however, caveats the term in a way that Rand's definition doesn't. Here, selfishness is being "devoted to or concerned with one's own advantage or welfare to the exclusion of regard for others." *Webster's New Collegiate Dictionary* similarly defines it as "regarding one's own comfort, advantage, etc., in disregard, or at the expense, of that of others." Peter Schwartz, author of a provocatively entitled, Objectivism-influenced book, In Defense of Selfishness, claims that the term "selfishness" is commonly used as a straw man and argues that "defining selfishness in this manner makes it seem that the harming of others is an integral part of the concept."[58] Indeed, feminist Rand scholars Mimi Gladstein and Chris Sciabarra explain that "Rand [...] opposed 'brute' selfishness, which posits the sacrifice of others to one's own ends."[59] A key precursor of this idea of a rational selfishness is German philosopher Max Stirner, assumed to be an influence on Friedrich Nietzsche and the existentialists, who wrote in 1844 of a kind of rational egoism in which "self-ownership" of the individual is a moral and psychological good. Stirner theorized that the "willing" egoist satisfies their own desires while imagining those desires to be greater than the self, or transcendent, while the "unwilling" egoist is aware that the exercise of their will is in pursuit of their subjective needs, but achieves a kind of transcendence through it. This transcendence is not theistic, but is one in which the exaltedness of the human is realized.[60] One aspect that many commentators ignore in critiquing or defending selfishness or egoism, however, is that both the moral-value-judgment-laden dictionary definitions of selfishness and Stirner's and the Randians' (albeit very different) attempts to achieve a descriptive version of it, that frees it from its association with vice or sin in a Judeo-Christian tradition, have particular significance when applied to women that they do *not* have when applied gender neutrally (or indeed to the bearer of the masculine pronoun that Rand and her followers relentlessly – and regressively – use as their universal).

If, for the moment, then, we take "selfishness" to mean no more than "concern with one's own interests" or "self-interest," it opens up two obvious questions, that are at the heart of both philosophy and feminism: (1) What is meant by "self" and (2) how are we to know if a given action or decision is in the interests of that elusive "self," especially in the light of analyses that argue that, in the present moment, the neoliberal machine co-opts the possibility of perceiving real self-interest? Much work in feminist philosophy has problematized what Cynthia Willet, Ellie Anderson and Diana Meyer describe as the "dominant modern western view of the self."[61] This hegemonic figure is modelled on a white, male, heterosexual, upper-class subject (though this is not, of course, acknowledged in the Ür-texts) following broadly two models: first, that of Kant's ethical subject, who uses reason and will to transcend the norms imposed by culture; second, the "homo economicus," discussed by Foucault in the context of the birth of neoliberalism, who operates strategically and hierarchically within a market-based field to satisfy selfish desire.[62] Both of these models are of individuals existing apparently in isolation, seeking their own ends. Feminist philosophers have recognized that a cultural dimension obtains in the formation of the idea of self. This is key not only to understanding the bias written into the concept, but also to identifying the lack of awareness of such bias on the part of those who did the defining. Willet et al write: "It is precisely the failure to acknowledge that the question of the self is not narrowly metaphysical that has led to philosophy's implicit modelling of the self on a male subject."[63] They argue that a notion of self, devoid of cultural contextualization and devoid of an awareness of power relations, is perforce partial.

While some liberal thinkers (including non-feminist-identified theorist of selfishness, Ayn Rand) would merely wish to make the existing category of self flexible enough to incorporate women too, where historically it has legally and practically excluded them in the context of their status as chattel, others have declared this "masculine" idea of "self" unfit for purpose for women, since it has been constructed not to exclude women *accidentally* or *contingently*, but rather to do so *systematically* and *structurally*. As Simone de Beauvoir writes, borrowing the Hegelian logic of the master–slave dialectic: "He is the Absolute. She is the Other,"[64] and "Man dreams of an Other not only to possess her, but also to be validated by her."[65] Beauvoir identified the absence of a fully conceptualized female self as a given in Western thought and culture to be the key ontological and political problem facing women. Woman, as "complement," has by definition not been in possession of self. Since the female subject is defined in contradistinction to what man is, Willet et al. point out that: "one corollary of selfhood is that women are consigned to selflessness – that is to invisibility, subservient passivity, and self-sacrificial altruism."[66] It is according to this understanding, then, that a selfish woman is culturally apprehended as unnatural. She is filled with something she properly *ought not to have*; she is, to use my term, too "self-ful."

Some feminist philosophy has attempted to rethink selfhood in ways that more adequately represent female experience than the available Western models of an atomized self described above. Drawing on Beauvoir's claim that it is the strong association between woman and body, and especially woman's role as childbearer, that traps her in the realm of immanence (socio-historical and personal contingency), rather than allowing her equal access to the transcendental (the realm of radical freedom with regard to one's capacity to make one's life into a chosen project), attempts have been made to revalue the bodily realm of experience as central to selfhood. This is not Beauvoir's strategy to respond to the problem she identifies, it should be noted. Beauvoir instead urges both men and women to renegotiate their positions with regard to immanence and transcendence, allowing the maximum potential for freedom, while contesting the radical independence of the Kantian model of self for any one of us, since we are all socially, historically located subjects.

Some philosophers working in the traditions of Continental philosophy, such as Luce Irigaray, and Africana philosophy, such as Patricia Hill Collins, have proposed in place of the model of sovereign individualism an "ethics of eros."[67] This describes a connected, affective mode of being in which the self is understood as relational. In the Anglophone analytical tradition, a parallel "ethics of care" emerged through the work of Carol Gilligan, Sara Ruddick, Hilde Lindemann, and others. These parallel paradigms from different traditions highlight the relational self, the self that comes into being through giving birth, being born, and interacting in social networks. They foreground the notion of bondedness that is seen as essential to subjectivity and as disavowed by what is perceived to be the masculinist model of individualism. The varieties of eros ethics discussed here draw on the idea that the damaged or severed social bond may be repaired through the freeing of libidinal drives, taking inspiration both from psychoanalysis (in Irigaray's case) and from non-white traditions of "othermothering" (i.e. nurturing bonds beyond biological kinship), in the case of Africana feminisms. This strategic way of thinking female selfhood emphasizes the properly agentic nature of childbirth and caregiving. Critiques of the "masculinist" concept of a radically independent self point to the extent to which such models tend to involve a negation of being woman-born and brought into the world by another. In the North American tradition in particular, much emphasis is placed in ethics of care literature on decisions that women have to make around pregnancy, birth, and/or abortion, leading to the creation of what Lindemann describes as the "practice of personhood." This is the practice of "initiating human beings into personhood and then holding them there."[68]

While these are valuable ways of redressing and relativizing the dominant model of Western subjectivity, taking on board both biological female lived experience and the realities, priorities, and differences of non-white cultures, these models may risk overvaluing the ethical import of female biological processes to a degree that may seem essentializing, normative, and regressive to many of us today. While I fully appreciate the creative attempt to redeploy *against the grain* the masculinist view of what self is, and what women as not-quite-selves are, and to value that which has been despised for being related to femaleness and femininity, one objection I have to feminist projects of this kind is that they assume that the experience of women under patriarchy is the expression of a "self" that will also best be suited to the freedom from patriarchy that is feminism's aim.

If the self is indeed more mutable and less absolute than the masculinist phantasy of it,[69] it seems unhelpful in some ways to base the revised feminist self on an iteration of woman's subordinate role. Another objection is that while we are all – whatever our gender – indisputably *born* and therefore linked through birth to others, not all women give birth, want to care for others, or – taking on board concerns from disability, intersex, and trans activisms and theory – are biologically equipped to give birth or to feed a child, even if they wished to do so. One of the dangers, then, of basing selfhood on normative female biological behaviours is that it excludes non-normative women. A concept of personhood that depends on biological reproduction cannot help but feel somewhat reductive, essentialist, Darwinian, and unfriendly to a more queer-inflected view of self.

Finally, to emphasize *feeling* when re-imagining female selfhood is already to be in the position of repeating, and so having to recuperate, a patriarchal, binary discourse that puts women on the side of emotion or unreason. As Laura Sjoberg and Caron E. Gentry posit in their study of violent women, "Very few researchers actually depict violent women as rational actors."[70] The same can be said, as we shall examine in this book, of selfish, individualistic, and exceptional women, whose violence is only *symbolic*. And, more generally and damningly, the same can be said of women *in general*. To adopt rationality as a strategic part of a re-imagined female selfhood can be seen as an audacious riposte to the original masculinist co-opting of reason for men and ascription to "the other" – to women – of emotionalism. It is for this reason that when emphasizing the *strategic use of reason* in the construction of female lives I shall borrow Rand's favoured term "self-interest," in preference to "selfishness" or "self-fulness."

Methods and contents

In the analyses that follow in this book, I will employ, borrowing a term from the writings of Foucault, a diverse "toolkit" of critical and analytical methods for interrogating the concept of gendered selfishness and the discourses that treat it, rather than a single, unified theoretical framework. The first tool in my kit is a particular feminist lens. This whole book is underpinned by a definition of feminism that I particularly like, namely "the radical notion that women are people," coined by Marie Shear.[71] Such a definition centres on women as human beings, who are just as complex in their tastes, needs, political affiliations, and so forth, as men. Some women will be caring, but others will be self-interested, ambitious, and power-seeking. It is my assertation that an imposed ontological category label – "woman" – should not be permitted to sanitize and excise such *human* differences (individuality). On the other hand, the analyses in the book are critical of certain tenets of some branches of feminism. These include the feminist suspicion around the notion of exceptionality, encapsulated in the pejorative concept of "exceptional woman syndrome." The argument goes that "by making a point of the exception, the rule is reinscribed,"[72] such that female excellence becomes the object of suspicion, considered as something with which to keep down other, "ordinary" women, rather than as something that could be inspirational or transformative. It is to this degree that Julia Kristeva, in considering the power of "female genius," wonders whether she can even call herself a feminist since she celebrates and valorizes exceptional women.[73] Another discourse issuing from feminism about which I have some concerns is the exhortation, made in some contemporary branches of feminism that have taken up (and, I would argue, deformed), the notion of "intersectionality" to "decentre" the self and one's self-interest in an effort always to raise up the interests of any perceived more vulnerable sub-group or sub-category than the one to which you "belong." I shall examine my objections to this trend at length in Chapter 5. Thus, while feminist analysis is one of my tools, it is also one of the objects of my scrutiny, and different branches of feminism, where they undermine a message of female self-fulness, will be critiqued in these terms.

My second major tool, drawing on my long-standing Foucauldian leanings, will be a specific kind of discourse analysis that is especially sensitive to, and aware of, the reverse-discursive function that concepts such as "selfishness" may serve. This means that when female selfishness is embraced as a good, this has to be understood in the context of a political-discursive field in which female altruism is the coerced norm, and in which selfishness attracts knee-jerk vilification. In such a context, the weight of "selfishness" is counter-normative and resistant. My approach to selfishness itself, then, is not value-judgment-laden in any straightforward way. The term is used descriptively, not prescriptively, though I will also suggest at moments throughout the book that it may be further strategically redeployed and that it should remain open to repurposing and expanding via my concept of "self-fulness."

The data to be analyzed in the book include psychiatric, philosophical, political, literary, print and online media texts. A broadly cultural studies-informed methodological approach is used. However, for reasons already set out, the assumed left-wing bias of cultural studies methods (that have led latterly to paranoid alt-right accusations of a "cultural Marxism" issuing from the humanities departments of universities – and taking over broader culture[74]) will not be a feature of my reading method or underpinning ideology. In an attempt to set aside the approximate and often unhelpful left-right dichotomy, I will interrogate both Marxian-influenced, class-based analyses, such as those produced by radical feminism, and pro-individualistic ideology, such as that produced by Rand and her followers, with the aim of breaking down the workings of the deployment of "selfishness" as rhetorical and moral marker. If this book has a political leaning at all, it is perhaps only an anti-authoritarian one that asks that we be open to reading all texts, and considering all ideas and taking them seriously on their own terms, rather than narrowing debate and analysis to a small number of "approved" views, ideologies, and texts. The book actively seeks out the words and ideas of prominent women commonly considered unpalatable and rebarbative and asks what they may contribute to debates about the meaning of "woman" and "self" in an epoch in which both are matters of urgency.

Over five chapters, via case studies from a range of European and Anglophone contexts and from different disciplines and discursive sites, the book explores how female selfishness has come to be constituted as aberrant, and how it is currently understood. The first chapter examines the historical construction of the pathological version of selfishness – "narcissism" – and its gendering, from Freudian psychoanalysis to late-twentieth-century American psychiatric and popular psychological accounts, paying particular attention to the figure of the "narcissistic mother," which has entered everyday parlance. Chapters 2 and 3 present case studies of two prominent selfish women who proudly claim individualism as a virtue or are strongly associated with having done so: in Chapter 2, Ayn Rand, who declared that "there is no such entity as 'society', since society is only a number of individual men"[75] and, in Chapter 3, Margaret Thatcher, who would take this very idea as central to her whole political message and agenda (without attributing it to Rand). In undertaking these case studies, I pay close critical attention to the specific ways in which discourses of selfishness, gender, and ideas about the political right wing intersect in the cultural imagination to create meanings and reinforce assumptions. The last two chapters of the book ask what gendered selfishness means currently, and has meant in modern times, for the lives of women. Chapter 4 considers the place of "self" in pervasive popular cultural and media narratives about women's personal and professional lives. It explores the double standards and double binds involved in both motherhood *and* child-free life choices (both of which can, by misogynistic sleight of hand, carry implications of inappropriate female selfishness), and examines the imperative to care that is intensely gendered, by revisiting the literature of "ethics of care," especially Carol Gilligan's classic text, *In a Different Voice* (1982). It also interrogates discourses of female ambition and female leadership, which fail to conform to a specifically gendered expectation of self-sacrifice. Creative – but not necessarily feminist – selfish or self-ful forms of resistance to these gendered expectations are explored via the writings of controversial novelist and journalist Lionel Shriver. Finally, Chapter 5 considers feminism's fraught historical – and present – relationship with the idea of selfishness, self-interest, and individuality. It looks at branches and philosophies of feminism – radical, intersectional, and postfeminist – that each treat the self-other dynamic and the ethics that accrue to it in different ways. It examines the ways in which a feminist agenda might be seduced by, or resist, recent narratives of "empowerment," and it asks if it is possible to articulate a vision of the feminist self – of feminist self-fulness – beyond the bounds of the freighted and over-simplistic dichotomy of collectivism and individualism.

In short, then, this book both explores how avowedly and vocally "selfish women" in history have viewed self, feminism, and, indeed, women, and examines the character of both feminist *and* mainstream cultural, political, and psychological discourses about women who refuse an ethical commitment to collectivism and to the other. The book is also interested in the rhetoric of "extremism" when it comes to women expressing strongly held opinions. Writing, speech giving, and discourse that are highly polemical and uncompromising often risk being dubbed totalitarian or fundamentalist when they are authored by subjects who are not supposed to express decided conviction. When women write this way, they tend to face criticism from men, for being "unfeminine," and from feminists for being bad sisters. Along with Rand and Thatcher, radical feminist writing of the "second wave" shares this tendency, and is also often rejected by contemporary forms of feminism for being too doctrinaire and uncompromising.[76]

The book is aware of, and celebrates, the audacity of thinking about selfishness neutrally, or even in strategically positive terms, in an epoch in which the term is most often linked to global capitalism and punitive austerity policies, seen as the cause of increasing misery for the majority. Politically, selfishness is generally assumed to be of the right. Yet, I would argue, those considering themselves feminist and/or progressive might do well to understand and take more account of strategic self-interest rather than simply considering it, unquestioningly, as a moral evil.

Notes

1 See Lisa Downing, "The Body Politic: Gender, the Right Wing, and 'Identity Category Violations'," *French Cultural Studies*, 29:4, 2018, 1–11.

2 Mary Wollstonecraft, *A Vindication of the Rights of Women with Strictures on Political and Moral Subjects* [1792] (London: Unwin, 1891), p. 73.

3 I acknowledge the West-centrism of this project. I am examining here the subjects produced in specific contexts: Anglo-American and European modernity. I fully acknowledge that non-Western models of self may well signify and function in very different ways, and that a study of the gendered self in other cultural contexts would be productive, both on its own terms and in a comparative perspective, but this lies outside the scope of my expertise, and hence outside the remit of this book.

4 Meghan Daum (ed.), *Selfish, Shallow, and Self-Absorbed: Sixteen Writers on the Decision Not to Have Kids* (New York: Picador, 2015).

5 Michael Copeman, "The Rise of the Selfish Woman," *Quadrant Online*, 2 August 2017, https://quadrant.org.au/opinion/qed/2017/08/rise-selfish-woman/

6 Copeman, "The Rise of the Selfish Woman."

7 Copeman, "The Rise of the Selfish Woman."

8 Copeman, "The Rise of the Selfish Woman."

9 Copeman, "The Rise of the Selfish Woman."

10 Copeman, "The Rise of the Selfish Woman."

11 Christina Hoff Sommers, *The War against Boys: How Misguided Policies are Harming our Young Men* [2010], new edition (New York: Simon and Schuster, 2013), p. 2.

12 This is a phenomenon that has been seriously addressed by educational researchers. See, for example, Christine Skelton, "The 'Feminisation of Schooling' or 'Re-masculinising' Primary Education?," *International Studies in Sociology of Education*, 12:1, 2002, 77–96. Her research findings suggest that: "the greater number of female teachers in primary education does not create a 'feminised' environment. Indeed, the perception that schools are 'feminised' in any way can be seen to be inaccurate" (p. 92).

13 Copeman, "The Rise of the Selfish Woman."

14 Copeman, "The Rise of the Selfish Woman" (My emphasis).

15 Copeman, "The Rise of the Selfish Woman" (My emphasis).

16 Caroline Rogus, "Conflating Women's Biological and Social Roles: The Ideal of Motherhood, Equal Protection, and the Implications of the Nguyen v. Ins Opinion," *Journal of Constitutional Law*, 5:4, 2003, 803–830, p. 803.

17 Rogus, "Conflating Women's Biological and Social Roles," p. 807.

18 Rogus, "Conflating Women's Biological and Social Roles," p. 807.

19 Rogus, "Conflating Women's Biological and Social Roles," pp. 807–808.

20 Copeman, "The Rise of the Selfish Woman."

21 See María Puig de la Bellacasa, *Matters of Care: Speculative Ethics in More Than Human Worlds* (Minneapolis: University of Minnesota Press, 2017) and Helen Hester, *Xenofeminism* (Cambridge: Polity, 2018).

22 The past ten years have, in fact, seen a glut of scholarly and journalistic articles from a feminist perspective on the unadulterated ills of neoliberalism and its incursion into feminism. See, as an exemplary sample, Nancy Fraser, "Feminism, Capitalism and the Cunning of History," *New Left Review*, 56, 2009, 97–117; Nanette Funk, "Contra Fraser on Feminism and Neoliberalism," *Hypatia*, 28:1, 2013, 179–196; Catherine Rottenberg, "The Rise of Neoliberal Feminism," *Cultural Studies*, 28, 2014, 418–437;

Elizabeth Prügl, "Neoliberalising Feminism," *International Feminist Journal of Politics*, 20:4, 2015, 614–631.

23 Sara Farris and Catherine Rottenberg, "Introduction: Righting Feminism," *New Formations*, 91, 2017, 5–15, p. 11.

24 Farris and Rottenberg, "Introduction: Righting Feminism," p. 11.

25 For a careful historical analysis of the deployment of the political language of selfishness and its intersection with austerity, see Anita Biressi and Heather Nunn, "Selfishness in Austerity Times," *Soundings: A Journal of Politics and Culture*, 56, Spring 2014, 54–66. For an analysis of how neoliberal policies disproportionately impact women negatively see Hester Eisenstein, "Hegemonic Feminism, Neoliberalism, and Womenomics: 'Empowerment' Instead of Liberation?," *New Formations*, 91, 2017, 35–49.

26 Kean Birch, *A Research Agenda for Neoliberalism* (Cheltenham: Edward Elgar, 2017), p. 69.

27 Birch, *A Research Agenda for Neoliberalism*, p. 69.

28 Christopher May, *Book Review: A Research Agenda for Neoliberalism by Kean Birch*, 14 February 2018, http://blogs.lse.ac.uk/politicsandpolicy/book-review-a-research-agenda-for-neoliberalism-by-kean-birch/

29 On the role of think tanks in furthering the neoliberal project, see Daniel Stedman Jones, *Masters of the Universe: Hayek, Friedman, and the Birth of Neoliberalism* (Princeton: Princeton University Press, 2012). ·

30 Damon Linker, "What Neoliberals Get Right," *The Week*, 5 February 2016, http://theweek.com/articles/603539/what-neoliberals-right

31 Michel Foucault, *The Birth of Biopolitics* (Basingstoke: Palgrave, 2008).

32 See Nicholas Gane, "Foucault's History of Neoliberalism," in Lisa Downing (ed.), *After Foucault: Culture, Theory, and Criticism in the 21st Century* (Cambridge: Cambridge University Press, 2018), 46–60.

33 Foucault, *The Birth of Biopolitics*, p. 67.

34 Foucault, *The Birth of Biopolitics*, p. 116.

35 Foucault, *The Birth of Biopolitics*, p. 217.

36 Foucault, *The Birth of Biopolitics*, p. 223.

37 Foucault, *The Birth of Biopolitics*, p. 226.

38 Gane, "Foucault's History of Neoliberalism," p. 51. Gane also points out here that this idea can be traced to an earlier text and set of ideas – Ludwig von Mises's assertion in *Epistemological Problems of Economics* (Princeton: Van Nostrand, 1960) that – to quote Gane's summary – "all forms of human action obey an economic principle." (p. 51).

39 Gane, "Foucault's History of Neoliberalism," p. 52, citing Foucault, *The Birth of Biopolitics*, p. 244.

40 For those proposing Foucault as a crypto-neoliberal, see Philip Mirowski, *Never Let a Serious Crisis Go To Waste: How Neoliberalism Survived the Financial Meltdown* (London: Verso, 2013) and Michael Behrent, "Liberalism without Humanism: Michel Foucault and the Free Market Creed, 1976–1979," in Daniel Zemora and Michael Behrent (eds), *Foucault and Neoliberalism* (Cambridge: Polity, 2016), 24–62.

41 See Wendy Brown, *Undoing the Demos: Neoliberalism's Stealth Revolution* (New York: Zone Books, 2015).

42 Gane is exemplary in this regard. He comments: "There is no argument here *for* the sovereignty of 'the market,' but rather an analysis of the discourses that have made such understandings and commitments possible." Gane, "Foucault's History of Neoliberalism," p. 56.

43 See Behrent, "Liberalism without Humanism," p. 75.

44 Gane, "Foucault's History of Neoliberalism," p. 57.

45 Gane, "Foucault's History of Neoliberalism," p. 57.

46 Rosalind Gill and Shani Orgad, "Confidence Culture and the Remaking of Feminism," in Farris and Rottenberg (eds), "Righting Feminism," 16–34.

47 Gill and Orgad, "Confidence Culture," p. 20.

48 Gill and Orgad, "Confidence Culture," p. 17.

49 Angela McRobbie, "Notes on the Perfect," *Australian Feminist Studies*, 30:38, 2015, 3–20, p. 4.
50 McRobbie, "Notes on the Perfect," p. 4.
51 McRobbie, "Notes on the Perfect," p. 9.
52 McRobbie, "Notes on the Perfect," p. 4.
53 McRobbie, "Notes on the Perfect," p. 4.
54 Gill and Orgad, "Confidence Culture," p. 32. My emphasis.
55 Foucault, *The Will to Knowledge: The History of Sexuality 1* [1976], translated by Robert Hurley (Harmondsworth: Penguin, 1990), pp. 95–96.
56 Ayn Rand, "The Virtue of Selfishness," in Ayn Rand (ed.), *The Virtue of Selfishness: A New Concept of Egoism* (New York: Signet, 1964), p. 142.
57 Rand, "The Virtue of Selfishness," p. 121.
58 Peter Schwartz, *In Defense of Selfishness: Why the Code of Self-Sacrifice is Unjust and Destructive* (Basingstoke: Palgrave MacMillan, 2015), p. 22.
59 Mimi Reisel Gladstein and Chris Matthew Sciabarra, "Introduction," in Mimi Reisel Gladstein and Chris Matthew Sciabarra (eds), *Feminist Interpretations of Ayn Rand* (Pennsylvania: The Pennsylvania State University Press, 1999), 1–21, p. 7.
60 Max Stirner, *The Ego and Its Own* [1844], edited by David Leopold (Cambridge: Cambridge University Press, 1995).
61 Cynthia Willet, Ellie Anderson and Diana Meyer, "Feminist Perspectives on the Self," *Stanford Encyclopedia of Philosophy*, https://plato.stanford.edu/entries/feminism-self/
62 Recent Kantian ethicists offer a more nuanced view of Kant's subject of reason. Onora O'Neil charges earlier readers of Kant with idealizing his view of human beings as autonomous and decontextualized, arguing that this is only one way of reading his work. See Onora O'Neill, *Bounds of Justice* (Cambridge: Cambridge University Press, 2000).
63 Willet, Anderson and Meyer, "Feminist Perspectives on the Self."
64 Simone de Beauvoir, *The Second Sex*, translated by Constance Borde and Sheila Malovany-Chevallier (London: Vintage, 2012), loc. 465. When citing electronic books that do not provide page numbers, the location of the quotation is indicated by "loc.".
65 Beauvoir, *The Second Sex*, loc. 4234.
66 Willet, Anderson and Meyer, "Feminist Perspectives on the Self."
67 For more, see Tina Chanter, *Ethics of Eros: Irigaray's Rewriting of the Philosophers* (New York: Routledge, 1995) and Patricia Hill Collins, *Black Feminist Thought* [1990], tenth anniversary second edition (New York: Routledge, 2000).
68 Hilde Lindemann, *Holding and Letting Go: The Social Practice of Personal Identities* (Oxford: Oxford University Press, 2014), p. ix.
69 The spelling of "phantasy" with "ph" in place of "f" is a convention from psychoanalytic criticism. It suggests a deep, unconscious, often collectively-held idea, rather than a conscious construction or a daydream.
70 Laura Sjoberg and Caron E. Gentry, *Mothers, Monsters, Whores: Women's Violence in Global Politics* (London; Zed Books, 2007), loc. 368.
71 The definition is often misattributed to Cheris Kramarae and Paula A. Treichler, as Shear used it in her review of their *Feminist Dictionary* (1986). See Deborah Cameron's blog post: https://debuk.wordpress.com/2019/01/26/radical-notions/?fbclid=IwAR0rEEa-3_K3QLx7IFORaMfpgwUm7B0yhGln-Xt0ysCJTturjTL1yqDVctw. See also: Marie Shear, "Media Watch," *New Directions for Women*, 15:3, 1986, p.6. Can be viewed at: https://voices.revealdigital.com/cgi-bin/independentvoices?a=d&d=DGBHBCA19860601.1.6&srpos=23&e=-------en-20-DGBHBCA-21--txt-txIN-mar ie+shear--------------1#
72 Jean F. O'Barr, *Feminism in Action: Building Institutions and Community through Women's Studies* (Chapel Hill: The University of North Carolina Press, 1994), p. 275.
73 Julia Kristeva, *This Incredible Need to Believe* (New York: Columbia University Press, 2009), p. 38.

74 For an explanation of the term (from a critical point of view), see, for example, Jason Wilson, "'Cultural Marxism': A Uniting Theory for Rightwingers Who Love to Play the Victim," *The Guardian*, 19 January 2015, https://www.theguardian.com/commentisfree/2015/jan/19/cultural-marxism-a-uniting-theory-for-rightwingers-who-love-to-play-the-victim

75 Rand, "*The Virtue of Selfishness*," p. 195.

76 The metaphor of "waves" to describe the history of feminism is a much-debated and contentious one, since it can assume a straightforward generational trajectory, rather than acknowledging overlaps, traces, and discontinuities in feminist activism. For practical purposes, however, in this book I will use the shorthand "first wave" to describe the liberal, rights-based feminism of the nineteenth and early-twentieth century, including the activism of the suffragettes; "second wave" to describe the politics of the 1960s, 1970s, and 1980s that focused on both the radical critique of patriarchy (radical feminism) and more reform-based agendas (liberal feminism); "third wave" to describe 1990s responses to these earlier feminist agendas and gains, often known as "postfeminism;" and "fourth wave" to describe the contemporary, online forms of feminism that have sparked such movements as "#metoo." There is, however, considerable overlap between the third and fourth waves, and both are associated with "intersectionality." For critiques of the wave metaphor, see Clare Hemmings, "Telling feminist stories," *Feminist Theory*, 6:2, 2005, 115–139 and Linda Nicholson, "Feminism in 'Waves': A Useful Metaphor or Not?," in Carole R. McCann and Seung-Kyung Kim (eds), *Feminist Theory Reader: Local and Global Perspectives* (New York: Routledge, 2017), 43–50.

1

THE PSYCHOPATHOLOGY OF SELFISHNESS

On narcissism and norms of gender

> The vices attributed to individualism by its critics are self-absorption, narcissism, unscrupulous competition, alienation, atomism, privatism, deviance, rationalization, worship of objectivity, relativism and nihilism.
>
> (Alan Waterman, *The Psychology of Individualism*, 1984)

> Much of our distress comes from a sense of disconnection. We have a narcissistic society where self-promotion and individuality seem to be essential, yet in our hearts that's not what we want. We want to be part of a community, we want to be supported when we're struggling, we want a sense of belonging. Being extraordinary is not a necessary component to being loved.
>
> (Pat MacDonald, cited in *The Guardian*, 2 March 2016)

> I think writers and artists are the most narcissistic people. I mustn't say this, I like many of them.
>
> (Sylvia Plath, interview with Peter Orr, 1962)

Narcissism is one of those terms that has both a lay meaning and a technical one. In everyday social discourse, narcissism has come to mean vanity, toxic self-obsession, egotism, and – most literally – excessive self-love. In the psy sciences its definition has evolved over time from Freud's turn-of-the-century Vienna, where it is understood as a failure of mature, adult "object love" to its current manifestation as a "personality disorder" in twenty-first-century psychiatry. It is a fascinating and timely concept, as it is at once an individual diagnosis of pathology with a discrete clinical history, and yet also it has become a metaphorical descriptor of our modern and post-modern Western cultural Zeitgeist. Certain periods of European and North American history have been characterized as eras with an especially narcissistic character. These include the nineteenth-century fin de siècle, characterized by the rise of the modern individual and by Decadent solipsism, the "permissive" post-1960s era (with the 1970s being dubbed the "Me Decade"[1]), and most recently, the decades characterized by what is often known as "neoliberalism," an economic philosophy of free markets that has allegedly led, according to critics, to selfish, atomized, unhappy citizens who view themselves first as consumers and a generation of young people obsessed with image and surface. (Psychologist Oliver James and psychoanalyst Paul Verhaeghe have both written searing critiques of the effects of this worldview on the subjects living with it.[2]) In 2000, psychoanalytic critic Jessica Benjamin stated that in our consumerist and celebrity-obsessed culture, "Narcissus has replaced Oedipus as the myth of our time."[3] Yet, while there may be some validity to seeing narcissism as a description of the collective character of our culture, it is also the case that both diagnoses of individual narcissism as a pathological clinical entity and accusations of cultural narcissism as a more widespread phenomenon can reveal much about attitudes to gender in contemporary culture, since narcissism has a particularly gendered history.[4]

In this chapter, I will explore the history of the gendering of the clinical concept of narcissism in the psy sciences. My history will cover narcissism in the foundational texts and ideas of psychoanalysis that were produced in Europe at the turn of the century, in twentieth-century American ego-psychology (which both built on and deviated from psychoanalysis), and in the American Psychiatric Association's diagnostic schema which first included "narcissistic personality disorder" in the *Diagnostic and Statistical Manual of Mental Disorders* in *DSM III*, published in 1980. I will also read the foundational text of psychoanalytic theory about narcissism, Sigmund Freud's "On Narcissism: An Introduction" (1914), with and through historically contemporaneous literary portrayals of female "narcissism" by the French Decadent writer Rachilde (Marguerite Vallette-Eymery, 1860–1953). I will then contextualize later psychological and psychiatric theories of narcissism by reading them alongside social commentary about cultural narcissism in order to further our understanding of the process of subjectification of the gendered narcissistic subject. I mean this, of course, in the broadly Foucauldian sense of a "specified individual,"[5] who comes about, can be thought, and can think themselves only as a result of the meeting of particular historical epistemological disciplines and discourses. In this case, those discourses are clinical psychology and psychiatry, the rise of economic/philosophical ideologies of individualism, and the socially changing gender roles brought about by the women's liberation movement and the branches of feminism which have followed on from it. I will conclude by making some broader points about the ways in which the conceptualization of specifically female narcissism may say as much about attitudes to women in modern Western culture, as about the so-called narcissistic women in question. I want to ask what notions of female narcissism reveal about the forms of female selfhood that are psychosocially allowed for. I also want to explore the extent to which narcissism really can be understandable as self-love or self-regard (the focus of this book), as distinct from their opposite – a compensation for damaged self-regard – since narcissism is a knotty concept that seems, according to those experts who write on it, to have as much to do with fragility as self-valuation, and to be far from a straightforward synonym for extreme selfishness or self-interest. Indeed, for Nathaniel Branden, the father of the modern self-esteem movement and Ayn Rand's sometime intellectual heir, narcissism is not a manifestation of genuine self-worth – excessive or otherwise – but, rather, a counterfeit form of it.[6]

Freud's female narcissist – a deviation from a myth

The figure who lent his name to the concept we are considering, Narcissus, the beautiful youth of Greek mythology, is a tragic and a cautionary one. Cursed by Nemesis, a goddess whose remit was to guard against hubris, Narcissus was compelled to fall in love with his own image, glimpsed in a pool. Unable to leave self-contemplation, even for a moment, or to accept the advances of other would-be lovers, Narcissus pined to death as the result of unrequited desire for his own image. The gendering of the Narcissus myth is telling. The vain and self-loving figure is male. Ovid's *Metamorphoses* introduced the female figure of Echo, who came upon Narcissus while out walking. When Narcissus called out "who's there?" Echo was compelled to repeat his words, fell in love with the beautiful youth, and became henceforth nothing but an echo when he rejected her, deprived of the ability to voice her desire. In Ovid's version, Nemesis's punishment of Narcissus came as a direct result of his treatment of Echo. In a 1988 book that reads the Narcissus and Echo myth as a structuring model for the relationships between the sexes drawn in a selection of modern French literary narratives, Naomi Segal argues that, archetypically, male figures function as narrative doubles, while female characters function as mere echos.[7] She argues for the need to restore Echo's desire, and to acknowledge the silenced voice of female, here heterosexual, desire that is cast into shadow by the grandiosity of Narcissus's self-focused plight. While, as I will explore in what follows, the psychological diagnosis to which Narcissus lent his name has little to do with the more fanciful details of the myth, something of the gender power play and politics of Ovid's version of the myth, as brought out by Segal's innovative reading, can indeed be discerned.

In his essay "On Narcissism: An Introduction" Freud attributes the first coining of the term, understood as a psychological pathology, to Paul Näcke, the Russian-born, German-based criminologist and sexologist, who used it in 1899.[8] Subsequently, Freud acknowledged that Havelock Ellis had used the term "narcissus-like" to describe a psychological attitude in 1898, a year earlier than Näcke.[9] Significantly, Näcke's 1899 account of "Narzissmus" categorized it primarily as a sexual perversion rather than as the regressive ego disturbance it would become for Freud. In Näcke's version, the narcissistic pervert desires, eroticizes, and stimulates his own body and derives complete satisfaction from this autoeroticism, in the very way, he says, that a "normal" person would with a sexual partner. In this respect, Näcke's version of narcissism is close to the autoerotic and romantic inspiration provided by the figure of Narcissus, who eschewed Echo's wooing in favour of complete, all-consuming self-love to the point of annihilation. Freud's essay is groundbreaking in that it deviates from Näcke's classification of narcissism as one of the sexual perversions and provides the point of origin for the way in which subsequent iterations – both clinical and cultural – of narcissism would be understood (whether in the form of a building-upon or reacting-against its tenets).

The essay proceeds according to a rather typical Freudian method and logic. Freud begins by seeking evidence of pathological narcissistic phenomena before arriving at the conclusion that there is also such a thing as healthy or normal narcissism. The ego comes into being, Freud speculates, by taking the self as the first love object (supplanting primary mother-love). This is primary narcissism. This is in line with Freud's major contribution to our understanding of human psychology, which holds that all of us are, to some degree, sick – at the very least neurotic – as a result of the trauma of socio-psychical development through which we all pass: the so-called "psychopathology of everyday life." Freud locates the child's earliest developmental stage as the autoerotic stage that precedes both the primary narcissism that gives birth to the ego, and the establishment of object relations. So, Freud remarks, "we are bound to suppose that a unity comparable to the ego cannot exist in the individual from the start; the ego has to be developed. The auto-erotic instincts, however, are there from the very first ..."[10] He highlights primary narcissism as a "normal" stage in psychosexual and ego development, but one that could be subject to arrest or regression in adulthood, and which could become psychopathological. For Freud, the growing child must choose between self and mother (and later mother-substitute) as sexual object. Freud writes:

> We say that a human being has originally two sexual objects – himself and the woman who nurses him – and in doing so we are postulating a primary narcissism in everyone, which may in some cases manifest itself in a dominating fashion in his object choice.[11]

Freud goes on to differentiate between male and female narcissism in a way that seems at first glance to suggest that *women* are more likely than men to be narcissistic. Men over-value their sexual object, he says, drawing on their latent primary narcissistic energy that has been diverted into son-to-mother-love (his translator, James Strachey, calls this the "anaclitic" type of love. In the original German "anaclisis" is *Anlehnung*). Women, on the other hand, develop their affect differently, owing in part to genital difference and penis envy. Woman, as the embodiment of lack, compensates for her insignificant genitalia with the satisfaction gained from her ability to attract and be attractive; she eroticizes her own desirability. Additionally, the ambivalence that Freud insists girls feel with regard to their mothers – that original love object who will become both erotic rival and source of disappointment on learning of the fact of sexual difference, means that she has no object to idealize unproblematically in the way that sons do. This leads women to what Freud calls the narcissistic type of love:

> With the onset of puberty the maturing of the female sexual organs [...] seems to bring about an intensification of the original narcissism, and this is unfavourable to the development of a true object-choice with its accompanying sexual overvaluation. Women, especially if they grow up with good looks, develop a certain self-contentment [...] Strictly speaking, it is only themselves that such women love with an intensity comparable to that of the man's love for them. Nor does their need lie in the direction of loving, but of being loved...[12]

Unlike our Classical mythical version of Narcissus, so in love with himself that it is of no interest to him how others may perceive him, Freud's female narcissists are described as having at best a "self-contentment" and a self-love based precisely on how attractive they are (i.e. how attractive others find them), so that their attitude to themselves is as an object; that is, a part of their psyche worships their physical being *as if that part were a man admiring a woman*. The heteronormative logic of Freud's discussion of female narcissism is striking. As has been much discussed in gay and lesbian studies, Freud sees gay men as essentially acting on a version of a narcissistic form of love, cathecting the image of themselves narcissistically in the other, rather than loving another separate person maturely, as he claims heterosexual men do.[13] It is very telling, however, that Freud has nothing whatsoever to say about narcissism and lesbians.[14]

Freud goes on to say that men will find female narcissists the most attractive among women because: "another person's narcissism has a great attraction for those who have renounced part of their own narcissism and are in search of object-love."[15] Freud's claim that men are attracted to narcissistic women is made using the most dubious and curious of analogies. Consider the following:

> The charm of a child lies to a great extent in his narcissism, his self-contentment and inaccessibility, just as does the charm of certain animals which seem not to concern themselves about us, such as cats and the large beasts of prey. Indeed, even great criminals and humorists, as they are represented in literature, compel our interest by the narcissistic consistency with which they manage to keep away from their ego anything that would diminish it.[16]

This is a bizarre and ambivalent passage in which narcissistic women are charming and fascinating for men because they resemble either small children or beasts; they are both infantilized and dehumanized. But, second, Freud calls on the discursive figure of the conscience-free, criminal genius or artist – the exceptional figure who falls outside of the usual codes of common morality and who was the subject of a previous book of mine.[17] This is the figure whom today we might call the psychopath. Freud does this in order to mythologize the narcissistic woman's disinterest in the desperate affections of the man who, he claims, would idolize and idealize her for having retained the narcissism he has renounced. What is notable here is that Freud seems to be suggesting at first glance that the gender of Narcissus and Echo might well be reversed, with a heterosexual male Echo pining for a self-absorbed female Narcissus – or Narcissa.

Yet, misogyny, whether in the form of dehumanization or of pedestal placing, is nevertheless misogyny. And, perhaps aware of some sexist projection in the terms he uses, Freud goes on to reassure us that he doesn't wish to "depreciate" all women,[18] and he backtracks to state that these love-styles are masculine and feminine *positions* not male and female immutable identities. There are even some women who love according to the mature, masculine, anaclitic type, he tells us – but these are the exceptions. In her feminist essay on Freud's account of female narcissism, "The Narcissistic Woman" (1980), Sarah Kofman asks:

> In the name of what would woman's narcissism be capable of depreciating her? In the name of what if not of a certain ethics which identifies narcissism with an egoism which must be overcome and not only because it would be a fixation or regression to an infantile libidinal stage?[19]

Kofman asks this intriguing question, but rather than going on to answer or discuss it, it remains rhetorical in her text. My reading of Freud's essay in answer to Kofman's question would suggest that Freud is guilty of disparaging so-called narcissistic women because egoism is something that it is incumbent upon women to overcome, as this is in the interests of *fulfilling their social role*, as well as of acquiring *his idea* of psychological and emotional maturity. It strikes me that one can glean a certain indignation in Freud's account of women who remain "cold and indifferent" to men, such that he has to reduce any *genuine* self-esteem, self-love, or self-interest a woman might possess to a pathology of immaturity. Thus, to answer Kofman's question, it would be in the name and in the interest of *masculine ego*. It is crucial to note that, if the female narcissist that Freud identifies "loves herself," it is not in a way that reflects genuine self-worth or self-esteem – much less rational self-interest. Rather it is as a result of the image of herself *as desirable to the other*, seen in Freud's insistence on female narcissism being a flaw especially of the conventionally good-looking. It seems that a synonym for Freud's version of female narcissism would simply be "female vanity." And all of this may, in short, betray little more than bitterness that women are not willing to make themselves sexually available, all of the time, to the men who desire them. The incumbency I allude to above thus takes on the cultural weight of an ethical imperative in patriarchy, as well as a mental health imperative in psychoanalysis, while it may in fact be no more than a revelation of male entitlement.

Freud's whole view of the "masculine type of love" and the "feminine type of love" is at best the result of a rather bizarre logic, and at worst it is a misrepresentation of the reality of the social power disparity between the sexes, possibly as a result of projection. If we accept for a moment – as a thought experiment – the model of male (anaclitic) and female (narcissistic) love that Freud suggests, we might look for reasons other than genital security or insecurity (a claim that is just so Freudian it is almost self-parody) to account for it, and we may ask why men might be secure enough to form attachments in which they overvalue a love object outside of themselves while women are not. We might then posit that this would surely be because, historically, male children have been valorized as subjects, citizens, *selves*, with an active social role which patriarchy traditionally allocates them, while women have not.

Moreover, the language of Freudian discourse which talks of "objects," even as this doesn't explicitly mean "objectification" in the contemporary ethical or feminist sense of turning a person into a thing via dehumanization, never the less reveals an underlying truth about the logic of the Freudian system. When Freud says that "men over-value their sexual object," he implies that (heterosexual) men overvalue the silly, vain, pretty little women they choose because women are perceived socially, culturally, psychically, politically as *less than* and precisely as "for being desired." That is, women in the society Freud describes *are* objects. The famous Freudian contention, from another of his papers, that it is not possible to desire and to identify with the same other (logically precluding the possibility of homosexuality), may be empirically untrue as an absolute, but in the context of heteropatriarchal eros, it reveals a fundamental structural truth. Men are raised to objectify women as other, not to see women as "selves" comparable to them. And, subject to the same heteropatriarchal currents, it would be utterly unsurprising if some women did as Freud claims they do, and internalized the notion that beauty and desirability is what they are for – is all that they are. In the system described, women are estranged from processes of reciprocal desire from the standpoint of subject-to-subject equality, and from genuine self-esteem or self-interest. Though Freud may not have intended it, reading him in this way allows us to see a critique of the heteropatriarchal desiring system *tout court*.

To raise one final point regarding Freud's essay: if the ennobling model of male love as other-oriented and mature, while female love is seen as vain and selfish, is not problematic enough, Freud then drops the following bombshell:

> Even for narcissistic women, whose attitude towards men remains cool, there is a road which leads to complete object-love. In the child which they bear, a part of their own body confronts them like an extraneous object, to which, starting out from their narcissism, they can then give complete object-love.[20]

So, women may overcome their unseemly narcissistic love by means of fulfilling their presumed biological and psychical destiny as mothers. Freud extends this principle (to some degree) to fathers as well, writing "Parental love, which is so moving and at bottom so childish, is nothing but the parents' narcissism born again, which, transformed into object-love, unmistakably reveals its former nature."[21] So, the implication is clear: women are especially childlike, vain, petty and immature. Via parenthood, they might just convert these qualities into the secondary, socially acceptable, form of narcissism that seeks to elevate one's child into the most special and precious object. Freud refers to parents' typical idealization of their child in the phrase "His Majesty the Baby,"[22] which he renders in English in the original German text. This also slyly, and perhaps unconsciously, conveys which sex he assumes is likely to be the most treasured. The message with which Freud leaves narcissistic women is therefore the following: "In order to escape the malady of selfishness, have a baby!"

Rachilde: A female narcissist before (and against) Freud

As has been argued in much of my previous work, and in work by scholars such as Peter Cryle, Rachel Mesch, and Anna Katharina Schaffner,[23] literature in the modern period, produced at the same time, and under the same historical conditions, as the burgeoning psy sciences, may in many cases offer alternative forms of sexual knowledge to the medical disciplines of sexology and psychoanalysis (just as psychoanalytic texts can be read "as literature"). Of especial interest here is the fact that the turn of the century in Europe has been described as an especially narcissistic epoch and the literature it produced thus provides a rich resource to mine for imaginings of desires and subjectivities that we might retrospectively call "narcissistic."

Diana Holmes has described the Decadents at the turn of the century in France as "instinctively more right- than left-wing" in their "rejection of democracy [which they understood as] the reign of the barbarians"[24] Yet, unlike the establishmentarian French right wing, they were also anarchic and counter-cultural in their critique of bourgeois mores and morality, and in their morbid and ambivalent celebration of the perceived grand decline of society. The European Decadents were that paradox: *a group of individualists*. Robert Ziegler associates the Decadent mindset of the turn-of-the-century with narcissism: "For the Decadents who believed themselves confined to their individual perceptions, narcissism is as much a curse as a psychological predisposition;"[25] while, in *The Hysteric's Revenge*, Mesch points out a gendered dimension to fin-de-siècle narcissism, when she writes that: "in the shorthand of [the] Belle Époque ... femininity was associated with inferiority, excess of emotion, *narcissism*."[26]

A key figure to consider with regard to narcissism and femaleness in this period is Rachilde, the only French female Decadent writer whose works have survived to the present day (and enjoyed something of a resurgence of popularity latterly). Writing just before Freud's essay on narcissism, but in terms that sometimes read uncannily as if they are a direct riposte to him and to it, Rachilde offers a number of reflections on female selfishness, an investment in vanity that resembles Freud's narcissism, and the condition of being female. Literary critics writing on Rachilde have been keen to note the narcissism of her characters. Melanie Hawthorne notes that "several [...] works by Rachilde open with [female] characters looking in mirrors," a "motif" commonly used to "illustrate the narcissism of the hero."[27] And in her study of female perversions in literature of the nineteenth century, Julie Lokis identifies two potentially narcissistic Rachildian characters: Éliante Donalger in *La Jongleuse* (The [female] Juggler) (1900) and Mary Barbe in *La Marquise de Sade* (1887).[28]

In *La Jongleuse*, the heroine, Éliante, a widow and amateur juggler with knives, eschews sexual relations with her younger suitor, Léon Reille, instead reaching orgasm alone as she masturbates using a life-size, human-form statue while he looks on. Léon's words, the first time this happens, summarize the horror of the spectacle of female self-sufficiency for the turn-of-the-century male: "But it's scandalous! There ... in front of me ... without me? No, it's just abominable."[29] He makes this comment even as he himself articulates a philosophy of narcissism: "Believe me, darling; one is not in love with anyone other than oneself."[30] That self-love is acceptable for the male but forbidden (and abominable) in the female is the message against which Rachilde's text works. Éliante resists Léon's sexual advances and his proposals of marriage throughout the novel, attempting instead to persuade him to marry her young niece, Missy. In the climactic scenes of the novel, Éliante tricks Léon into going to bed with Missy by pretending to be her. As she watches them engage in sexual relations, Éliante stabs herself fatally using one of her juggling knives in what Mesch has described as a "joyful suicide."[31]

This female protagonist's refusal of heterosexual intercourse is explained in her words "I'm disgusted by intercourse. It weakens me, and does not satisfy me erotically."[32] Her pleasure instead is described as: "being happy, all alone, arms tightly crossed over my chest, thighs hermetically sealed, smiling like a virgin taking communion."[33] The self-satisfaction that this suggests is described by Rachilde's biographer Holmes as "narcissistic pleasure."[34] And Lokis writes: "The authority Éliante holds over her own body allows her to resist men's sexual advances and displace male sexual identification," while "juggling with knives is a means [...] to create her own world and her own fantasy."[35] The properly self-contained woman, whose vanity is not in the interests of seeking recognition from men, offers a psycho-sexual female figure that pre-dates and contradicts Freud's model of narcissistic femininity as paradoxically all about being for the other – as an object to be desired.

Rachilde's *La Marquise de Sade* imagines the *éducation sentimentale* of a female sadist, Mary Barbe, the daughter of a military father and a neurasthenic mother who dies giving birth to Mary's brother. Mary is a heroine who, throughout the novel, uses her feminine beauty to manipulate men in the service of obtaining greater freedom in a patriarchal social order in which women belong to men. To escape the guardianship of her uncle, following her father's death, Mary marries Louis de Caumont, whom she will later murder by poisoning, leaving her financially independent and socially free in the role of widow. (The role of widow as one allowing for exceptional female self-fulness is explored in many of Rachilde's novels and in Lokis's psychoanalytic reading of them.) Yet, despite appealing to men by means of her beauty and feminine grooming, like Éliante, Mary's sexuality and sense of self are not rooted in the dependent feminine narcissism of finding pleasure in the desire men have for her as object, in the Freudian sense. Instead, being sexually appealing is a consciously calculated means of advancing socially, while she finds her sexual thrills in active sadism and her existential thrills in murder.

Moreover, Mary's is a female selfishness that refuses – as an act of rational will – the Freudian exhortation for women to find their proper object-love in a baby. Consider Mary's words to her husband on their wedding night:

> Louis, I have decided not to give you an heir. [...] I do not want to get ugly nor to suffer. What is more, *I am enough*, JUST BY BEING, and if I could take the world with me when I die, I would do so.[36]

The rareness of the position being articulated here is borne out by Rachilde's insistence on the typographical peculiarities seen in the piece of dialogue. The italics and upper-case letters that appeared in the manuscript were to be scrupulously replicated in published editions of *La Marquise de Sade*. Words which express what is not habitually expressed appear in a form that sets them visibly apart from regular speech. The "I am enough" bespeaks disobedience to three discourses about what women are supposed to be: first, subject to a psychological need to bear children in order to justify their own lives and overcome their own inadequate, childlike vanity, pace Freud; second, the complements of men, in a heteropatriarchal logic that is as self-serving as it is tendentious; and third, profoundly social animals, natural carers for others and essentially predisposed to be for the interests of collectivity. It is in this third regard that Mary's gesture of refusal of female selflessness – her insistence instead on self-*ful*-ness – is most pertinent for the larger argument I am making in this book.

At the time of its publication, Rachilde's work was not critiqued as immoral in terms of its Decadent thematics or its individualistic, anti-social, narcissistic ideals per se; rather it was critiqued in specifically gendered terms. The themes in Rachilde's work – gender inversion, sexual perversion, autoeroticism, and baroque violence – were not at all unusual in the context of Decadent writing. But, whereas in response to the works of her male contemporaries, critics like Jules Boissière and Henri Fouquier espied subtle parody and social critique in such tropes, they instead termed Rachilde and her work variously "sadistic", "ghoulish", and "perverted."[37] For a woman to have imagined the strong, perverse, female protagonists against society who populated her novels led to her being (unofficially) diagnosed as suffering from a specifically feminine kind of neurosis. Even Maurice Barrès, a professed admirer of Rachilde's writing, wrote in the preface of her novel of gender inversion, *Monsieur Vénus* in 1884, that it was the product of "the malady of the century," i.e. hysteria, and that Rachilde, then a young woman of 20, should be understood as "a neurotic" and "a feverish woman," who was "uniquely governed by instinct."[38]

In her 1928 tract *Pourquoi je ne suis pas féministe* (Why I am not a feminist), Rachilde explains that "I've always acted as an individual, never thinking of founding a society or overturning the one that exists."[39] Adopting wholesale the discourses about women that characterize her cultural moment, and that coloured the pathologizing and reductive critical reception of her own work, Rachilde figures women as physiologically and psychologically weaker than, and therefore inferior to, men: "Women are the inferior siblings of men simply because they have physical weaknesses."[40] And, echoing the logic of feminine nervous frailty and hysterical neurosis voiced by male literary critics in judgment of her, she writes: "I am a creature endowed, like all women, with excessive neurosis."[41] Rachilde, then, seems to have operated a schizoid view of women and of herself. On the one hand, she argued for her right to freedom as an individual social and creative agent who claimed "I love logic above all things"[42] and allowed herself to imagine the audacious, self-focused, society-defying female characters who populate her fiction. On the other hand, she accepted that, insofar as she was biologically and psychologically a woman, she was irredeemably less robust – and therefore *less* – than a man. That the notion of identifying proudly as a woman writer or a feminist should have been unthinkable to Rachilde is understandable in light of this cognitive dissonance, and it is unsurprising that her calling card bore the legend: "Rachilde: Homme de lettres" (Rachilde: Man of Letters).

However, in more reflective and measured mode, Rachilde wrote:

> I've always regretted that I wasn't a man, not because I value one half of humanity more than the other half, but because, obliged by duty or taste to live like a man, to carry all alone the heavy burden of life during my youth, it would have been preferable to have at least had the privileges of being male.[43]

This strikingly insightful comment shows Rachilde's frustration with the fact that, in her culture, the only way to operate as a functional, agentic subject and to have one's strengths recognized would be to be male. Yet she does not conclude from this that the way to achieve her desired right to personhood would be to make common cause with other women with the same ambitions and sense of injustice, and attempt to change society's views of men and women. Rather she believes that, in preferring logic and desiring an active social role, she must take up the mantle of honorary man in three ways: by cross-dressing while out in the public sphere; by revelling in the titles of "Man of Letters" and "Mlle Baudelaire," a sobriquet given to her by Maurice Barrès; and by consciously embracing and identifying with a stereotypical masculine perspective, including the denigration of women as inferior.

Regardless of Rachilde's own, real-life, ambivalence about women's abilities and qualities, what is of particular note here is that, while Rachilde's heroines are (of course) fictional, literary female authorship demonstrates that self-sufficient and eccentric female subjects can be *thought* and *imagined* despite the lack of psychological models to do them justice.[44] They also came to life on the page despite the fact that their reception – and that of their author – were inevitably subjected to pathologizing, reductive understandings. The label "hysteric," levelled at both Rachilde and her heroines, is nothing but an example of a misogynistic projection onto, and the desire to exert control over, excessively self-ful women who flout understandings of what women are. The real sadness, in the case of Rachilde, is that she too seems, at the deepest level of her personal reflections, to have internalized the prevailing view of female lack.

Post-Freudian views of narcissism

In studying diagnoses that produce subjects of psychological and sexual peculiarity, it is often observed that there is shift in the concentration of activity from the Northern Europe of the late-nineteenth century to the Anglophone USA by the mid-twentieth century. The most prominent psychoanalytic writers on narcissism after Freud were two Austrian-Americans, Heinz Kohut and Otto Kernberg, whose theories of, and treatment protocols for, narcissism differed considerably, leading to schisms and disagreements between them and their adherents. Both were most active in their research and writing on narcissism in the decade of the 1970s. This may not be coincidental since, as I shall go on to explore below, social commentators deemed this the "Me Decade." Where Kernberg synthesized the ego-psychology then popular in the USA with psychoanalytic relations theory, especially the work of Melanie Klein and W.R.D. Fairbairn, Kohut, on the other hand, eventually repudiated ego-psychology altogether and founded a new school of psychoanalysis called "self-psychology," incorporating the methods and insights of the Hungarian school represented by Sandor Ferenczi and Michael Balint. Both psychoanalysts began to use the language of "personality disorder," which had not appeared in classical Freudian psychoanalysis and which would ultimately be borrowed by the American Psychiatric Association for its system of diagnostic classification in 1980.[45]

In his book *The Analysis of the Self: A Systematic Approach to the Psychoanalytic Treatment of Narcissistic Personality Disorders* (1971), Kohut argued that in order to develop secure attachment and self-image, children need to idealize admired figures and have that admiration mirrored back to them by empathic parent figures (a role that may also be played by therapists in later life). Narcissism for Kohut is therefore the result of inadequate attachment. Crucially, while saying little about specifically female narcissism itself, Kohut implied that the increased employment of women outside the home was a factor in the creation of narcissistic children with insecure attachment, inaugurating a fashion for blaming selfish women for their children's sufferings that is still with us today.

For Kernberg, by contrast, the self consists of multiple self-representations which it must work to integrate. He theorized three types of narcissism: normal infantile narcissism, normal adult narcissism, and pathological adult narcissism. Normal or healthy adult narcissism occurs as a result of erotic investment in the self, mediated equally by the involvement of the ego, superego, and id, such that the self is integrated. Pathological narcissism for Kernberg is the result of id-driven libidinal investment in an undeveloped, pathological, and unintegrated self, or a self against which the subject feels a degree of unworked-through hostility in combination with erotic attachment. Severe pathological narcissism is characterized for Kernberg by the perception of having obtained "a sense of superiority and triumph over life and death."[46]

Works by Kohut and Kernberg and their followers formed the canon and consensus on narcissism to which those writing in the psychoanalytic tradition and within the field of the psychology of women would respond. Within the tradition of object relations theory, feminist sociologist and psychoanalyst Nancy Chodorow both worked within the terms of and argued against the grain of the gender-neutral aspects of the attachment theory propounded by Kohut. She argues that it is observable that children tend in all cases to be socialized differently according to their sex, such that girls and women are encouraged to develop a stronger sense of relatedness and capacity for interpersonal attachments and empathy, in comparison to boys and men who are socialized to prize autonomy and individuation.[47] Where empathy is absent or deficient (in parenting or relating to others), Chodorow attributes this to a particular relationship to self, characterized by lack. She borrows from the words of psychoanalyst Enid Balint to describe "a state she calls 'being empty of oneself' – a feeling of lack of self or emptiness."[48] She goes on to specify that "women are more likely [than men] to experience themselves this way. Women who feel empty of themselves feel that they are not being accorded a separate reality nor the agency to interpret the world in their own way."[49] Unfortunately for mothers everywhere, Chodorow concludes: "This feeling has its origins in the early mother-daughter relationship."[50]

In an article from 1985 entitled "Gender and Narcissism," Ilene Philipson critiques much existing psychological and psychoanalytic writing on narcissism for making it "gender neutral."[51] She suggests that family dynamics lead to expressions of narcissistic psychopathology that are different in boys and in girls. Following Kohut, she argues that narcissism is a result of inadequate attachment and results primarily from narcissistic mothers who respond with a lack of empathy to the child's developing sense of self. Philipson argues that, while low self-esteem and a deficient psychic structure are at the root of both male and female narcissism, and "while both males and females may experience mothers' emotional inconsistency or faulty empathy, their characteristic ways of reacting to this are different,"[52] resulting in specifically gendered narcissistic outcomes. She claims that narcissistic mothers are more likely to treat their daughters as extensions of themselves, resulting in the daughters suffering from a particularly insecure self-image and seeking the narcissistic compensation of attaching themselves to outstanding figures, such as rich or powerful male partners, in order to boost their sense of esteem and narcissism by proxy. (She does, however, also make mention of Annie Reich's theory "that the attempt to become 'one with a grandiose love partner was related to the original homosexual object, the mother, primitive attachments to whom had never been relinquished',," in a rare example in this literature of acknowledging female homosexuality – even as unconscious phantasy.[53]) Sons of such un-empathic mothers, on the other hand, will themselves desire to *be* those outstanding, rich, successful figures. This relates back to Chodorow's psychological claim that women in general understand their "self" as in relation to others, while men see themselves as starkly individuated (even if as a narcissistic defence against childhood insecure attachment). In the case of so-called narcissists, then, girls seek self-esteem through fusion and merger with omnipotent others (as the mother has encouraged such fusion and blurring of boundaries during early years) while sons seek defensive separateness from the mother, resulting in behaviour that is grandiose and self-centred.

It is worth pointing out here the fact that the focus is consistently placed upon mothers in both classical Freudian and this later psychoanalytically informed literature for *creating* narcissistic children as well as for *being* narcissistic – or at least selfish – mothers (while at the same time insisting on the benefits of motherhood for women as the route to maturity). And this obtains in two senses. First, according to the logic of Freud's model, we have seen the theory that all parenting involves the re-orienting of narcissism from self into that extension of self that is the majestic offspring, but that this is psychologically more important for mothers than for fathers. (This is the idea against which Rachilde's heroine Mary Barbe rails, *avant la lettre* and against the grain.) Second, we see that the psychological writing on narcissistic children from the 1970s and 1980s focuses on the parenting and empathic deficiencies of mothers. Even if Philipson is clear that "a mother could be feeling abandoned, frustrated, harried, or helpless and still her child may experience her as simply angry or rejecting and unavailable,"[54] nevertheless, the burden of perfect, patient, empathic benevolence in creating the child's stable sense of self falls to the mother, and the role of the father is seldom even mentioned.

The "Me Decade"

At the same time as debates in psychoanalysis and ego-psychology about the correct aetiology, definition, and diagnostic criteria of narcissism were active, a range of cultural commentators, also mainly located in the USA, described and critiqued what they perceived to be an increasingly narcissistic society. These included, prominently, the founder of New Journalism, Tom Wolfe, who, in 1976, dubbed the 1970s the "Me Decade," a catchphrase that would appear on the front of *New York Magazine* on 23 August of that year, along with a photograph of a number of men and women wearing T-shirts emblazoned with the word "ME." (See Figure 1.1) Wolfe attributes the rise of a culture of self-interest and instant gratification to the post-War economic boom, thanks to which "ordinary people" could pursue material betterment and leisure. He writes: "once the dreary little bastards started getting money in the 1940s [...] they took their money and ran. [...] They've created the greatest age of individualism in American history!"[55]

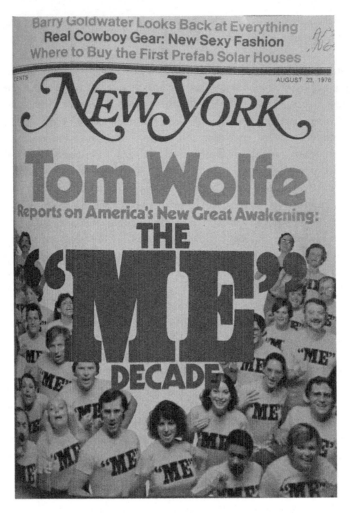

FIGURE 1.1   Cover of *New York*, 23 August 1976. Photograph by Erna Cooper.

Influenced by Wolfe's coining, albeit coming from a radically different political perspective, perhaps the most influential commentator on what was dubbed "the new narcissism" was Christopher Lasch, ostensibly a Marxist. His book *The Culture of Narcissism* (1979), a reflection on social changes in America over the past decade, charts a "narcissistic decline" precipitated by an attack on patriarchal values and seen as having a disastrous effect on the population. Men become effeminate and narcissistic as a result of eroded social authority and an insufficiently authoritarian ego-ideal; they do not identify with "work ethic […] and responsibilities," but with "an ethic of leisure, hedonism, and self-fulfilment."[56] The model laid down by Kohut in particular is visible in Lasch's cultural analysis: society as a whole is failing to give its children, i.e. its citizenry, the strong boundaries needed for healthy adaptation.

Ilene Philipson asks:

> When Christopher Lasch speaks of a world populated by exploitative, com-
> petitive, and emotionally impoverished narcissists, our vision is of men and
> women who mutually exploit and compete with each other in a society in
> which mere psychic survival has replaced any desire for achievement, suc-
> cess, or intimacy. [...] Women and men share equally in their culpability
> for the existence of the culture of narcissism and in the emotional isolation
> and psychic misery of the narcissistic personality. But is this really the case?
> Are women as likely to be narcissistic as men?[57]

Where Lasch refers to women living in this narcissistic dystopia at all, it is in
the context of sex role transgression, abandonment of their traditional place in
the family unit, and "unladylike" behaviour (the latter being an odd choice of
epithet for a Marxist in its classed, if not its sexed, implications). So, to quote
Lasch: "Women smoke and drink in public, move about freely, and assert their
right to happiness instead of living for others."[58] Women, increasingly independent in the wake of the so-called sexual revolution and the birth of second-wave
feminism, begin to behave in "self-indulgent" ways that propriety had previously proscribed. As Michèle Barrett and Mary Mcintosh have pointed out in a
feminist-leftist critique of Lasch, his book returns a "total silence on the oppression of women in the patriarchal family he so admires."[59]

Moreover, certain non-conforming female types are singled out for particular
opprobrium by Lasch: sex workers (Lasch writes that "the happy hooker stands in
place of Horatio Alger as the prototype of personal success"[60]), feminists, career
women, lesbians, and – of course – bad mothers. Imogen Tyler, in an important
feminist article from 2007 on the political trend for ascribing cultural narcissism
to 1970s American mores, locates the discourse in a climate of white middle-class
male unease with the rise of feminism, the gay rights movement, black rights
movements, and socio-economic mobility. She writes:

> We can read claims of cultural narcissism, and the denigration of identity
> politics that formed a central part of these claims as part of a growing dis-
> content among those sections of the American population who felt threat-
> ened by the radical social politics of the 1960s and the 1970s.[61]

This socio-political case study from 1970s America is useful as it tells us several
things about the ascription of narcissism to a population and selfishness to an
individual – and it tells us that such ascriptions are not necessarily themselves
selfless, altruistic, or coming from a place of concern with genuine collectivity
or social justice. Largely, in this case, what is at stake is the question of *who is
allowed to be* a subject or "self," and to have their self-interest legitimated or even
recognized at all. For Wolfe and then Lasch, social cohesion is threatened when
those (women, black people) who traditionally worked for the good of others

(socio-economically advantaged white men) take account of their own interests and start to act in the service of them. Similarly, the activism of the lesbian and gay rights movement was seen as a selfish assertion of identity politics by threatening the heterosexual privilege of the majority. The individual or group labelled "narcissistic" in such social commentaries, then, may well be an individual or group whose interests are not perceived as legitimate, and who is understood to be expressing unseemly and demanding behaviour in suddenly attending to them.

The American Psychiatric Association's narcissistic personality disorder (NPD)

It is notable that, with the glut of theorization of psychological narcissism in the 1970s, and against the backdrop of the "Me Decade" rhetoric used by Wolfe and Lasch to describe the period, it was in the year of 1980 that Narcissistic Personality Disorder (hereafter NPD) entered the American Psychiatric Association's manual with the publication of *DSM-III*. Personality disorders had not appeared at all in the second edition (1968), suggesting that between the two dates, individual *personalities*, and the ways in which they could deviate from accepted social collective norms, became the focus of intense psy science interest. So, it might be said that *a personage* in the Foucauldian sense – that of "the personality-disordered subject" – was *produced* at this time. The formulation of NPD in *DSM-III* owes much to the ideas of Kohut and Kernberg, who both used the language of "personality disorder." However, if we are to be precise – and as was pointed out by Philipson[62] – the *DSM* version resembles the specifically *male* manifestations of narcissism as discussed above.

The definition of NPD in *DSM-III* is as follows: "The essential feature of this disorder is a pervasive pattern of grandiosity (in fantasy or behavior), hypersensitivity to the evaluation of others, and lack of empathy that begins by early adulthood and is present in a variety of contexts."[63] The definition changed little in the fourth and fifth editions, with the following wording being used identically in both *DSM-IV* and *DSM-5*: "Narcissistic personality disorder is a pattern of grandiosity, need for admiration, and lack of empathy."[64] The *DSM* version of this diagnosis does not differentiate between female/male narcissistic traits emphasized in psychoanalysis and bases its diagnosis only on the "male version," identified by Philipson, which is concerned with grandiosity and single-minded lack of empathy. The single possible exception to this is the second descriptor, to do with "sensitivity to others' views," which may fit with some of the traditionally "feminine" narcissistic traits described above.

It is a commonplace in psychiatric circles to note that there is a lower incidence rate of female patients than male patients diagnosed with NPD. Eric Plakun remarks upon the "apparent absence of a female preponderance in NPD."[65] In an attempt to account for this, Philipson writes:

> Once the gender specificity of the narcissistic diagnosis is recognized, it becomes tautological to say that the incidence of narcissism is higher in

males than females. Since the definition of narcissism is founded on men's developmental experience more than women's, it seems only logical that men would more frequently fit the description of a narcissistic personality than women.[66]

And it is not coincidental that there are, similarly, fewer female patients diagnosed with Antisocial Personality Disorder (APD) as the American Psychiatric Association (APA) defines it. Both these disorders – NPD and APD – are characterized by grandiosity and an egoistic lack of empathy, with the addition of low impulse control and likely criminal behaviour in the case of APD. By contrast, Histrionic Personality Disorder and Borderline Personality Disorder (more recently renamed by some psychiatrists as "Emotionally Unstable Personality Disorder") – which are characterized by attention-seeking, flirtatious behaviour, insecure attachment, and uncontrolled emotionalism – are disproportionately diagnosed in women. It is immediately obvious that the APA personality disorders appear as caricatures or exaggerations of gender stereotypes. This is an argument that has been made in recent scholarship, particularly by critics of the borderline diagnosis, such as Lisa Johnson in *Girl in Need of a Tourniquet* (2010). Ironically, too, Borderline and Histrionic qualities – flirtatiousness, vanity, valuing the self primarily according to estimation as a sexually attractive object – sound rather close to Freud's original version of the female narcissist.

Where instances of female NPD *are* discussed in the American psychiatric literature, it is again usually in the context of the deleterious effects of female narcissism on the nurturing of children (echoing both Freud's preoccupation with adult women as mothers rather than as selves, and the post-Freudian focus on mothers who hinder their children's development). And, interestingly, it is here that female narcissism in the APA sense has slipped from medico-legal terminology and into lay discourse, with the term "narcissistic mother" (or "narc mom") having entered popular cultural Anglophone parlance. A glut of self-help books and confessional memoirs treating the phenomenon have been produced over the past ten years including, to name but a few: Karyl McBride's *Will I Ever Be Good Enough?: Healing the Daughters of Narcissistic Mothers* (2009), Susan Forward's *Mothers Who Can't Love: A Healing Guide for Daughters* (2014), and Danu Morrigan's reassuringly entitled *You're Not Crazy – It's Your Mother: Understanding and Healing for Daughters of Narcissistic Mothers* (2012). Making an industry out of women's failings and marketing its products primarily at women can be read as a somewhat cynical gesture at a particular moment in a longer history of mother-blaming.

The relative shortage of scholarly consideration of narcissism in women and lower incidence of psychiatric diagnoses of women with NPD in the contemporary APA system are facets of a larger cultural phenomenon in which women's relationship with the whole concept of *self* is imagined differently from that of men. The insistence in more recent discourse on seeing women as narcissistic primarily in relation to bad mothering illustrates the persistence of narratives of women's nature and social roles. Philipson explains that the condition of low self-esteem which many women experience can lead them to the behaviours thought to produce narcissistic children: "Women's low self esteem – structured in their own childhoods and exacerbated by the particular social historical environment in which they mother – is the basis of their overidentification and fusion with their own children." In this way, "children are used as the missing part of the self, allowing women to recapitulate the feeling of attachment and/or merger with a loved and valued other."[67] It is a pity that psychoanalysis and cultural commentary have largely focused on *describing* the effects of women's poorly developed sense of self on their own mental health and that of their children, rather than on imagining ways of shoring up women's relationship to self. Though, to be fair to Philipson, she does conjecture that:

> The more we celebrate exclusive mothering by women and place a premium on the intensity of the mother–child bond, the more we are likely to raise males who are narcissistic and females who attempt to locate their missing sense of self-esteem through merger with and dependency on others.[68]

We are also reminded that the phantasy of the masculine/male self is of an isolated individual (as pointed out by Chodorow), while the model of female selfhood is understood only in terms of how a woman navigates her relationships and manages her connectedness, particularly to partner, family, and child. Hence, a woman "malfunctions" when she fails to place the interests of others above her own.

Frequch feminist Élisabeth Badinter has written in *The Conflict: Woman and Mother* (2010), of the dual disapprobation and suspicion of mental ill health that accrue to women who refuse this connectedness by choosing not to have children, a phenomenon that, she notes, is becoming more common in this so-called age of individualism, especially in Anglophone countries. She writes:

> For a very long time and perhaps still to this day [...] explanations for not wanting children were considered unseemly rationalisations of unresolved subconscious conflict. Childlessness was a negative choice that suggested psychological issues: a poor relationship with the mother, a rejection of womanhood, "questionable narcissistic motivations," depressive tendencies or low self-esteem. This was a pathological rejection that only psychoanalytic treatment might be able to sort out.[69]

Badinter's book carefully parses the discourses surrounding maternity, childlessness, and being childfree and takes seriously the question of female individualism and its effect on motherhood. She points out that *both* becoming a mother *and* refusing to become a mother are frequently ascribed to narcissism, noting that: "the individualism and hedonism that are hallmarks of our culture have become the primary motivations for having children, but also sometimes the reason not to."[70] Badinter draws attention to the by now familiar idea of our age as an atomized, individualistic one, but in a non-judgmental mode that does not assume that all was better when women accepted their identity as identical to that of caregiver. It is worth pointing out the rarity of this, since the commonplace understanding of women as defined by her capacity for relationality is not just a patriarchal edict or a norm contrived by medical authorities. It is a supposed female quality that some feminists also espouse and valorize.[71]

Towards a conclusion: On the age of selfies and selfish capitalism

Using terminology similar to that favoured by 1970s commentators Wolfe and Lasch, discussed above, who believed that social change had ushered in an era of cultural narcissism – a "Me Decade" – the 2000s saw Oliver James's publication of *The Selfish Capitalist* (2008), which critiqued twenty-first-century culture as one that produced both selfish and unhappy subjects – victims (and perpetrators) of the scourge of what he calls "Affluenza." This is the malaise created by a consumer-oriented environment in which instant gratification and the pursuit of self-fulfilment are placed above other, more communitarian, values. In the system James constructs, capitalists or "materialists" are discussed in similar terms to those we have seen used to describe narcissists:

> Materialists have been shown to be more likely to be distressed than non-materialists, and there are a number of reasons why it has this effect. Materialists are more emotionally insecure, have poorer quality personal relationships, are more inauthentic and lacking in a sense of autonomy, and have lower self-esteem.[72]

It has become something of a cliché to assert, as James does, that, since the turn of the millennium, individuals have become more superficial and dissatisfied, while increased self-indulgence has resulted in lower self-esteem.

One particularly gendered, and oft-criticized, cultural phenomenon that is seen to exemplify these claims is the popularity of the "selfie" (self-portrait photographs, usually taken with the cameras inside mobile phones and then posted to social networking sites, most often by girls and young women). The title of Will Storr's book *Selfie: How We Became So Self-Obsessed and What It Is Doing to Us* (2018) takes the name of this practice to highlight his claim that the era of "hyper-individualism" in which we find ourselves makes us both more self-obsessed – or "narcissistic" – and unhappier than previous generations. What such accounts ignore, perhaps, is that with online activity and social media replacing other ways of socializing for many, especially young people, the form and medium in which this alleged narcissism is played out has changed, but the phenomenon being criticized is at least as old as the nineteenth century and is, in many ways, understandable as a self-renewing and shape-shifting moral panic.

Some feminist scholarly accounts of selfie culture argue precisely against an interpretation of the practice as symptoms of youthful narcissism. In an article from 2015, Anne Burns argues that the cultural censure expressed towards young women who like to photograph themselves and/or share their image is at least as much a "regulatory social mechanism" as are the *presumed* peer pressure to take selfies and the young women's unthinking compliance with it. Burns contends:

> By naturalizing certain knowledge – such as the narcissistic nature of selfies – as "truth," the discussion of selfies acts as a subtle yet significant form of social control and a means for maintaining gendered power relations. I argue that by devaluing selfies and by identifying them as feminine, popular discourse serves to direct disdain at young women openly – and largely without challenge.[73]

We can see very easily reflected in the phenomenon of the selfie the Freudian notion that the beautiful, narcissistic woman gains satisfaction in being the object of desire of the (male) other and making herself her own object in the process. And the over-simplification inherent in Freud's heteronormative logic and the single motivation he ascribes to "vain" women finds a parallel in the single meaning ascribed to selfie-taking as analyzed by Burns. Burns argues: "Once the selfie is established as connoting narcissism and vanity, it perpetuates a vicious circle in which women are vain because they take selfies, and selfies connote vanity because women take them."[74] In this understanding, practices of female vanity – regardless of the particular modern moment or cultural mode in which they are carried out – are abjected. While I see selfies neither as just another compulsory neoliberal technique of self-regulation, pace Gill and McRobbie, nor as necessarily a liberating or "empowering" practice for women, what the phenomenon *does* draw to our attention is the continued misogyny that is directed towards women who are perceived to be *focusing on themselves*.

In different, but comparable ways, the danger posed to the whole of society by *female forms of self-regard* is a theme that runs through Belgian Lacanian psychoanalyst Paul Verhaeghe's book *What About Me?* (2012). The book became an international bestseller, translated from the original Flemish into numerous languages. It critiques the effects on our psyches of the neoliberalism that arose from the Reaganism and Thatcherism of the 1980s. Verhaeghe's book is notable especially for the value judgments about collectivity and individuality that it contains, sometimes dressed in the language of sociology, sometimes in that of biological science. Just as Lasch mourned the weakening of the institution of the family, as critiqued by Barrett and Mcintosh, so Verhaeghe writes:

> It is in the sphere of relationships that I see the most distressing effect of this trend [of individualization]. The double whammy of excessively competitive individualism and the obligation to seek pleasure at all costs [...] spells disaster for lasting relationships.[75]

And, "[b]iology shows that we are social animals; if a member of our species lives a solitary life, he or she is either diseased or has been ostracised."[76] The prescriptive normativity of Verhaeghe's statements here is illustrated by the extent to which collective social agendas can tend towards the oppressive for those – regardless of gender – who are, in fact, personally strengthened and creatively fuelled, by solitude. The desire to reject the *specific, so-called neoliberal* version of individualism has led to a denigration of individualism in all its forms, including those that can be benign and promote creativity. It has, instead, been tarred with pathology. When Virginia Woolf argued in 1929 for women's need for "a room of one's own," it was as a reaction against the relentless imperative of being-with and being-for that characterized the lives of those socially allotted the roles of daughter-wife-mother – and never that of individual.

Verhaeghe also promotes a version of identity that is heavily predicated on family belonging, writing: "[t]he content of our identity is, as we know, bound up with those closest to us: we are the child of, partner of, parent of, or sibling of someone."[77] The psychoanalytic determinism that states that family (romance) is destiny also has gendered consequences that are elided here. To be *firstly* a daughter and defined as such by social convention, to be *firstly* a mother, with all the baggage that that carries (and which is not conveyed by the gender-neutral "parent" or "guardian"), is to define oneself in the terms of heteropatriarchal institutions that have historically been in the business of oppressing women. It is also to uphold roles which psychoanalysts have considered may cause a great deal of psychical harm, as seen by the difficulty of defining how the mother might be just "good enough"[78] so as to preclude instilling narcissism in the child. And Verhaeghe abandons any pretence at neutrality with regard to sex roles and gender stereotyping at all in his statement which complains: "[t]here are no fathers any more because the system has done away with symbolic authority figures,"[79] a point he clearly feels to be so important that he makes it a second time in almost identical terms: "There are no fathers any more. They disappeared because their function was undermined."[80] One is left with an irresistible mental image here of the patriarch shouting into the abyss that his authority is being undermined.

That the call for a return to more social connectedness risks falling into a nostalgic, masculinist longing for a retro-utopia of 1950s family values, and a shoring up of the most literal embodiment of the patriarchy at the expense of feminist gains in independence, is a very real danger of the backlash against a supposed age of selfishness. Giving up "self" cannot be the answer to the perceived problems of "neoliberalism" for those who, as discussed in this chapter, have never been permitted a full relationship to self – a relation of self-fulness – that the default male subject is permitted to enjoy. Feminists of colour, who experience oppression and threats to their very existence as both women and as people of colour, have perhaps articulated this problem most clearly in their calls to prioritize "care for self" as an ethical feminist imperative. Audre Lorde famously stated: "Caring for myself is not self-indulgence, it is self-preservation, and that is an act of political warfare."[81] And Sara Ahmed in 2014 suggests that this problem persists today, when she invokes the figure of "willful subjects"[82] to draw out the ways in which willfulness, a related concept to selfishness, has been a charge made by the powerful against those – women, queers, people of colour – whose subjectivities are subaltern, and whose desired freedoms are perceived to compromise those of the established elite. It is in the context of claims such as Verhaeghe's for the healthfulness of a connected society as one in which everyone knows their role and implicitly their rung on a hierarchical ladder that a form of resistant gendered selfishness becomes an ethical necessity. It may not yet be appropriate to throw the squalling baby of female selfishness out with the fetid sludge of the neoliberal bathwater. The horror of these much vaunted "connected societies," when seen from the viewpoint of women, is that they were societies *in which women knew their place.*

Notes

1 Tom Wolfe, "The Me Decade and the Third Great Awakening," *New York Magazine*, 23 August, 1976.

2 Oliver James, *The Selfish Capitalist: Origins of Affluenza* (London: Random House, 2008); Paul Verhaeghe, *What About Me: The Struggle for Identity in a Market-Based Society* [2012], translated from the Flemish by Jane Hedley-Prôle (Melbourne and London: Scribe, 2014).

3 Jessica Benjamin, "The Oedipus Riddle," in Paul Du Gay, Jessica Evans, and Peter Redman (eds), *Identity: A Reader* (London: Sage, 2000), 231–247, p. 233.

4 In "Who Put The 'Me' in Feminism? The Sexual Politics of Narcissism," Imogen Tyler examines how charges of "narcissism" are often, throughout the twentieth and twenty-first century, issued at feminists in particular and at women in general (while the "beauty industrial complex" appeals to women's desire to live up to an ideal of vanity constructed by the industry). *Feminist Theory*, 6:1, 2005, 25–44.

5 Michel Foucault introduced the concept of the "specification of individuals" to describe the construction of a taxonomy of aberrant individuals in the first volume of the *History of Sexuality*, Foucault, *The Will to Knowledge*, pp. 42–43.

6 Nathaniel Branden, *The Art of Living Consciously: The Power of Awareness to Transform Everyday Life* (New York: Simon and Schuster, 1997).

7 Naomi Segal, *Narcissus and Echo: Women in the French Récit* (Basingstoke: Palgrave Macmillan, 1988).

8 Many accounts of the history of narcissism suggest, incorrectly, that the clinical concept originates with Freud himself. See, for example, James L. Sacksteder, "Psychological Conceptualizations of Narcissism from Freud to Kernberg and Kohut," in Eric M. Plakun (ed.), *New Perspectives on Narcissism* [1990] (e-Book, International Psychotherapy Institute, 2016), 13–102.

9 Sigmund Freud, "On Narcissism: An Introduction" [1914], translated by James Strachey, in *On Metapsychology: The Theory of Psychoanalysis* (Harmondsworth: Penguin, 1984), 59–97, p. 65, n. 1.

10 Freud, "On Narcissism," p. 69.

11 Freud, "On Narcissism," pp. 81–82.

12 Freud, "On Narcissism," p. 82.

13 Freud writes: "We have discovered, especially clearly in people whose libidinal development has suffered some disturbance, such as perverts and homosexuals, that in their later choice of love-objects they have taken as a model not their mother but their own selves. They are plainly seeking *themselves* as a love-object, and are exhibiting a type of object-choice which must be termed 'narcissistic'. In this observation we have

the strongest of the reasons which have led us to adopt the hypothesis of narcissism."
("On Narcissism," p. 81.)

14 Teresa de Lauretis's *The Practice of Love: Lesbian Sexuality and Perverse Desire* (Bloomington and Indianapolis: Indiana University Press, 1994) attempts to formulate a psychoanalytic theory of lesbian desire. Through an analysis of several lesbian literary texts and films, she concludes that what desired in lesbianism, and largely unrepresented in culture, *is the desiring/desirable female body*, not that of the mother, but that of the narcissistic little girl.

15 Freud, "On Narcissism," pp. 82–83.

16 Freud, "On Narcissism," p. 83.

17 Lisa Downing, *The Subject of Murder: Gender, Exceptionality and the Modern Killer* (Chicago: University of Chicago Press, 2013).

18 Freud, "On Narcissism," p. 83.

19 Sarah Kofman, "The Narcissistic Woman: Freud and Girard," *Diacritics*, 10:3, Autumn 1980, 36–45, p. 40.

20 Freud, "On Narcissism," p. 83.

21 Freud, "On Narcissism," p. 85.

22 Freud, "On Narcissism," p. 85.

23 See, for example, Peter Cryle, *The Telling of the Act: Sexuality as Narrative in Eighteenth- and Nineteenth-Century France* (Newark: University of Delaware Press, 2001); Rachel Mesch, *The Hysteric's Revenge: French Women Writers at the Fin de Siècle* (Nashville: Vanderbilt University Press, 2006); Anna Katherina Schaffner, *Modernism and Perversion: Sexual Deviance in Sexology and Literature, 1850–1930* (Basingstoke: Palgrave Macmillan, 2012).

24 Diana Holmes, *Rachilde: Decadence, Gender, and the Woman Writer* (Oxford: Berg, 2001), p. 56.

25 Robert Ziegler, *Asymptome: An Approach to Decadent Fiction* (New York and Amsterdam: Rodopi, 2009), p. 18.

26 Mesch, *The Hysteric's Revenge*, p. 193. My emphasis.

27 Melanie Hawthorne, *Rachilde and French Women's Authorship: From Decadence to Modernism* (Lincoln: University of Nebraska Press, 2001), p. 166.

28 Julie Lokis, *Deadly Desires: A Psychoanalytic Study of Female Sexual Perversion* [2013] (Abingdon: Routledge, 2018), pp. 130–131.

29 Rachilde, *La Jongleuse* [1900] (Paris: des femmes, 1981), p. 51. My translation.

30 Rachilde, *La Jongleuse*, p. 51. My translation.

31 Mesch, *The Hysteric's Revenge*, p. 153.

32 Rachilde, *La Jongleuse*, pp. 49–50. My translation.

33 Rachilde, *La Jongleuse*, p. 167. My translation.

34 Holmes, *Rachilde*, p. 138.

35 Lokis, *Deadly Desires*, p. 148.

36 Rachilde, *La Marquise de Sade* [1887] (Paris: Gallimard, 1996), p. 285. My translation; the typography is retained from the original text: "Louis, je suis décidée à ne pas vous donner d'héritier [...] Je ne veux ni enlaidir ni souffrir. De plus, *je suis assez*, EN ÉTANT, et si je pouvais finir le monde avec moi, je le finirais."

37 Mesch, *The Hysteric's Revenge*, p. 138.

38 Cited in Mesch, *The Hysteric's Revenge*, p. 138. My translations.

39 Rachilde, *Pourquoi je ne suis pas féministe* (Paris: Les Éditions de France, 1928), p. 6. My translation.

40 Rachilde, *Pourquoi je ne suis pas féministe*, p. 10. My translation.

41 Rachilde, *Pourquoi je ne suis pas féministe*, p. 7. My translation.

42 Rachilde, *Pourquoi je ne suis pas féministe*, p. 6. My translation.

43 Rachilde, *Pourquoi je ne suis pas féministe*, p. 6. My translation.

44 For an account of the history of the gendering of eccentricity in France, see Miranda Gill, *Eccentricity and the Cultural Imagination in Nineteenth-Century Paris* (Oxford: Oxford University Press, 2009). Commenting on the rise of individuality in the

nineteenth century, she writes: "Female individualism was portrayed [negatively] since the model of selfhood implicit in nineteenth-century philosophical, legal, medical, political, and psychological discourse was gendered as masculine." (p. 34).

45 See Sacksteder, "Psychological Conceptualizations of Narcissism."
46 Otto Kernberg, *Severe Personality Disorders: Psychotherapeutic Strategies* (New Haven: Yale University Press, 1984), p. 195.
47 See Nancy Chodorow, *The Reproduction of Mothering: Psychoanalysis and the Sociology of Gender, with a new preface* [1978] (Berkeley: University of California Press, 1999).
48 Chodorow, *The Reproduction of Mothering*, p. 100.
49 Chodorow, *The Reproduction of Mothering*, p. 100.
50 Chodorow, *The Reproduction of Mothering*, p. 100.
51 Ilene Philipson, "Gender and Narcissism," *Psychology of Women Quarterly*, 9, 1985, 213–228, p. 214.
52 Philipson, "Gender and Narcissism," p. 225.
53 Annie Reich, "Narcissistic Object-Choice in Women," *Journal of the American Psychoanalytic Association*, 1, 1953, 22–44. Cited in Philipson, "Gender and Narcissism," p. 223.
54 Philipson, "Gender and Narcissism," p. 214.
55 Tom Wolfe, "The Me Decade and the Third Great Awakening," *Mauve Gloves and Madmen, Clutter and Vine* (Toronto and London: Bantam Books, 1976), 111–147, p. 146.
56 Christopher Lasch, *The Culture of Narcissism: American Life in an Age of Diminishing Expectations* (London: Norton, 1979), p. 221.
57 Philipson, "Gender and Narcissism," p. 214.
58 Lasch, *The Culture of Narcissism*, p. 74.
59 Michèle Barrett and Mary Mcintosh, "Narcissism and the Family: A Critique of Lasch," *New Left Review*, 1:135, September–October 1983, https://newleftreview.org/I/135/michele-barrett-mary-mcintosh-narcissism-and-the-family-a-critique-of-lasch
60 Lasch, *The Culture of Narcissism*, p. 53. Horatio Alger (1832–1899) was an American writer whose *Bildungsromans* charted the social rise of male protagonists from humble backgrounds, owing to their courage, honesty, and strong work ethic.
61 Imogen Tyler, "From 'The Me Decade' to 'The Me Millennium': The Cultural History of Narcissism," *International Journal of Cultural Studies*, 10:3, 2007, 343–363, p. 357.
62 Philipson, "Gender and Narcissism," p. 226.
63 American Psychiatric Association, *Diagnostic and Statistical Manual of Mental Disorders (DSM-III)*, 3rd ed. (Washington: APA, 1980), p. 349.
64 American Psychiatric Association, *Diagnostic and Statistical Manual of Mental Disorders (DSM-IV)*, 4th ed. (Washington: APA, 1994), p. 629; American Psychiatric Association, *Diagnostic and Statistical Manual of Mental Disorders (DSM-5)*, 5th ed. (Arlington: APA, 2013), p. 645.
65 Plakun, "Empirical Overview of Narcissistic Personality Disorder," in Plakun (ed.), *New Perspectives on Narcissism*, 142–202, p. 179.
66 Philipson, "Gender and Narcissism," p. 226.
67 Philipson, "Gender and Narcissism," p. 225.
68 Philipson, "Gender and Narcissism," p. 228.
69 Élisabeth Badinter, *The Conflict: Woman and Mother* [2010], translated from the French by Adriana Hunter (Melbourne: Text Publishing, 2011), loc. 1573.
70 Badinter, *The Conflict*, loc. 52.
71 Perhaps the most famous example of this is the work of psychologist and ethicist Carol Gilligan, whose study *In a Different Voice* (1982), which I shall discuss in detail in Chapter 4, compared male and female styles of ethical problem solving. It noted that women tend to favour an "ethic of care and responsibility," when weighing up a moral dilemma, asking who would be affected and how, while men valorize an "ethics of rights," echoing Chodorow's claim that women operate psychologically from a position of connectedness not individuality and separateness.

72 James, *The Selfish Capitalist*, p. 5.
73 Anne Burns, "Self(ie)-Discipline: Social Regulation as Enacted through the Discussion of Photographic Practice," *International Journal of Communication*, 9, 2015, 1716–1733, p. 1716.
74 Burns, "Self(ie)-Discipline," p. 1720.
75 Verhaeghe, *What About Me*, loc. 2503.
76 Verhaeghe, *What About Me*, loc. 1061.
77 Verhaeghe, *What About Me*, loc. 2696.
78 The phrase "good enough mother" was first coined in 1953 by Donald Winnicott, a British pediatrician and psychoanalyst, in an attempt to counter the excessive societal pressure on women, compounded by psychoanalytic discourse, to be a perfect mother.
79 Verhaeghe, *What About Me*, loc. 2595.
80 Verhaeghe, *What About Me*, loc. 2589.
81 Audre Lorde, "Epilogue," *A Burst of Light and Other Essays* [1988] (New York: Ixia, 2017), p. 130. The radical notion of "care for self" propounded by women of colour has been appropriated in recent years for what many would call a "neoliberal" agenda. That is, it has been stripped of political content and racial context, and commercialized. When "self-care" is evoked now, it is often in the service of selling beauty products, spa days, etc. (We might recall make-up brand L'Oréal's well-known advertising soundbite: "Because I'm worth it"). See, for example, Holly Smith, "Your Appropriation of 'Self-Care' is Terrifying. And it Must Be Stopped," *Medium*, 25 April 2017, https://medium.com/@hesmith/your-appropriation-of-self-care-is-terrifying-andit-must-be-stopped-e1d0f7731606
82 Sara Ahmed, *Willful Subjects* (Durham: Duke University Press, 2014).

2

THE PHILOSOPHY OF SELFISHNESS

On Ayn Rand and rational self-interest

I believe that women are human beings. What is proper for a man is proper for a woman. The basic principles are the same. I would not attempt to prescribe what kind of work a man should do, and I would not attempt it in regard to women. There is no particular work which is specifically feminine. Women can choose their work according to their own purpose and premises in the same manner as men do.

(Ayn Rand interview in *Playboy*, 1964)

I [regard] man as a superior value.

(Ayn Rand, cited by her biographer Barbara Branden)

Ayn Rand is among the most controversial figures of our age. The sense of vehemence emanating from the pens and mouths of her critics is matched only by the devotion she commands from her admirers.

(Douglas Den Uyl and Douglas Rasmussen,
The Philosophic Thought of Ayn Rand, 1984)

Despite the fact that Ayn Rand died more than 35 years ago, her name and the ideas with which it is associated have been frequently on the lips of political commentators in recent years. Rand's philosophy of "Objectivism" is a theory of rational self-interest that offers a moral argument in favour of individual self-interest as a good, and free-market capitalism as the system in which this can be achieved. Rand writes:

The basic social principle of the Objectivist ethics is that just as life is an end in itself, so every living human being is an end in himself, not the means to the ends or the welfare of others—and, therefore, that man must live for his own sake, neither sacrificing himself to others nor sacrificing others to himself. To live for his own sake means that the achievement of his own happiness is man's highest moral purpose.[1]

Objectivism is cited as a major influence on contemporary right-wing American – and world – politics. Figures such as senator Rand Paul, Republican congressman Paul Ryan, and late US president Ronald Reagan all openly professed admiration for Rand's writings.[2] Donald Trump claimed during his campaign for US president that he admired Rand's novel *The Fountainhead* (1943), and that he identified with its protagonist Howard Roark (despite Roark being an exceptionally talented, self-made man from a poor background rather than the heir to a fortune, much of which was squandered).[3] Rand's best-known novel, *Atlas Shrugged* (1957), has frequently been described as the most influential book in America after the Bible. And, as noted in the epigraph above, Ayn Rand has been described by philosophers Douglas Den Uyl and Douglas Rasmussen as one of "the most controversial figures of our age."[4]

At the most obvious level, the controversy surrounding Rand's name and work can be attributed to the headline of her agenda: a single-minded pursuit of the ideals of "rational selfishness" and capitalism, while denouncing altruism in deliberately emotive terms as an "evil." Rand clearly set out to be seen as a *provocatrice* and as a thinker aiming to overturn some of the most naturalized assumptions of the consensus her day, regardless of whom that may upset. She claimed "Objectivists are not 'conservatives.' We are *radicals* for capitalism."[5] And when asked "Why do you use the word 'selfish' to denote various qualities of character, when that word antagonizes so many people to whom it does not mean the things you mean?", Rand replies: "For the reason that makes you afraid of it."[6]

Rand's concerted attempt to inspire strong reactions in her readers has certainly succeeded. She has been rewarded by both adoration and vilification in equal measures from different quarters. Critic Lisa Duggan has recently described Rand as "the writer whose dour visage presides over the spirit of our time [...] the original Mean Girl," and described the books that present her worldview as "theaters of cruelty."[7] The emotively worded title of Duggan's book, *Mean Girl: Ayn Rand and the Culture of Greed*, typifies progressives' view of Rand. The book sets out to read Rand's writings as precursors of the obsessions of our age, including her influence – both direct and indirect – on the big names and major events of capitalist modernity and postmodernity. This is in keeping with a raft of titles that chart the impact of Rand for trends in US politics, and often attribute developments in economic and political policy to the reception of her work.[8] One work, Darryl Cunningham's graphic book, *Supercrash: How To Hijack the Global Economy*, even manages to attribute the 2007 financial crash to the influence of Rand's thought.[9] Yet, we might also wonder whether the fact that the architect of such a radical and ruthless philosophy was a woman might contribute to the strength of the reactions she elicits, since the refusal of self-sacrifice is such a transgression of conventional, feminine virtue and the vocal, uncompromising style in which Rand writes and speaks run contrary to stereotypes of her sex.

Also notable is that despite the tremendous and unquestionable influence of Rand's work, and the number of words written about it, many critics are keen to dismiss the seriousness of her intellectual contribution in all of the fields to which she contributed. Her philosophy is often debunked as logically flawed or as "not a real philosophy."[10] Scott Ryan's *Objectivism and the Corruption of Rationality* (2003) includes the witheringly dismissive section title "Why Bother?",[11] implying that Rand barely deserves the effort expended by the male philosopher in analyzing her system. He notes that, as well as committed Objectivists (who cannot be expected to know better?), she is also read by "classical liberals and libertarians" who, on the contrary, "ought to know better."[12]

Similarly, Rand's fiction writing is seldom accorded serious literary critical attention. In an essay on "Ayn Rand Literary Criticism," Mimi Reisel Gladstein notes that "lamenting the lack of critical attention paid to Rand's creative writing is almost a cliché."[13] There may also be some truth to Michael Prescott's claim that "Rand has not made great inroads into the academic establishment, in part because of whatever philosophical and literary weaknesses she possesses, but in part also because of the liberal bias of humanities professors."[14]

Finally, despite the fact that Rand's writing on the economic theory and practice of capitalism directly influenced Alan Greenspan, who, in 1974, was sworn in as Chairman of Ford's Council of Economic Advisors (and photographed with Rand at the event), and despite the number of articles and books that attribute the currently dominant economic philosophy to Rand, she is seldom included in any histories or overviews of economic philosophy. Books that explain "neo-liberalism," including Kean Birch's work to which I have referred in the Introduction of this book, fail to include a mention of Rand's name alongside those of Friedrich Hayek and Ludwig von Mises. This omission is all the more striking given that Rand and Mises admired each other and corresponded, as seen when he wrote to her in 1958:

> You have the courage to tell the masses what no politician told them: you are inferior and all the improvements in your conditions which you simply take for granted you owe to the effort of men who are better than you.[15]

A woman's influence can be blamed for doing perceived economic and social harm, it seems, but she must not be acknowledged for her contribution to knowledge or accorded authority.

Finally, it is a commonplace to dismiss Rand's writing as childish and as naively melodramatic – as appealing to the puerile, rather than to mature thinkers. Duggan repeatedly states that it is not the presentation of Rand's *ideas* in the form of philosophical treatises or *romans clés* that accounts for the fascination and enthusiasm her followers feel for her, but rather her ability to infuse an eroticism into her presentation of those ideas in fiction. Duggan argues that Rand's dramatic novels appeal to the dual emotions of lust and a mean-spirited enjoyment of feeling superior, rather than the rationality that Rand consciously extols as her raison d'être. She writes: "Rand's *sense of life* combines the libido-infused desire for heroic individual achievement with contempt for social inferiors and indifference to their plight."[16] This reading is commensurate with the often expressed view that Rand's target readers are upper-middle-class college boys driven by a mixture of social entitlement and horniness, as memorably personified by "mean boy" Robbie Gould (Max Cantor) in the film *Dirty Dancing*, set in America in 1963.[17] Robbie, who believes that "some people matter and some people don't," advises "Baby" (Jennifer Beale) that she should read *The Fountainhead*, a well-thumbed copy of which he has under his arm – but tells her "bring it back. I have notes in it."[18]

This association between Rand's work and immaturity is particularly intriguing, as the combination of selfishness and being female has tended to make selfish women the objects of pathologizing discourses of immaturity throughout the history of the psy sciences, as seen in the previous chapter. For Freud, as noted, a mature woman is defined in psychoanalytic discourse as the child-bearer and doting mother, whose narcissism has passed from superficial vanity and found its proper – that is secondary – form. Ayn Rand's sexually selfish and childfree personal life, in combination with her audacious system of thought, are thus illegible as mature, female attitudes. In this way, Rand is a transgressive figure. The Lacanian cultural theorist Slavoj Žižek has commented on the sexual affair between Rand and her younger disciple Nathaniel Branden that it was "*ethical* in the most profound meaning of the word."[19] He means "ethical" here in the Lacanian rather than in the Randian sense of the word, as in the former system, ethics is the principle of being true to the real of one's desire. There is a long-standing tradition of dismissing unrepentantly selfish women such as Ayn Rand as less than full adult subjects, and as doubly aberrant but, as Žižek shows here, Rand's life and philosophy can justifiably be read to constitute an audacious ethical and philosophical experiment in *desire* as much as in *will*.

In what follows I shall attempt an honest assessment of Rand's fraught and often contradictory project of being a selfish woman, one who claims, as seen in the first epigraph above, that women are individuals who need and are capable of self-actualization as much as men, while also holding the contradictory position that – in Rand's words – "I [regard] man as a superior value,"[20] making her sexual politics as much a problem for feminists as her pro-capitalist politics are for leftists.

Who is Ayn Rand?[21]

Ayn Rand (1905–1982) was born Alissa Zinovievna Rosenbaum in St. Petersburg, Russia.[22] Following the Soviet revolution, and the degradation of her family's fortunes under the new regime, she travelled, alone, to the USA aged 21 in 1926. She lived initially with cousins and managed to find work as a screenwriter for Cecil B. DeMille. In 1929, she married aspiring actor Frank O'Connor, a man whose attraction for her she would attribute sometimes to the simple fact that he was "so beautiful,"[23] while at other times she insisted that he was an intellectual soulmate, despite strong evidence that Frank had little interest in philosophical and literary questions.[24]

Rand published her first novel, the quasi-autobiographical *We the Living*, in 1936. Set in Soviet Russia, its central theme is the struggle between individual will and the state. Her novella *Anthem*, which takes place in a dystopian future in which the concept of individuality has been eradicated and the pronoun 'I' replaced by 'we,' was rejected by scores of publishing houses before being published to indifferent critical attention in the UK in 1938. (It would be published for the first time in the USA in 1946, after the publication, to some acclaim, of Rand's breakthrough novel, *The Fountainhead* in 1943.)

The Fountainhead was initially intended to be titled *The Second-Handers*, as a nod to its theme of the parasitism of the mediocre. It tells the story of the brilliant and maverick modern architect, Howard Roark, who dynamites a building he has agreed to design for a less talented colleague, the ultimate "second-hander," Peter Keating. Roark destroys The Cortlandt Building – a tenement block for social tenants – because his plans for it have been altered, in violation of the one condition he had placed on agreeing to design the building anonymously for Roark to pass off as his own. *The Fountainhead* is also notorious for the rape/forced sex scene between Roark and Dominique Francon, a cynical, irritable, and self-destructive high-society aesthete. About the contentious scene, condemned by feminists including rape theorist Susan Brownmiller, Rand claimed during a radio interview "if it's rape – it's rape by engraved invitation."[25]

The influence of *The Fountainhead* was sufficient to make Rand's name. A film adaptation of it, starring Gary Cooper as Roark, was made in 1949 under the directorship of King Vidor. Rand wrote the screenplay for the adaptation and, unusually for Hollywood at the time, insisted on having final approval of the words spoken in the film – and obtained it. *The Fountainhead* also made Rand a cult figure for young right-wing students, intellectuals, and aspiring politicians, who found themselves out of step with the prevailing political climate of "New Deal" America, characterized by a brief admiration for "the Russian Experiment," which Rand's childhood experiences led her to abhor. A group of these young followers clustered around Rand, led by psychologist Nathaniel Branden and philosopher Barbara Weidman (who would become Nathaniel's wife – a marriage strongly encouraged by Rand who saw them as ideal intellectual partners). They would call themselves, with heavy irony, "The Collective"[26] or "the Class of '43" (after *The Fountainhead*'s date of publication). This group also would include names that are now prominent in American political and intellectual life, including Greenspan and Barbara Branden's cousin, the philosopher Leonard Peikoff, who would go on to co-found The Ayn Rand Institute with Ed Snider in 1985, three years after Rand's death. The members of "The Collective" were Rand's intellectual companions, as she battled to complete the epic, 1,000-plus-page fictional manifesto of Objectivism, *Atlas Shrugged*, published in 1957. During this time, Rand also began an affair with Nathaniel who was 25 years younger than her, with the knowledge and (grudging) agreement of Frank and Barbara.

Atlas Shrugged, written under the working title of *The Strike*, tells the story of a strike undertaken by the most brilliant and productive of society's individuals, at the behest of the mysterious John Galt, the man who would "stop the motor of the world."[27] The movers and shakers withdraw from the world in protest against their instrumentalization by an administration of mediocre, welfare-state bureaucrats managing a socialist government. The story is told in the third person but closely aligned to the perspective of the beautiful and dynamic Dagny Taggart, COO of Taggart Transcontinental Railway, who battles to keep her trains running despite the increasing collapse of society and the incompetence of her brother James, a mooching ally of the government. Dagny also attempts to solve the mystery of where the great innovators are disappearing to, before herself being invited to join them in "Galt's Gulch," their retreat from the world where they have built their own ideal society, innovating, creating, and producing for their own ends. It is only at the end of the novel that the inhabitants of the Gulch consent to return to the world where, finally, following a speech by Galt broadcast over the airwaves justifying the importance of productive and creative exceptional individuals, their excellence will be appreciated.

A subplot of *Atlas Shrugged* concerns Dagny's sex life. In the course of the novel she has sexual encounters with three handsome, successful men: Francisco d'Anconia, CEO of his family's copper mining company; Hank Reardon, a steel manufacturer who produces an innovative new material, "Reardon Metal" that is used for both the tracks on her railway and to fashion her a bracelet in the shape of a chain; and – ultimately – her ideal man, engineer and philosopher of self-interest, John Galt. Dagny's sexually liberated attitude and the respect in which her suitors hold her and each other offers a genuinely striking model of sexual politics for the time in which it was written. The genre of *Atlas Shrugged* is difficult to define. It is at once a Romantic treatment of meritocracy, a romance with melodramatic elements, a thriller, a philosophical novel, and a fantasy or science fiction-influenced work, with the inclusion of "Galt's Gulch" effectively removing the action from realism.

Atlas Shrugged took Rand approximately a decade to write, with Galt's climactic, 60-odd-page-long, speech about the nature of man's ethical existence alone taking her almost two whole years. Rand predicted that *Atlas Shrugged* was "going to be the most controversial book of this century; I'm going to be hated, vilified, lied about, smeared in every possible way."[28] Following publication, Rand's book was indeed largely vilified by reviewers, with a few voices speaking up for its bravery and originality. Her ambitions for it, however, were no less than that it should be a book that would alter the philosophical, economic, and political paradigm guiding society at the time. Many have commented on the fact that Rand would have been delighted by the free market ideology that would go on to characterize the politics of the 1980s, but *Atlas Shrugged* came out before the world was ready for it. This led Rand to a period of several years of depression, during which her sexual relationship with Nathaniel ceased. In her distressed state, possibly exacerbated by effects of the amphetamines she had taken for years to aid the writing of *Atlas Shrugged*, Rand chided herself for her inability to deal with what she perceived as failure: "John Galt wouldn't feel this," she is alleged to have said. "He would know how to handle this. I don't know [...] I would hate for him to see me like this."[29]

Rand foreswore fiction writing henceforth, resolving to focus instead on philosophical essays and lectures. Indeed, she devoted her remaining years to disseminating her ideas as a public philosopher. Accordingly, and to this end, in 1958, The Nathaniel Branden Institute was set up to deliver courses designed to spread the understanding of Rand's thought. It produced "The Objectivist Newsletter," later renamed "The Objectivist." In 1968, Rand discovered that Nathaniel had commenced a sexual relationship with model and student, Patrecia Scott. Despite their own sexual relationship having long since ground to a halt, Rand professed herself "betrayed" and distanced herself from Nathaniel, accusing him of plagiarism and embezzlement and "disinheriting" him in favour of Leonard Peikoff. She subsequently would sever ties with Barbara and with several other members of The Collective whom she suspected of wavering in their loyalty to her or of supporting Nathaniel. Having co-written the book *Who Is Ayn Rand?* in 1962, both Nathaniel and Barbara would later go on to write their own, sole-authored accounts of their years with Rand, including the adulterous affair, the described events of which largely corroborate each other.[30]

Ayn Rand's last years appear to have been lived in ill health and loneliness. She was diagnosed with lung cancer in 1974 (a medical event which she would claim had no causal relationship to her lifetime of chain smoking). Throughout the 1970s, she made several appearances on American television, talking about the legacy of her ideas. During one particularly memorable appearance on *The Phil Donahue Show* in 1979, she lost her temper and angrily berated a woman in the audience who had the temerity to suggest that her one-time admiration of Objectivism had been a folly of youth.[31] In November 1979, Frank O'Connor died, leaving behind a grief-stricken Rand. By the end of her life, of her followers, only Peikoff remained a close companion and confidant, called to Rand's deathbed but arriving moments too late to say goodbye. Ayn Rand died on 6 March 1982. In death, as in life, her values were ostentatiously displayed, in defiance of convention and taste. An article in *The New York Times* noted: "Ayn Rand's body lay next to the symbol she had adopted as her own – a six-foot dollar sign."[32] In 1999, a drawing approximating Rand's most recognizable and often used author photograph appeared on a US postage stamp.

The sentimental education of a selfish woman

A number of existing biographical accounts of Rand, both authorized and unauthorized, as well as her own notes and journals that have been edited for publication, offer crucial insights into her development as a thinker, writer, and persona from childhood to old age. Her adherence to an ethic of selfishness can be traced to her earliest memories (though we should not underplay the possibility of retroactive self-construction of a childhood personality of which the reminiscing adult approves). Speaking to her authorized biographer and close friend Barbara Branden of her childhood attitudes towards songs, books, and other things that she held passionately dear, Rand claimed:

> I didn't want others to share this value. I felt: This is my value, and anyone who shares it has to be extraordinary. I was extremely jealous—it was literal jealousy—of anyone who would pretend to like something I liked, if I didn't like that person. I had an almost anxious feeling about it, that it wasn't right. They have no right to admire it, they're unworthy of it.[33]

Female socialization militates strongly against a girl first holding herself in such high esteem, and second jealously guarding to herself the things she values, rather than sharing them. While no doubt rebarbative to many readers for the attitude of arrogance and superiority it displays, Rand's sentiment here is – albeit unwittingly, since she does not evaluate them through the lens of gendered expectations and sex stereotyping – a radical violation of the attitude that girls are encouraged to hold towards themselves and towards what is theirs. Second-wave radical feminist Shulamith Firestone has pointed to this phenomenon when she reminisces in her manifesto *The Dialectic of Sex* (1970) of her girlhood love for those Donald Duck comics that featured Uncle Scrooge McDuck in the following terms: "I loved the selfish extravagance of his bathing in money. (Many women – deprived of Self – have confessed the same girlhood passion.)"[34] That a Marxian radical feminist should confess to this desire, and should articulate the lack of permission to be selfish – or better self-ful – as a girl, demonstrates the extent to which such a radical example of girlhood self-valorization as demonstrated by Rand is vanishingly rare and exceptional.

"Exceptionality" was, in fact, the quality with which Rand most closely identified herself. She recalls her childhood self as an intellectual prodigy and, speaking of her parents' and teachers' response to her, she claimed: "They all seemed to see something unusual in me."[35] She also recalled resenting being treated as a child and the restrictions it placed on her freedom:

> I did not like being a child. I did not like being attached to a family. I resented enormously the implication that anything to do with the family was binding on me – or anything to do with anybody – I had no obligation to unchosen values.[36]

Again, according to conventional values, there is no doubt something shocking about this renunciation of the principle of family duty. Rand would leave Russia for the USA in 1926 and never again attempt to make contact with her parents or siblings, remaining unaware even of whether they had perished under the oppressive regime she had left behind. Along similar lines, Rand never even considered having children herself, and recounted having written a story in which a woman chose to save her husband over her child, an attitude of which Rand approved.[37] The socially prescribed close association between women and family makes the ruthlessness of Rand all the more striking, precisely because it appears as *unnatural*. Yet of course it is perfectly in keeping with the central tenet of the philosophy she would go on to articulate and would place in the voice of her ultimate hero John Galt: "I swear by my life and my love of it that I will never live for the sake of another man, nor ask another man to live for mine."[38] The demands of family duty and parental – especially maternal – responsibility are perforce the very epitome of "living for another."

The quest for self-sufficiency and independence that seems to have been the hallmark of Rand's personal and philosophical credo is reflected in the following anecdote:

> Elayne Kalberman once asked her, "If you could do anything you wanted, or be anywhere you wanted, what would you choose?" "I'd choose to be on a cloud," Ayn answered wistfully, "just floating by myself, with nothing and nobody to bother me ... drifting serenely above the whole world."[39]

Barbara Branden also recalled that Ayn "had often quoted the saying: 'it is not I who will die, it is the world that will end.'"[40] The "narcissistic" self-regard and solipsistic ambition that so abundantly characterize Rand's view of herself translated also to an early fascination with (other) exceptional subjects and (anti-) heroes – yet tellingly, these were without exception male. Rand idealized an archetypical male hero whose primary characteristics were that he pleased only himself, to the exclusion of the views of others, and held conventional morality in disregard. Her literary career would be characterized by numerous attempts to incarnate this ideal male hero, most famously personified by Howard Roark, protagonist of *The Fountainhead*, the maverick architect whose devotion is to his project of designing perfect buildings without care for fame, fortune, or the recognition of others, and John Galt, genius engineer and leader of the strike in *Atlas Shrugged*.

In her early writing journals, Rand muses on the qualities of her ideal hero and the role she wishes the hero to play in her writing. A main aim of depicting the "ideal man" is to show up – by means of extreme contrast – the debased values of the society in which she lived and the perceived mediocrity of the everyday. One inspiration for the selfish hero was found in a figure I have explored at length elsewhere – the exceptional masculine criminal-genius of Romanticism, whose crimes, in that aesthetic philosophy, are understandable as cries of rebellion and independence against an indifferent and banal world.[41] In light of Rand's fascination with exceptional outsiders, it is unsurprising that she held Romanticism to be the ideal aesthetic mode or that Victor Hugo was her favourite writer (notwithstanding his socialist principles, so obviously contrary to her own political leanings). In particular, the young Rand documented in her journals her fascination with the figure of William Edward Hickman, the defendant in a highly publicized murder trial in the 1920s. Hickman was found guilty of kidnapping and murdering a young girl and was hanged on 20 October 1928. He was a vocal rebel who made statements to the press about his state of mind and crimes. Rand reported: "Hickman said 'I am like the state: what is good for me is right.' That is the boy's philosophy. (The best and strongest expression of a real man's psychology I have ever heard.)"[42]

The figure of Hickman was a source of inspiration for Rand's creation of the character of Danny Renahan in an early, never-published work, *The Little Street*. Rand stated that it was not Hickman's crimes that inspired her characterization, but rather "what Hickman suggested to me."[43] She noted: "[Renahan] is very far from him, of course. The outside of Hickman but not the inside. Much deeper and much more. A Hickman with a purpose. And without the degeneracy."[44] Hickman and Renahan, then, stand as the figure of a superior individual against a banal society, or the "Outsider," before Colin Wilson's immortalization of that existential heroic type in 1956.[45] Wilson's book is a study of those literary authors and their creations who are at odds with the norms of society and are unrepentantly independent. Unsurprisingly, given the gendering of exceptionality in culture, the authors and the fictional characters Wilson discussed are all male. That Rand's *The Fountainhead* does not make it into his pantheon is both anomalous and telling. Rand and her character Roark are at least as ruthless and as independent as many of Wilson's examples. Both Rand and Wilson draw in their fascination with "the outsider" on Friedrich Nietzsche, creator of the "Superman," a figure of aspiration for humankind. Rand writes in connection with her concept for the story, *The Little Street*, "I think of the man who said: 'Oh, that their best is so very small! Oh, that their worst is so very small'! And oh, how horrid it is to be small!"[46] Harriman notes that this is a paraphrase of a quotations from Nietzsche's *Also Sprach Zarathustra* (*Thus Spake Zarathustra*, 1883–1891).

Rand writes of her Hickman/Danny hybrid: "He was born without the ability to consider others [...] his emotions are entirely controlled by his logic" and that he experienced "the absolute lack of social instinct or herd feeling."[47] The key characteristics of both killer Hickman and character Danny, then, are recognizable as belonging to that empathy-impaired psychopathological type that criminologists and psychiatrists have called "the psychopath."[48] The psychopath is on one side (the pathological side) of the discursive coin on the other side of which is Wilson's and Rand's idealized subject who is *above* morality (the Romantic side). Rand's fascination with this figure is in keeping with her aesthetic and intellectual sense of wishing to transcend the ordinary – a near pathological fear, perhaps, of being "ordinary." This seems to be related to her horror of the familiar – and the familial. She describes "family-life" as "the glorification of mediocrity"[49] and states that in her writing she sets out to demonstrate "the real, one and only horror – the horror of mediocrity."[50] Extending this, she writes: "the idea of the 'extremist' is splendid. We should have more extremists – then life wouldn't be what it is,"[51] and "Extremist beyond all extreme is what we need."[52] The young Rand's fascination with the notion of "extremism" was later tempered and rationalized as she observed that its usage was often in the service of "smearing." In *Capitalism – The Unknown Ideal* (1966), Rand identified extremism as an "anti-concept," that is, "an unnecessary and rationally unusable term designed to replace and obliterate some legitimate concept."[53]

While the very extreme outsider embodied by Danny Ranahan was perhaps tempered in later incarnations of the Randian hero, the notion of perfect masculine heroism is a feature of the whole of Rand's oeuvre. And a facet of Rand's obsession with Romantic heroes is the inescapable fact that, while extoling a philosophy of reason, and claiming her male protagonists as objectively perfect, her creative writing can on one level be seen as little more than a kind of – to use an anachronistic term – "fan fiction." Rand's novels are erotic fantasies featuring the kind of man that Rand could not find in life, a man to look up to. Moreover, Rand went some way towards admitting this. When her lover Nathaniel Branden asked her why there were a number of heroic men in *Atlas Shrugged*, but only one heroic woman – Dagny Taggart – Rand responded "That didn't interest me. And after all, this is *my* fantasy."[54] In similar vein, she allegedly commented to a friend, "Do you know what it's like to have no one to look up to – always to look down? Can you understand what it means still to hope, always to hope, and never to find it?"[55] Moreover, the heroines of both *The Fountainhead* and *Atlas Shrugged* – Dominique Francon and Dagny Taggart – can plausibly be read as "Mary Sues," that is as fictional stand-ins for an idealized Rand in the novels. Of Francon, Rand claimed: "The key to Dominique is that she is myself in a bad mood;"[56] whereas Dagny Taggart is:

> myself with any possible flaws eliminated [...] myself without my tiredness, without my chronic slightly anti-material feeling, without that which I consider the ivory tower element in me, or the theoretician versus the man of action [...] Dagny is myself without a moment of exhaustion.[57]

The receptions of Rand

Both of Rand's major novels, *The Fountainhead* and *Atlas Shrugged*, received very polarized reviews from professional literary reviewers, many of which are worth mining for the language used to describe and critique them. In a review of *The Fountainhead* for *The New York Times*, Orville Prescott writes in exaggerated terms:

> All the betrayals, all the dirty crawling, scheming malice, all the lust and lechery in *The Fountainhead* give it an atmosphere so luridly evil and conspiratorial that Cesare Borgia, the Marquis de Sade and Adolf Hitler could walk right in and feel cozily at home. The result is disastrous to what I am sure are Miss Rand's high and solemn intentions.[58]

Striking an entirely contrary note, *The Fountainhead* received its most positive reception in another review for *The New York Times*, this time by feminist reviewer Lorine Pruette. As Barbara Branden points out, Pruette's gender and politics may not be coincidental to her admiration of Rand's book.[59] Pruette describes it as "the only novel of ideas written by an American woman that I can recall," with characters who are "amazingly literate, romanticized as larger-than-life representatives of good and evil."[60] And of Rand, she writes: "Ayn Rand is a writer of great power. She has a subtle and ingenious mind and the capacity of writing brilliantly, beautifully, bitterly."[61] But, in terms of official critical reception, Pruette's view was the minority one.

To the lukewarm official critical reception of *The Fountainhead*, we cannot help but contrast the enthusiasm bordering on fanaticism that prompted the formation of Rand's group of followers "The Collective." Rand was adamant that the intended audience of her books were its readers, not professional critics. Yes, it is undeniable that the unfavourable reception of her books, particularly *Atlas Shrugged*, deeply impacted her mental health and outlook, as noted above. Perhaps the most notorious review of *Atlas Shrugged* was written by Whittaker Chambers, a former communist spy turned right-wing Christian, in the *National Review*. Chambers writes with outrageous hyperbole, and echoing Prescott's evocation of Godwin's law in his review of *The Fountainhead*: "from almost any page of *Atlas Shrugged*, a voice can be heard from painful necessity, commanding: 'to a gas chamber, go!'"[62] The misogyny subtending Chambers's critique reveals itself as the review progresses. Rand's "dictatorial" tone suggests to Chambers that "children probably irk the author and may make her uneasy."[63] That such a comment would be made of a male author is simply unthinkable. What is being taken to task here is Rand's failure to present herself and her ideas in a way that displays appropriate femininity. And, in equally exaggerated tones, Gore Vidal wrote of *Atlas Shrugged* that: "Ayn Rand's philosophy is nearly perfect in its immorality," noting with prescience that this "makes the size of her audience all the more ominous and systematic as we enter a curious new phase in our society." He goes on: "Moral values are in flux. The muddy depths are being stirred by new monsters and witches from the deep. Trolls walk the American night."[64] Gore's opinion of Rand's politics notwithstanding, it is hard to see how anyone can attribute the mention of "witches" to anything other than misogyny.

According to Barbara Branden, Rand consistently denied that the often brutally hostile critical responses elicited by her published work had anything at all to do with her status as a female thinker and author. Yet, Barbara believed that, in the business of being a published writer and philosopher, "Ayn Rand was in fact greatly hindered by being a woman."[65] She opines that the "savage and accusatory"[66] critical responses to Rand's novels have as much to do with their author being female, as with the arguably rebarbative elitism of her message and its uncompromising vision of individualism. Indeed, if one thinks of the kinds of individualistic, violently misogynistic, and male-glorifying material written by contemporary male American authors, such as Henry Miller and Norman

Mailer (who explicitly likened the psychopath to "the hero of our age"[67] in an essay published the same year as *Atlas Shrugged*), one recalls that their authors faced much less moral and aesthetic condemnation in reviews. Indeed, they are often given the title of "genius," a status historically accorded uniquely to men. It becomes clear that it is, at least in part, Rand's sex that leads to *The Fountainhead* and *Atlas Shrugged* being likened to perfect immorality and to Nazi propaganda (the latter being particularly unfair, as Rand consistently named fascism along with communism as extreme resorts of the philosophy of collectivism that she despised). That Rand repudiated feminist analysis entirely led her, as Barbara Branden has argued, to a partial understanding of her own reception.

The recent resurgence of interest in Rand in light of the financial crisis and latterly of Trumpism has led to a number of critical articles and retroactive reviews of her works in the press. Prominent left-wing writer George Monbiot authored a sensationally titled piece for *The Guardian* to mark the 30-year anniversary of Rand's death on 5 March 2012: "A Manifesto for Psychopaths."[68] Echoing the hyperbole that characterized views of Rand in her own time, Monbiot writes that Objectivism "has a fair claim to be the ugliest philosophy the post-war world has produced." The critical receptions of Rand's work, from the publication of *The Fountainhead* and *Atlas Shrugged* to the present day, then, share certain stylistic features – among them an exaggeration of Rand's immorality and a misattribution of *fascism* to her (intellectual) *elitism*. More recent accounts and reviews of Rand, however, exemplified by Monbiot's text, also feature the tendency to map direct real-world events – such as the financial crisis – onto her novels and philosophy in a causal manner. This is somewhat ironic, in that the attribution of a relationship of direct causality between fiction and real-world effects is often downplayed as unverifiable by writers of a more progressive bent in other contexts. (Consider debates about the real-world implications of "video nasties," violent computer games, and "extreme" pornography. In each case, those arguing against life aping art in a direct way are broadly on the left.) An exception is made, it seems, for the cultural production of right-wing women writers, which is imagined to have the power to "bewitch" – to refer back to Vidal's imagery – real-life right-wingers and to impel them to translate ideas straight from the page into action. However, as we have seen, Rand herself was that rare beast, a self-avowed female extremist. Thus, it is maybe not surprising – and indeed, perhaps, fitting – that the language she inspires in others is, in turn, so extreme.

Rand and feminism

The relationship between Ayn Rand and feminism is a fraught and far from simple one. About feminism, Rand wrote: "Every other pressure group has some semi-plausible complaint or pretence at a complaint, as an excuse for existing. [...] Women's Lib has none."[69] Yet, she made many statements in favour of the equality of the sexes and woman's right to work (see the epigraph of this chapter), and argued that "the notion that 'a woman's place is in the home' is an ancient, primitive evil."[70] To attempt to shed light on this tension, Nathaniel Branden has written that:

> As far as her view of women and human rights is concerned, Rand's work is entirely compatible with the dominant direction of nineteenth-century feminism. Historically, feminism was born of a demand, not for special entitlements provided by means of political coercion, but for equal treatment with men before the law. [...] These women were individualists who fought to be treated as such: treated as *persons*.[71]

While the tenets of equality feminism associated with first-wave ideas and aims may indeed have been wholly in keeping with Rand's view on the potential of both sexes, conversely, she objected to the second-wave feminism that was contemporaneous with her later years. Her objection to this radical feminism was made precisely on the grounds of her perception that feminists elevated their sex *above* their individuality, creating a form of collectivism that she associated with the hated Soviet communism of her childhood. For this reason, Rand was unwilling to support the idea of women *as a group* sharing a claim to any particular rights or agenda, while she would have robustly upheld the right of an individual woman to pursue her ambition.

To complicate matters further, Rand also, simultaneously, seems to have been invested in a surprisingly traditional view of psychological femininity that was entirely at odds with her assertions that career and worldly achievement should be just as important to women as to men, and that they were equally capable of excellence in the creative and productive spheres. It may simply be, as some have suggested, that Rand's *rational* belief in the rightness of equality was undermined by an *erotic* ideal. Rand argued that for a "woman qua woman," "the essence of femininity is hero worship," which she defines as "the desire to look up to man."[72] In light of this, consider the following conversation remembered by Nathaniel Branden:

I asked her "Don't men worship women? I mean the women they love?"

> "Oh, I suppose so, but that's not how I would think of it. By 'worship', I mean our highest capacity for admiration, reverence, looking up. I see man as superior to woman and ..."
> "Oh Ayn," I protested. "You don't. You're joking!"
> "I am not joking," she answered seriously.
> "Superior in what? Intelligence? Creativity? Moral worth?"
> "No, of course not. In spiritual or intellectual matters the sexes are equal. But man is bigger, stronger, faster, better able to cope with nature."[73]

Rand thus seems to hold an essentialist view of female inferiority based on biology, that may remind us of that earlier anti-feminist, arch-individualistic woman writer Rachilde's statements about men's greater physical robustness leading to their advantage in the previous chapter. Yet, unlike Rachilde, Rand actively *eroticizes* male physicality, and the physical power imbalance between heterosexual partners, in a way that is corroborated by her drawing of the relationship between Roark and Francon in *The Fountainhead*, that led Brownmiller and others to accuse her of being a rape apologist, and in her reflections on her own romantic life. She reportedly said to Nathaniel, "Don't you understand that a truly strong woman *wants* to see man as stronger? Certainly *her* man [...] for the pleasure of surrendering."[74] But when asked whether that meant that Rearden, d'Anconia or Galt would have viewed Dagny as inferior, her immediate answer was "*Of course not* [...] it would not be proper for a man to think in such terms."[75]

At other times, it seems that rather than dwelling on the (masochistic) pleasures of (what she perceived as) female/feminine nature, Rand wished instead (like Rachilde), to be seen as "like a man." In the Introduction of the one existing book devoted to the subject of feminist interpretations of Ayn Rand, editors Gladstein and Sciabarra contextualize that "for many contemporary feminists, Rand might be viewed as a masculinist in her exaltation of the role of consciousness and reason."[76] This refers to Brownmiller's opinion that Rand is "a traitor to her own sex,"[77] "spiritually male,"[78] and "an example of the ways in which a strong, male-directed woman accommodates herself to what she considers to be superior male thought."[79]

In light of these observations, Barbara Branden recounts the following anecdote:

> Henry Hazlitt said to Ayn one day: "I just talked with Lu Mises a few days ago. He called you 'the most courageous man in America'." "Did he say man?" asked Ayn. "Yes," he replied. Ayn was delighted.[80]

And in *Atlas Shrugged*, Rand's strong female protagonist, Dagny, responds to her sister-in-law's announcement: "I'm the woman in the family now" with the words "that's quite all right [...] I'm the man."[81] When James Taggart, her brother, attempts to insult Dagny by telling her "even though you were named after her, you really look more like Nat Taggart [their grandfather] than like that first Dagny Taggart, the famous beauty who was his wife", we are told that "Dagny accepted it happily as a compliment".[82] Yet the very problem of a woman having to be *like a man* in order to express agency or to be *full of self* is one of the issues of central concern to this book, and one that the case of Ayn Rand exemplifies particularly well. To extol reason as a virtue, as she does, Rand has to be "the man", since masculinity has long been linked with reason and with genius, as Christine Battersby has shown in her tour de force work *Gender and Genius* (1994), and as Julia Kristeva has attempted to subvert via her triptych of female genius.[83] How to reconcile reason as *proper to women,* as something *from which men have alienated women* is one of the problems I consider it well worth grappling with.

In some, if not all, of Rand's fiction we may find some accommodation of her insistence that women are not inferior to men, despite her less-than-enlightening comments on female psychology as defined by the principle of "hero worship." In an article from 1978, Mimi Gladstein discusses her controversial choice to set *Atlas Shrugged* as a core text on her women's studies syllabus under the rubric of "The Liberated Woman" or "She Who Succeeds," on the basis of the rareness of Dagny Taggart.[84] Gladstein bemoans a dearth of American literature that depicts a female character who "is active, independent, professionally successful, sexually emancipated, and doesn't pay for it by dying in childbirth [or] going mad."[85] Gladstein and her women's studies students are not alone in celebrating the character of Dagny. Tennis stars Billie Jean King, Martina Navratilova, and Chris Evert have independently cited the fictional female railroad hero as an inspiration, King commenting "like Dagny Taggart, I had to learn to be selfish, although selfish has the wrong connotation. As I see it, being selfish is really doing your own thing."[86]

Rand has also stated that Dagny Taggart is her "ideal woman", writing "I had always been somewhat frustrated by my presentation of women, and eager to present *my* kind of woman."[87] It is also via Dagny that Rand allows herself to articulate the fact that an agentic woman in the public sphere may find herself facing extra biases and barriers that have to do, not with her individual competence, but with the role society expects women to play – an admission that, as Barbara Branden explains, Rand had refused to make about her own career trajectory and critical reception. Consider the following passage from *Atlas Shrugged* concerning the messages the young Dagny received about her attitude and socially prescribed future destination:

> "You're unbearably conceited", was one of the two sentences she heard throughout her childhood, even though she never spoke of her own ability. The other sentence was "you're selfish". She asked what was meant, but never received an answer. She looked at the adults, wondering how they could imagine that she would feel guilt from an undefined accusation.
>
> She was twelve years old when she first told Eddie Willers that she would run the railroad when they grew up. She was fifteen when it occurred to her for the first time that women did not run railroads and that people might object. To hell with that, she thought – and never worried about it again.[88]

And it is left to mouthpiece Dagny to articulate some of the complexities of negotiating between contemporary cultural expectations of domestic femininity and individual (heterosexual) desire – complexities that Rand *qua* Rand often downplays. Despite her blanket dismissal of feminism, Rand would place in Dagny's voice ideas that are prescient and offer pre-echoes of key works of second-wave feminism, such as Betty Friedan's *The Feminine Mystique* of 1963, which critiqued compulsory domesticity and debunked the "mystique" of the title – namely, women's natural maternal instinct.[89] Already, in 1957, Rand has Dagny musing:

> There is a reason, she thought, why a woman would wish to cook for a man … oh not as a duty, not as a chronic career, only as a rare and special rite in symbol of … but what have they made of it, the preachers of woman's duty? … The castrated performance of a sickening drudgery was held to be a woman's proper virtue.[90]

The suspension points and disjointedness seen in this extract are atypical of Rand's prose style and of Dagny's thought processes. Both tend to favour precision and a lack of ambiguity; characteristics of the vaunted, if psychologically unliveable, pure rationality of Objectivism. I would suggest that the syntactical awkwardness here reveals the difficulty of articulating the position that Rand and Dagny gesture towards. When Rand acknowledges – through Dagny – that the constraints that society places upon women *may materially reduce their capacity to achieve greatness*, she admits, despite herself, that men and women do not face equal odds in their life struggles and that female individualism – female heroism – is actually socially much harder won than its male counterpart. The purely biological rationale that Ayn delivered to Nathaniel in defending her position of hero-worship (men are stronger and better adapted to nature) does not account wholly for the difficulties faced by women in comparison to men in the public and professional spheres.

Rand's reverse discourse and its limits

One of the fascinating and frustrating aspects of Ayn Rand's writing, for me, is that it is in some ways stultifyingly reactionary while, in others, genuinely radical and daring. Her reversal of the Christian morality of altruism as not only a philosophical error, but a form of *evil*; her insistence on selfishness as the highest virtue and on collectivism as tyranny; the money speech she included in *Atlas Shrugged*, placed in the mouth of Francisco d'Anconia, which reverses the saying "money is the root of all evil," to argue instead that "money is the root of all *good*" – all demonstrate a striking ability to think reverse-discursively in the Foucauldian sense, that is to turn ideas against the uses to which they are habitually put, in order to unsettle the dominant forms of reason and power. (That we are less used to seeing reverse discourse used in the service of pro-capitalist, selfish energies against a consensus of collectivity, does not alter the structure of the mechanism Foucault describes.) In his coruscating review of *Atlas Shrugged*, Gore Vidal effectively recognized this aspect of Rand's logic. He wrote: "Miss Rand now tells us that what we have thought was right is really wrong. The lesson should have read: One for one and none for all."[91] "One for one and none for all" is, indeed, a beautiful example of a kind of reverse-discursive thinking that seeks to upend and empty out conventional wisdom.

For all that, today, her political-economic values may seem familiar from observation of the world around us and in keeping with what many see as the worst excesses of capitalism, Rand was articulating her theory of free-market capitalism at a time when a welfare state project (the "New Deal"), implemented in the USA to remedy the effects of the Depression, constituted the political consensus. Thus, when Slavoj Žižek writes that Rand's subversiveness is that of the "overconformist," and an effect of her "very excessive identification" with "the ruling ideological edifice" – here capitalism[92] – I believe that he underestimates the extent to which Rand's politics were in fact wholly out of step and out of time with her milieu. As Nathaniel Branden put it, prior to the publication of *Atlas Shrugged* "sometimes I was uneasy [...] knowing how foreign Ayn's vision was to the culture in which we lived."[93]

And, despite her refusal to affiliate to feminism, Rand's provocative thinking against the grain or reverse discourse extended to issues of women's rights. Rand argued actively in the socially conservative 1950s for a woman's right to a career and equal pay. She supported access to abortion, calling it "a moral right which should be left to the sole discretion of the woman concerned,"[94] and she detested the dogmatic religiosity that was engulfing the US right. As Jennifer Burns points out in her biography of Rand, "in the 1940s Rand had been one of many intellectuals seeking a plausible grounding for individual rights and democracy. By the 1950s conservatives had found an answer in religion."[95] And, as late as 1980, Rand claimed she could not vote for Ronald Reagan owing to his bringing religion into the business of capitalism and his opposition to abortion.[96] It is the case still today that many of those American conservatives who profess admiration for Rand do so despite – or in ignorance of – her atheism and pro-reproductive rights ideology, as is acknowledged by even her most virulent critics, including Monbiot who writes: "ignoring Rand's evangelical atheism, the Tea Party movement has taken her to its heart"[97].

Finally, Rand created the one American female protagonist that a women's studies professor in the 1970s considered worthy of featuring in her university course as an example of a proper heroine. Yet, despite her own forms of genuine radicalness – shocking for her era – when it came to the capabilities of women, Rand, as we have seen, does not carry her oppositional discourse through to its logical endpoint. Superficial claims for equality aside, her writing is haunted by an abiding sense of female inferiority that she assumes to issue primarily from women's weaker physiology, rather than from historical oppression and the social conditioning of girls. Rand professes, in non-fiction, a belief in an essence of femininity, even if some of her fiction shows up, as illustrated previously by examples from Dagny's perspective in *Atlas Shrugged*, the constructed nature of femininity and the unreasonable expectations placed upon women precisely to act against our own self-interests.

The rigid, binary sex-gender logic to which Rand adheres also results in a stultifying heteronormativity. Rand assumes heterosexuality as an inevitable for her fictional heroines, and as a superior resort for the "natural woman", rather than being aware of it as a compulsory system. Instead, she assumes that its inevitability lies in nature. Nathaniel Branden reports:

> She was always pleased when someone told her she 'thought like a man.' And yet, when asked if she would have preferred to be born a man, she invariably answered 'God no! Because then I'd have to be in love with a woman!'[98]

The *have to* is puzzling – is it an assumption based on nature or morality? Rand suggests that the answer may be "both," when she writes of homosexuality that it is "immoral," "disgusting" and the "result of psychological flaws and corruptions."[99] What we are faced with, then, is a writer with an extraordinary capacity to think the unacceptable, to argue for the counter-intuitive, whilst also, sometimes, relaying on lazy and bigoted received ideas.

However, perhaps surprisingly, queer readings of Rand against the grain do exist. Rand's virulent and distasteful homophobia is in contradiction with the arguably erotic energies which animate her passion for women she perceived as being beautiful and powerful. Consider the terms in which Rand describes her reaction to a foreign girl she spied expertly playing tennis on a family holiday in the Crimea as a young girl, a figure who would go on to inspire Dagny Taggart:

> "It amazed me," she said. "It was a creature out of a different world, my idea of what a woman should be. She was a symbol of the independent woman from abroad. I felt what today I'd feel for Dagny Taggart. I only saw her that one summer, but the symbol was magnificent—I can still see her today, a very active, tall, long-legged girl in motion; I don't remember the face, only the long-legged agility, and black stockings worn with white tennis shoes. For years, her outfit seemed the most attractive I had ever seen ... I didn't long to approach her or to get acquainted, I was content to admire her from afar."[100]

The homoeroticism we might espy in Rand's biographical musings here are corroborated by a theory proposed by Slavoj Žižek. The rather eccentric conclusion to his psychoanalytic article on Rand is that her perverse (non-monogamous) sexual configuration, in fact, depicts not the hyper-heterosexual dynamic of superficial appearances, but rather a "disavowed lesbian economy,"[101] as Ayn Rand and Barbara Branden share a man between them – queerly – as a sort of sexual proxy. He writes: "contrary to the standard patriarchal procedure of men exchanging women among themselves, here, the exchange took place *among woman* – one woman borrowed a man from another one."[102] This is a neat gender inversion of what Eve Sedgwick describes as the model of homosociality in *Between Men* (1985).[103]

Most strongly, perhaps, Rand's radical inversions suggest a relic of her early reading of, and love for, Friedrich Nietzsche, which she would later deny with the claim that Aristotle alone of the philosophers had influenced her thought and writing. She would also claim in a lecture that philosophy consisted only of "the three A's – Aristotle, Aquinas, and Ayn Rand"[104] – a gesture of breathtaking arrogance, but also a rare and daring insertion of a female name into the pantheon of great dead white men. The errant and creative impulse to unsettle commonplaces and the slavish adherence to an ideal of rationality stand at odds and in stark tension with each other. In fact, the counter-intuitive alternative ethics that Rand deploys resembles nothing so much as the pronouncements of that other alternative moralist, Nietzsche's Zaroaster in *Also Sprach Zarathustra*. Here are the terms in which Zaroaster imagines joyous, virtuous selfishness:

> "Bestowing virtue"—thus did Zarathustra once name the unnamable.
> And then it happened also,—and verily, it happened for the first time!—that his word blessed SELFISHNESS, the wholesome, healthy selfishness, that springeth from the powerful soul:—
> —From the powerful soul, to which the high body appertaineth, the handsome, triumphing, refreshing body, around which everything becometh a mirror:
> —The pliant, persuasive body, the dancer, whose symbol and epitome is the self-enjoying soul. Of such bodies and souls the self-enjoyment calleth itself "virtue."
> With its words of good and bad doth such self-enjoyment shelter itself as with sacred groves; with the names of its happiness doth it banish from itself everything contemptible.[105]

And Rand describes selfishness thus, placing the words in the mouth of her ideal moral spokesman, John Galt:

> [T]he first precondition of self-esteem is that radiant selfishness of soul which desires the best in all things, in values of matter and spirit, a soul that seeks above all else to achieve its own moral perfection, valuing nothing higher than itself.[106]

This is one of many examples I could draw from Rand's texts where both a quasi-spiritual lexicon ("soul", "spirit" – strangely at odds with Rand's materialism) and discourses of psychological health and joy are deployed in relation to selfishness, in order to replace sacrifice with self-interest as the greatest moral good. In these ways, Rand's textuality parallels and overlaps with Nietzsche's formulations in both style and message.

What I am deliberately calling Rand's "reverse discourse" also renders her intellectual project, in numerous ways, not entirely dissimilar from the project of that other enthusiast of Nietzsche, Michel Foucault, whose term it is. Foucault's interest in tracing the history of the human, medical, psychological, and psychiatric institutions since the dawning of modernity stemmed from the fact that he saw in them, and was fascinated by, "a hermeneutics of the self that would substitute a 'positive' self for the self-sacrifice imposed by the Christian imperative of renunciation."[107] This could equally be a direct description of the aim of Rand's philosophy of rational selfishness.

Foucault's writings on the ethics of the "care of the self" reflect on two strands of ancient ethics that have received differing amounts of attention in modernity: "know yourself" and "take care of yourself." According to Foucault:

> There are several reasons why "Know yourself" has obscured "Take care of yourself." First, there has been a profound transformation in the moral principles of Western society. We find it difficult to base rigorous morality and austere principles on the precept that we should give ourselves more care than anything else in the world. We are more inclined to see taking care of ourselves as an immorality, as a means of escape from all possible rules. We inherit the tradition of Christian morality which makes self-renunciation the condition for salvation.[108]

He goes on: "our morality, a morality of asceticism, insists that the self is that which one can reject." Here, Foucault reasserts the moral value of centring and valuing the self, and understands renunciation of it as an effect of the development of Christian morality's logic. About the figure of Christ and the religious imperative of sacrifice, Rand writes:

> Christ, in terms of the Christian philosophy, is the human ideal. He personifies that which men should strive to emulate. Yet, according to the Christian mythology, he died on the cross not for his own sins but for the sins of the nonideal people. In other words, a man of perfect virtue was sacrificed for men who are vicious and who are expected or supposed to accept that sacrifice. If I were a Christian, nothing could make me more indignant than that: the notion of sacrificing the ideal to the non-ideal, or virtue to vice. And it is in the name of that symbol that men are asked to sacrifice themselves for their inferiors. That is precisely how the symbolism is used.[109]

For Rand, "sacrifice is the surrender of a value."[110] Rand takes for granted that the self – and self-interest – should, for every person, be their highest value. For both Rand and Foucault, then, what needs challenging in the morality developed and bequeathed by Christianity is the notion that the self is to be sacrificed – and that to care for it in Foucault's language, or hold it as the highest value in Rand's – is a vain or inappropriate project. Both writers attempt to imagine an ethics in which valuing/caring for the self is considered a valid endeavour. Yet, the closeness of Foucault's ideas to some of Rand's here is seldom commented on in the scholarship of either thinker.

In light of these similarities, one might ask then why, in my aim to take selfishness, self-interest, self-fulness seriously as ethical precepts in an era in which they are so unfashionable, I am primarily drawing on the politically abjected Ayn Rand, rather than on Foucault for this thought experiment. And indeed, one might further ask *why* Foucault is considered so much more palatable than Rand when their projects overlap in a number of ways, as suggested above. The answer to the first question is simply that Rand, as a female proponent of selfishness, is an obvious point of reference and case study for a book about selfish women, while Foucault has little to nothing to say about female selfhood (the masculine bias of his care-of-the-self writings being a critique often levelled at him by feminists). And to the second, I would answer that while Foucault flirts with selfishness and has a fascinatingly ambivalent relationship with the philosophy of neoliberalism, as discussed in the Introduction, he has largely been taken up by the left intellectual establishment, making him "respectable," in a way that Rand's blunt advocacy for capitalism precludes. As useful as I find Foucault for my work, the absence of women in his universe, which has frustrated me throughout my time working on him and using some of his models as key to my own analytical methodology, is just one of my reasons for writing this book.

Conclusion

As demonstrated throughout this chapter, and particularly in the previous section, some of Rand's texts come very close to making similar arguments to elements of the *œuvres* of both Friedrich Nietzsche and Michel Foucault. However, Rand is accorded nowhere near the intellectual respect of either of these canonical males of Continental thought. It is almost a cliché to insist that Rand was "not a qualified economist," that her philosophy was "not a real philosophy," and to paint her as a novelist whose characterization and plotting are at best – to use Duggan's preferred term – "cartoonish."[111] All of which points to a trend of refusing to take Rand seriously, on her own terms, as an intellectual. As Barbara Branden puts it:

> Can one doubt that, had Ayn Rand been a man she would at least have been taken seriously as a philosopher, however much her reviewers might have disagreed with her ideas? [...] It is as if most male reviewers said to themselves. 'I dislike her ideas on reason, individualism and free enterprise. Besides, who ever heard of a woman philosopher?'[112]

Regardless of one's view of Rand – from seeing her as a genuinely visionary prophetess to understanding her as the personification of all that is bad or cruel about the practices of capitalism – what is striking in receptions of Rand is that she is not accorded the same *kind* of criticism as male proponents of related ideas. Reception of her is instead *personalized* so that her ideas are often seen to reveal deviant facets of her personality and womanhood. This was visible in the reviews of Rand's books at the time of their publication. But it is also visible in recent works by critics, including left-leaning female scholars. According to Duggan: "It is difficult to resist rather crudely psychoanalyzing or otherwise diagnosing her, explaining her body of work as the compensatory fantasy life of a tortured soul who was perhaps a sociopath, but at least a malignant narcissist."[113]

While dismissing Rand's intellectual credentials, however, critics and journalists are especially keen to emphasize Rand's influence and indeed to blame her for many of the perceived ills of the modern world, from Reagan, through neoliberalism, to Trump. It is hard to view this pervasive gesture of hypocrisy of taking a woman seriously enough to *blame*, but not seriously enough to assess her contribution to literature and thought respectfully, as anything other than evidence of good old-fashioned misogyny. Yet the misogyny that accrues to Ayn Rand does not only come from external sources. I would argue that Rand's contradictory and confused perception of the nature and character of woman itself issued from an internalized misogyny, suggesting that the pervasiveness of sexism is the sticking point of a theory of rational selfishness that is as available to women as it is to men. Given her capacity for perverse thinking-against-the grain and audacious reverse-discursive argumentation, then, the fact that Rand leaves entirely intact the most garden-variety discourses of misogyny suggests more than anything the cultural and epistemological barriers to the task of imagining what it would mean truly to value the *female individual qua individual*.

I argue that an ethic of *specifically female selfishness* may, in fact, be so elusive as to be largely unarticulated. That would be a selfishness that fully comprehends the social constraints placed on women and is able to ask whether a given aim is in a woman's interests *not only as an individual, but also as a person who has been situated by the social order as a woman* – as "woman-function," regardless of whether she herself identifies with this role or not. Such a brand of selfishness – or self-*ful*-ness – is, in the words Rand used in another context, an "unknown ideal;"[114] something we have not yet properly tested.

That Rand should give us an ethical model that refuses sacrifice of the self in the interests of the other, and yet be both unable and unwilling to free the female subject from the self-sacrifice of man-worship, suggests the broader difficulty of thinking radical individualism in female terms and of imagining an individual woman as genuinely free from the constraints of culturally defined femininity. My fascination with Rand stems from the fact precisely that, not only external reactions to her, but also her own abreactions in the form of deflections, contradictions, and aporia when faced with the problem of theorizing true self-interest for and as a woman, tell us so much about the immensity of the task of valorizing *self* in the misogynistic culture that has defined *woman* against it.

Notes

1 Rand, "The Virtue of Selfishness," p. 454.
2 Rand herself, however, disapproved of Reagan. See Barbara Branden, *The Passion of Ayn Rand* [1986] (New York: Author & Company, 2013), loc. 9729. (As I will refer to various works by both Barbara and Nathaniel Branden, in each reference I will give their first name as well as surname to avoid ambiguity.)

3 See Robert Reich, "Trump's Brand is Ayn Rand," *Salon*, 19 March 2018. www. salon.com/2018/03/19/trumps-brand-is-ayn-rand_partner/

4 Douglas J. Den Uyl and Douglas B. Rasmussen (eds), "Preface," *The Philosophic Thought of Ayn Rand* (Urbana: University of Illinois Press, 1984), p. ix.

5 In Rand, "Check Your Premises," *The Objectivist Newsletter*, 1, 1962, 1. My emphasis.

6 Rand, *The Virtue of Selfishness*, p. 66.

7 Lisa Duggan, *Mean Girl: Ayn Rand and the Culture of Greed* (Berkeley: University of California Press, 2019), p. xi, p. 85.

8 See, for example, in addition to Duggan's recent title, Anne C. Heller, *Ayn Rand and the World She Made* (New York: Anchor Books, 2009) and Gary Weiss, *Ayn Rand Nation: The Hidden Struggle for America's Soul* (New York: St Martin's Griffin, 2012).

9 Darryl Cunningham, *Supercrash: How To Hijack the Global Economy* (Brighton: Myriad, 2014).

10 See, for a detailed excoriation of the logical flaws in Rand's system from the perspective of a Christian philosopher, John W. Robbins, *Without a Prayer: Ayn Rand and the Close of Her System* (Dallas: Trinity Foundation, 1997). See also Scott Ryan, *Objectivism and the Corruption of Rationality: A Critique of Ayn Rand's Epistemology* (New York: Writers Club Press, 2003). There are many other titles by philosophers showing how Rand got logic or reason wrong; the above are by way of example. Den Uyl and Rasmussen's book is a rare exception, in that it includes essays which consider seriously Rand's "attempt to provide a systematic, philosophical position," *The Philosophic Thought of Ayn Rand*, p. 224.

11 Ryan, *Objectivism and the Corruption of Rationality*, p. 1.

12 Ryan, *Objectivism and the Corruption of Rationality*, p. 1.

13 Mimi Reisel Gladstein, "Ayn Rand Literary Criticism," *The Journal of Ayn Rand Studies*, 4:2, Spring 2003, 373–94, p. 375.

14 Michael Prescott, "Shrugging Off Ayn Rand," blog post, n.d., http://michaelprescott. freeservers.com/shrugging-off-ayn-rand.html

15 Quoted in Jennifer Burns, *Goddess of the Market: Ayn Rand and the American Right* (Oxford: Oxford University Press, 2009), p. 177.

16 Duggan, *Mean Girl*, p. xv.

17 Directed by Emile Ardolino, 1987.

18 On the demographic of Rand's fans, see Claudia Franziska Brühwiler, "Pitiless Adolescents and Young Crusaders: Reimagining Ayn Rand's Readers," *Canadian Review of American Studies*, 46:1, Spring, 2016, 42–61.

19 Slavoj Žižek, "The Actuality of Ayn Rand," *The Journal of Ayn Rand Studies*, 3:2, Spring 2002, 215–227, p. 224.

20 Cited in Barbara Branden, *The Passion of Ayn Rand*, loc. 688.

21 The biographical information in this chapter is not based on original research but on existing published sources, including Barbara Branden, *The Passion of Ayn Rand* (1986); Nathaniel Branden, *Judgment Day* (1989); Jennifer Burns, *Goddess of the Market: Ayn Rand and the American Right* (2009); Anne Heller, *Ayn Rand and the World She Made* (2009); and Rand's journals published as *Journals*, edited by David Harriman, foreword by Leonard Peikoff (1990).

22 Rand's full Russian name appeared for the first time with the publication of Chris Matthew Sciabarra's *Ayn Rand the Russian Radical* (University Park: Pennsylvania State University Press, 2013).

23 Barbara Branden, *The Passion of Ayn Rand*, loc. 2250.

24 Biographer Barbara Branden notes: "They seemed so oddly mismatched as a couple – the handsome, elegant gentleman, quiet, unintellectual and passive, and the small, aggressive, ferociously intellectual woman." In: *The Passion of Ayn Rand*, loc. 2153.

25 Rand's words are cited in Barbara Branden, *The Passion of Ayn Rand*, loc. 3610, Note 20. See Susan Brownmiller, "Ayn Rand: A Traitor to Her Own Sex," in Gladstein and Sciabarra (eds), *Feminist Interpretations of Ayn Rand*, 63–65. For an excellent assessment of the convoluted logic of desire and rape in *The Fountainhead*,

critics' assessments of it, and Rand's responses to them, see Susan Love Brown, "Ayn Rand and Rape," *The Journal of Ayn Rand Studies*, 15:1, 2015, 3–22.

26 The notion of "a collective of individualists" finds a pre-echo in philosopher Max Stirner's theory of a "union of egos" in *The Ego and Its Own* (1844). As a political anarchist, Stirner saw this strategic collective as an alternative to the state.

27 Rand, *Atlas Shrugged* [1957] (New York: Signet, 1992), p. 671.

28 Nathaniel Branden, *Judgment Day: My Years with Ayn Rand* (Boston: Houghton Mifflin, 1989), p. 204.

29 Cited in Heller, *Ayn Rand and the World She Made*, loc. 6358.

30 Nathaniel Branden and Barbara Branden, *Who Is Ayn Rand?* (New York: Random House, 1962); Branden, *The Passion of Ayn Rand*; Nathaniel Branden, *Judgment Day: My Years with Ayn Rand* (Boston: Houghton Mifflin Harcourt, 1989), revised as *My Life with Ayn Rand* (New York: Wiley, 1999). Barbara Branden's book was adapted for the small screen as *The Passion of Ayn Rand*, directed by Christopher Menaul in 1999 with Helen Mirren in the starring role as Rand.

31 Barbara Branden, *The Passion of Ayn Rand*, loc. 9550.

32 Cited in Barbara Branden, *The Passion of Ayn Rand*, loc. 9830.

33 Barbara Branden, *The Passion of Ayn Rand*, loc. 486.

34 Shulamith Firestone, *The Dialectic of Sex: The Case for Feminist Revolution* [1970] (London: Paladin, 1972), p. 152.

35 Barbara Branden, *The Passion of Ayn Rand*, loc. 494.

36 Barbara Branden, *The Passion of Ayn Rand*, loc. 1086.

37 Nathaniel Branden, "Was Ayn Rand a Feminist?," in Gladstein and Sciabarra (eds), *Feminist Interpretations of Ayn Rand*, 223–230, p. 224.

38 Rand, *Atlas Shrugged*, p. 1069. The words appear four times throughout *Atlas Shrugged*, and are inscribed in granite in Galt's Gulch.

39 Barbara Branden, *The Passion of Ayn Rand*, loc. 9397.

40 Barbara Branden, *The Passion of Ayn Rand*, loc. 9822.

41 See Downing, *The Subject of Murder*.

42 Rand, *Journals of Ayn Rand*, edited by David Harriman, foreword by Leonard Peikoff (New York: Plume, 1999), loc. 773.

43 Rand, *Journals*, loc. 665.

44 Rand, *Journals*, loc. 664.

45 Colin Wilson, *The Outsider* (New York: Houghton Mifflin, 1956).

46 Rand, *Journals*, loc. 1074.

47 Rand, *Journals*, loc. 768.

48 The notion of "psychopathy" was first developed by J. C. Pritchard in the nineteenth century to describe the condition of being "morally insane" but otherwise technically "normal." See J. C. Pritchard, *A Treatise on Insanity and Other Disorders Affecting the Mind* (London: Sherwood, Gilbert, and Piper, 1835). It developed in the course of the twentieth century to refer to those without the capacity for empathy. The current idea of the "psychopath" is embodied in the extremely ruthless and successful CEO or else the remorseless criminal.

49 Rand, *Journals*, loc. 726.

50 Rand, *Journals*, loc. 738.

51 Rand, *Journals*, loc. 1062.

52 Rand, *Journals*, loc. 1076.

53 See http://aynrandlexicon.com/lexicon/anti-concepts.html.

54 Nathaniel Branden, "Was Ayn Rand a Feminist?" 224.

55 Barbara Branden, *The Passion of Ayn Rand*, loc. 9401.

56 Barbara Branden, *The Passion of Ayn Rand*, loc. 3335.

57 Barbara Branden, *The Passion of Ayn Rand*, loc. 5568.

58 Orville Prescott, "*The Fountainhead* by Ayn Rand," *The New York Times*, 12 May 1943, p. 23.

59 Barbara Branden, "Ayn Rand: The Reluctant Feminist," in Gladstein and Sciabarra (eds), *Feminist Interpretations of Ayn Rand*, 25–45, p. 27.

60 Lorine Pruette, "Battle against Evil: *The Fountainhead* by Ayn Rand," *The New York Times*, May 16 1943, p. 7.
61 Pruette, "Battle against Evil."
62 Whittaker Chambers, "Big Sister Is Watching You," *National Review*, 28 December 1957, http://whittakerchambers.org/articles/nr/bigsister/
63 Chambers, "Big Sister Is Watching You."
64 Gore Vidal, "Comment," *Esquire*, 1 July, 1961, https://classic.esquire.com/index.php/article/1961/7/1/comment
65 Barbara Branden, "Ayn Rand: The Reluctant Feminist," p. 26.
66 Barbara Branden, "Ayn Rand: The Reluctant Feminist," p. 26.
67 Normal Mailer, "The White Negro" (San Francisco: City Lights, 1957).
68 George Monbiot, "A Manifesto for Psychopaths", *The Guardian*, 5 March 2012, www.monbiot.com/2012/03/05/a-manifesto-for-psychopaths/85
69 Ayn Rand, "The Age of Envy, Part II," *The Objectivist*, August 1971, p. 1076.
70 Cited in Burns, *Goddess of the Market*, p. 263.
71 Nathaniel Branden, "Was Ayn Rand a Feminist?", p. 225.
72 Rand, "About a Woman President," [1968] reprinted in Leonard Peikoff (ed.), *The Voice of Reason: Essays in Objectivist Thought* (New York: New American Library, 1988), p. 268.
73 Nathaniel Branden, "Was Ayn Rand a Feminist?", p. 228.
74 Nathaniel Branden, "Was Ayn Rand a Feminist?", p. 228.
75 Nathaniel Branden, "Was Ayn Rand a Feminist?", p. 228.
76 Gladstein and Sciabarra, "Introduction," p. 3.
77 Brownmiller, "Ayn Rand," p. 65.
78 Brownmiller, "Ayn Rand," p. 64.
79 Brownmiller, "Ayn Rand," pp. 64–65.
80 Barbara Branden, *The Passion of Ayn Rand*, loc. 4662.
81 Rand, *Atlas Shrugged*, p. 396.
82 Rand, *Atlas Shrugged*, p. 102.
83 Christine Battersby, *Gender and Genius: Towards a Feminist Aesthetics* (London: Women's Press, 1994). Julia Kristeva wrote three volumes on the female genius of Hannah Arendt, Melanie Klein, and Collette designed to address the absence of a conception of female genius in Western thought. See *Le Génie féminin: La Vie, la folie, les mots*, 3 volumes (Paris: Gallimard, 1999–2002).
84 Gladstein, "Ayn Rand and Feminism: An Unlikely Alliance" [first published in *College English* in 1978] in *Feminist Interpretations of Ayn Rand*, 47–55, p. 48.
85 Gladstein, "Ayn Rand and Feminism," p. 48.
86 Billie Jean King, "Interview", *Playboy*, March 1976, cited in Gladstein, "Ayn Rand and Feminism," p. 49.
87 Cited in Barbara Branden, *The Passion of Ayn Rand*, loc. 5562.
88 Rand, *Atlas Shrugged*, p. 51.
89 A glowing review of Friedan's book appeared in *The Objectivist Newsletter*, authored by Nora Ephron, who described it as "brilliant, informative and culturally explosive". See "The Feminine Mystique," *The Objectivist Newsletter* 2:7, 1963, p. 26. And according to Barbara Branden, Rand herself read and enjoyed the book in 1963. See Barbara Branden, "Ayn Rand: The Reluctant Feminist," p. 25.
90 Rand, *Atlas Shrugged*, p. 775.
91 Vidal, "Comment."
92 Žižek, "The Actuality of Ayn Rand," p. 215.
93 Nathaniel Branden, *Judgment Day*, p. 203.
94 Rand, "Of Living Death," *The Voice of Reason: Essays in Objectivist Thought* (New York: Meridian, 1990), pp. 58–59.
95 Burns, *Goddess of the Market*, p. 196.
96 Rand stated: "anyone who takes that attitude has no right to claim that he is a defender of human rights." Cited in Jerry Schwartz, Interview with Ayn Rand, *Objectivist Forum*, 1:3, 1–6, p. 2.

97 Monbiot, "A Manifesto for Psychopaths".
98 Nathaniel Branden, "Was Ayn Rand a Feminist?", p. 224.
99 These were statements made by Rand during the Question-and-Answer session following her Ford Hall Forum Lecture, "The Moritorium on Brains," in November 1971. Cited and discussed in Chris Matthew Sciabarra, *Ayn Rand, Homosexuality, and Human Liberation* (Cape Town, South Africa: Leap Publishing, 2003), pp. 7–8. I am grateful to Chris Sciabarra for drawing this reference to my attention.
100 Branden, *The Passion of Ayn Rand*, loc. 478.
101 Žižek, "The Actuality of Ayn Rand," p. 225.
102 Žižek, "The Actuality of Ayn Rand," p. 224.
103 Eve Sedgwick, *Between Men: English Literature and Male Homosocial Desire* (New York: Columbia University Press, 1985).
104 Michael Prescott, "Shrugging Off Ayn Rand," http://michaelprescott.freeservers.com/shrugging-off-ayn-rand.html
105 Friedrich Nietzsche, *Thus Spake Zarathustra* [1883–1891], translated by Thomas Common (Mineola: Dove, 1999), p. 132.
106 Rand, *Atlas Shrugged*, p. 1021.
107 Monica Greco and Martin Savransky, "Foucault's Subjectivities," in Downing (ed.), *After Foucault*, 31–45, p. 42.
108 Foucault, "Technologies of the Self," in Luther H. Martin, Huck Gutman, and Patrick H. Hutton (eds.), *Technologies of the Self: A Seminar with Michel Foucault* (Amherst: The University of Massachusetts Press, 1988), 16–49, p. 22.
109 Rand, *Playboy* Interview [1964]. Reproduced in: Playboy, *50 Years of the Playboy Interview: Ayn Rand* (Playboy ebook), 2012, loc. 280.
110 Rand, "This Is John Galt Speaking," *For the New Intellectual*, 116–192, 1961, 140.
111 Duggan, *Mean Girl*, pp. 4, 14, 59, 73.
112 Barbara Branden, "Ayn Rand: The Reluctant Feminist," p. 27.
113 Duggan, *Mean Girl*, p. 4.
114 I refer to the title of Rand's co-authored collection (with Nathaniel Branden, Alan Greenspan and Robert Hessen), *Capitalism: The Unknown Ideal* (1966).

3

THE POLITICS OF SELFISHNESS

On Margaret Thatcher and exceptional women

They are casting their problems at society. And, you know, there's no such thing as society. There are individual men and women and there are families. And no government can do anything except through people, and people must look after themselves first.

(Margaret Thatcher, interview, *Woman's Own,* 1987)

Thatcherism is a self-addressed valentine card or a hymn in the key of me. [...] When they swot upon Thatcher the 'ism' they will find nothing but a one-woman band playing "I Did It My Way."

(*The Daily Mirror,* 1 March 1984)

I do take some small consolation that there is only one small vowel sound between ruin and run. The small vowel sound is "I."

(Thatcher, Speech to the Institute of SocioEconomic Studies, 1975)

The very notion of a "female leader" is, in many ways, historically speaking, an anomaly. Mary Beard's book *Women and Power* traces the silencing of women in political and public discourse back to the very origins of Classical literature, Homer's *Odyssey.* She highlights Telemachus's assertion to his mother Penelope that "speech will be the business of men," while women's work is "the loom and the distaff."[1] British Prime Minister Winston Churchill commented on the occasion of the election of the first female Member of Parliament, Nancy Astor, in 1919, that: "I find a woman's intrusion into the House of Commons as embarrassing as if she burst into my bathroom when I had nothing with which to defend myself, not even a sponge."[2] And in "About a Woman President" (1968), Ayn Rand expressed her view that there should never be a female President of the USA, and that she would certainly never vote for a female candidate. Rand wrote

> A woman cannot reasonably want to be a commander-in-chief. For a woman to seek or desire the presidency is, in fact, so terrible a prospect of spiritual self-immolation that the woman who would seek it is psychologically unworthy of the job.[3]

According to Randian logic, a female president may well have the capacity to be a good *president* but, in doing so, she would become a bad *woman*, or more radically *would logically not be a woman*. That Rand, a powerful, influential female individualist should have held these views is lamentable; that they are the views of her containing culture (an influence she would have claimed did not affect her) is undeniable. While we have still to see – despite a recent near-miss – the election of a female POTUS, Rand's words shed prescient light upon the particular form of misogyny both embodied in and produced in response to that consummate female commander-in-chief, Britain's first female Prime Minister, Margaret Thatcher.

In this chapter, I shall first examine the political and personal connotations of individuality and selfishness for Thatcher and Thatcherism, before considering how the figure of the UK's first female Prime Minister became a cultural repository for anxieties about gender and power. I shall explore how her own carefully contrived self-presentation embodied some of the contradictions and difficulties of propounding a discourse of selfishness or self-reliance while female. And I shall examine the ways in which many existing commentaries and critiques of Thatcher's female selfishness – including feminist ones – often perpetuate problematic assumptions about the degree to which ambition and self-interest can be "proper" to any woman.

Who was Margaret Thatcher?[4]

Margaret Hilda Roberts was born in Grantham, Lincolnshire, UK, on 13 October 1925. The daughter of a grocer and local alderman, Alfred Roberts, young Margaret was raised with the dual – and intertwined – values of Wesleyan Methodism and economic frugality, values that she would carry into adulthood and her political career. She would go on to state "Economics are the method; the object is to change the soul."[5] After completing her secondary education at Kesteven and Grantham Girls' Grammar School, Margaret would read Chemistry at Somerville College, Oxford. In 1946 she became President of the Oxford University Conservative Association. As a hard-working, academically gifted meritocrat from relatively humble beginnings, Thatcher came from a completely different socio-economic class than the majority of her fellow Party members. The Conservative Party traditionally favoured candidates from aristocratic backgrounds or with inherited wealth, who had been privately educated (often at Eton) followed by an Oxbridge degree, and with a professional grounding in finance, law, the military, or the church. Thatcher's premiership obviously departed from this tradition, both in class and gender terms, although Edward Heath's election as leader in 1965 would, in fact, mark the first rupture: He was the grammar-school-educated son of a Kent carpenter. For questions having as much to do with class as with his quiet, "confirmed bachelor" persona, Heath was often held up as an example of weak, middle-class leadership. In contrast, and ironically, Thatcher's style would be marked by a perceived virility.[6] But economic privilege was not only the mainstay of the MPs of the Conservative Party. Thatcher would later declare at the Party conference in 1977: "People from my sort of background needed grammar schools to compete with children from privileged homes like Shirley Williams and Anthony Wedgwood Benn."[7] (These were, respectively, a Labour MP turned Liberal Democrat peer who was responsible for the abolition of the grammar school system, and a far-Left Labour MP of considerable private means.)

In 1951, Margaret married Denis Thatcher, a wealthy factory-owner, whose financial backing would enable her to study for the Bar, and who would go on to support her emotionally and practically throughout her meteoric political ascendancy. Thatcher later allegedly commented to an old school friend visiting her for a tour of the Houses of Parliament that she would not have been able to have a career in politics had it not been for "Denis's money."[8] Thatcher's Parliamentary political career was launched in the 1959 General Election, when she became MP for Finchley, a safe Conservative seat. In October 1960 she was given the role of Parliamentary Secretary for the Ministry of Pensions and National Insurance. Throughout the 1960s, with the Conservatives in opposition, she held a number of posts in Edward Heath's shadow cabinet, including in Housing and Land (from 1965), Transport (1968), and Education (from 1969). In 1970, Heath's Conservatives defeated Harold Wilson's Labour Party in a General Election and Margaret Thatcher took her first cabinet post as Secretary of State for Education and Science.

In February 1975, following the Conservatives' recent defeat in the 1974 General Election, discontented members ousted Edward Heath as Party Leader and elected Margaret Thatcher in his place – a surprise result. She became the first woman to lead a British Political Party. On 3 May 1979, the Conservatives defeated James Callaghan's Labour Party with 44% of the vote and Thatcher became Prime Minister. She would go on to win two further General Elections in 1983 and 1987. By the time of her reluctant resignation on 28 November 1990, Margaret Thatcher would be the longest serving British Prime Minister of the twentieth century, with a term of 11 years, six months, and 24 days behind her. Thatcher embodied the "difficult woman," often expressing views that were oppositional to both prevailing social norms and the tendencies of her own Party. On taking up her premiership in 1979, she expressed her view that the country had become mired in an unproductive reliance on the Welfare State, a politics of envy, and "bourgeois guilt." She declared that she sought to revive "a sober and constructive interest in the noble ideals of personal responsibility."[9]

Throughout Thatcher's three terms as Prime Minister she pursued a strong leadership style and stuck to her brand as a "conviction politician," drawing simultaneous praise and vilification for policies such as the sale of council housing properties to tenants and her bellicose stance during the Falklands conflict with Argentina in 1982 (which saw her popularity among the electorate soar prior to the 1983 election, which she won with a resounding majority). Her ultimate defeat, in the form of her reluctant resignation in the face of significant pressure and leadership challenges from within her Party on 22 November 1990, came on the back of one of her most individualistic and unpopular policies: the introduction of the Community Charge, or "poll tax." The poll tax, introduced to Scotland in 1989 and to the rest of Great Britain the following year, replaced a tax on dwellings based on the value of the property with a single, flat-rate, per-capita tax on every adult in the country. It was heavily criticized for hitting the poorest hardest and for ignoring accrued wealth in the form of equity. Its introduction was chaotic and its implementation led to numerous refusals to pay and widespread protests throughout the country (the "Poll Tax Riots"). It was, however, a perfectly logical initiative for the Prime Minister in its Thatcherite insistence on the individual as the political and social unit and in some ways it is poignantly fitting that such a selfish policy should have been Thatcher's undoing. Images of the former Iron Lady, leaving Downing Street for the final time on 28 November 1990, uncharacteristic tears visible on her face, were broadcast across the world to widespread consternation. Her ousting was widely described as a "betrayal" of Thatcher by her Party colleagues, including by Thatcher herself. She would later write in the first volume of her autobiography:

> I was sick at heart. I could have resisted the opposition of opponents and potential rivals and even respected them for it; but what grieved me was the desertion of those I had always considered friends and allies and the weasel words whereby they had transmuted their betrayal into frank advice and concern for my fate.[10]

Thatcherism: "I Did It My Way"?

The rise of Thatcherism, and the way in which Thatcher's vision of a self-reliant population caught the imagination of the nation, can be at least partially explained by the fact that she emerged on the national scene at a time when public discontent was very pronounced. The post-War consensus in Britain had been characterized by the expansion of the Welfare State, a strong Trade Union movement, investment in nationalized industries, and high taxes. This state of affairs was broadly supported (or at least tolerated) by One Nation Conservative politicians, as well as Labour ones. When in government, Tories saw themselves as the guardians of the status quo, responsible for administering existing policies, in the spirit of "small 'c' conservatism," rather than for implementing large-scale reform. The fear of public insurrection and the wrath of the unions arguably attended their apathy. However, by the 1970s, many felt that the UK economy was stagnating. The three-day week, power cuts, and the strikes that brought parts of the country effectively to a standstill signalled a country that was barely functioning. Edward Heath had aspired to a lower tax, smaller state economy, but had not been perceived as having the vision or strength of personality to implement it. It fell to Thatcher, opportunistically, to make Heath's dreams a reality, with the warning that "where there is no vision, the people must surely perish."[11] She argued that the risk of greater unemployment and increased social inequality was worth taking if it led to greater long-term national wealth-creation overall and enabled those who made the effort individually to prosper.[12]

Marxist feminist Ros Brunt argued in 1987 that the implementation of this free-market, neoliberal ideology succeeded under Thatcher's premiership precisely *because* Thatcher was a woman. She claims:

> The effectiveness of Thatcher's femininity is the degree to which it serves as cover for what would otherwise be transparent Heathism, or its ultimate extension, "naked Tebbitry," where the full extent of the present government's devastating sleaziness and mean-minded corruption would be amply displayed.[13]

Thatcher's choice of language to describe and justify the policies she would implement suggests that Brunt may be right. To make her message relatable, Thatcher drew on the lexicon of housekeeping, of holding the country's purse-strings, and suggested that it took the shrewd common sense of the British housewife to carry out solid economic management:

> My policies are based not on some economic theory but on the things I and millions like me were brought up with. An honest day's pay; live within your means; put by a nest egg for a rainy day; pay your bills on time; support the police.[14]

A *Sunday Times* profile of Thatcher in 1978 commented on the "uncanny ease" with which she moved "between her roles as potential Prime Minister and superwife."[15] A recent doctoral thesis dedicated entirely to the topic of Thatcher's deployment of the trope of "domestic femininity" has proposed that "it was as a lower-middle class 'housewife'" that Margaret Thatcher "won the Conservative Party leadership in 1975 and the general election in 1979".[16] And in her psychoanalytic essay on Thatcher's violence, Jacqueline Rose comments on the incongruity of her "embracing of the most phallic of self-images (the iron lady) and an insistence on her femininity as utterly banal (the housewife managing the purse-strings of the nation)."[17]

Thatcher's claim that her economic package was based on the principles of good housekeeping rather than on any economic theory aside, the political

philosophy that would become known as "Thatcherism" was, in fact, characterized by a rejection of the model of post-War economics often assumed to
be dominant – Keynesianian[18] – and a robust explicit shift towards the style
of free-market capitalism espoused by Milton Friedman, with a focus on the
principles of privatization and profit.[19] Thatcher deliberately appealed to those
who were socially aspirational, as perhaps best epitomised by her "right to buy"
scheme which allowed council tenants to buy their social housing at a discount
price and thereby become "home-owners." She promised, in place of a state-
funded security blanket, independence, property ownership, and financial security for those who dared. She refused to acknowledge the determining factor
of one's class at birth on life chances, and argued that it was in the gift of the
"individual, family and nation" to make the decision to prosper. She appealed
directly to those who did not want to be dependent on the state, but rather to
be masters of their own destiny, stating "self-government is for those men and
women who have learned to govern themselves."[20] In July 1979, directly after
winning the General Election, Thatcher gave a lecture entitled "The Renewal
of Britain" at Cambridge University. In it she spoke of "the moral fallacy" that
"conscience" could be "collectivised" through the "wanton expansion of the
state's responsibilities."[21]

On her style of communicating about the matter of governing the country –
both with her fellow MPs and with the electorate – Thatcher insisted on the
importance of persuading others of the rightness of her vision. She stated:

> You've got to take everyone along with you ... You can only get other
> people in tune with you by being a little evangelical about it ... I'm not a
> consensus politician or a pragmatic politician: I'm a conviction politician.
> And I believe in the politics of persuasion: it's my job to put forward what
> I believe and try to get people to agree with me.[22]

And, she claimed: "I tend to look at things more logically than do my colleagues.
They come eventually to [my viewpoint] because there aren't any other ways to
go."[23] Thatcher's insistence on her superior logic and rationality in comparison
to her overwhelmingly male cabinet offers a striking inversion of the assumed
gendering of reason. In fact, the characteristics of independence, strength of will,
and individual achievement that marked Thatcher's message were perfectly and
seamlessly mirrored in her own public persona such that, for Thatcher, the political was absolutely the personal. Rumours of superhuman strength of personality and unnatural amounts of energy circulated around Margaret Thatcher and
contributed to her mythic status. Her ability to function on four hours of sleep
per night and the speed with which she was able to comprehend and complete
reports at extraordinary speed meant that she was held in awe by colleagues.

Thatcher's biographer, Hugo Young, described her "inexhaustible psychic energy"
as fuelled by the "desire to dominate."[24] "Exceptionality" thus became Thatcher's
brand, making her admired and feared by her foes in Parliament (those she derided

as "wets"), and hated by feminists, who perceived her unwillingness to lift other women up alongside her as the symptom of an underlying misogyny or identification with paternalistic and patriarchal values. In the 61 years of the British Parliament up to 1979, female MPs had constituted less than 5% of the House of Commons. Thatcher did little to change this. She only ever included one woman in her cabinet – Baroness Janet Young, who briefly served as Leader of the House of Lords. When asked in the course of an interview in *The Daily Telegraph* in 1966 why there were so few female peers, she replied, "The trouble is that there are still not many of us who have made the grade as men. Therefore we stand out more conspicuously."[25] And, in 1981, Thatcher claimed in an interview for Thames Television News that not much more could be done to prevent gender discrimination, stating "I don't think there has been a great deal of discrimination against women for years."[26]

Thatcher constructed for herself a dual and contradictory femininity. On the one hand, she appealed to an archetype of the good, traditional, Tory woman. According to Brunt, this had to do with "'making the best of yourself' and 'making do.' It belongs to the realm of the housewife, of putting the best face on it, of perfect grooming, smart but practical, of care with the household budget." In this guise, she balanced the country's budget as she would her household budget, and invited other hard-working, aspirational housewives of the electorate to identify with her.[27] On the other hand, she set herself apart from the common run of women, explaining the underrepresentation of women in politics and Parliament as the result of women's reluctance to step up, or lack of strength of character, rather than in terms of structural inequality of access. And the perception of her as an atypical woman (perhaps as "not really a woman") was precisely what enabled her to function as leader for so long. Conservative MP Iain Macleod commented, with regard to Thatcher as a female politician, that "this one is different," declaring her "quite exceptionally able. A first-class brain."[28] To the degree that "the grocer's daughter" was accepted within the ranks of the Tory Party, it was precisely owing to the difference perceived between her persona and that of other female MPs (and the fact that the vaunted qualities she possessed were ones coded as masculine, so that she was "like" – but better than – a man).

Thatcher's persona: Between virility and hyper-femininity

An observation that is often made about Margaret Thatcher has to do precisely with the way in which her persona and appearance alternated between hyper-femininity and a profound virility. Indeed, Heather Nunn opens her impressive psychoanalytic study of Thatcher and her place in Britain's national cultural fantasy with a discussion of the images of the Prime Minister test-driving a British-Built Challenger tank on a visit to Germany. Nunn writes:

> Swathed in white, with a headscarf trailing behind her in the breeze, white leather gloves upon her hands, she stood upright, seemingly guiding the

bulky armoured tank across barren, desert-like terrain [...] She appeared unafraid of imagined opposition, and at home with the machinery of war that carried her.[29]

Iconic images of the female warrior and symbol of the nation Britannia are simultaneously evoked by this description of Thatcher's upright bearing and warlike demeanour, while the mention of a white headscarf and gloves sharply recalls 1970s and 1980s middle-to-upper-class British femininity. Note that Queen Elizabeth the Second is often photographed wearing her head scarf. Further, drawing on the link between the female Prime Minister and the head of state, *Guardian* journalist Marion Bower wrote of Thatcher in 1989: "if she uses the Royal 'we' a lot, it's because she is a Queen Bee."[30] And an article in the Scottish *Herald* from 2013 described Thatcher as a "suburban Boadicea."[31]

Much published scholarship examining the expectations placed on female politicians and political activists, especially but not solely those on the right, focuses on the degree to which such women are expected to embody these two, contradictory, symbolic ideas of "the feminine": compliant motherly defender of family values and exceptional warrior queen.[32] While these are both caricatures and contradictions, they have become iconic, perhaps recalling legendary and mythic female symbols of nationhood (Britannia, Boadicea, Marianne, Joan of Arc). Where women leaders possess other qualities that appear to undermine this approved-of duality, they become illegible. I have written elsewhere of how far-right French leader of the *Front national* Marine Le Pen and UKIP leadership candidate turned founder of her own Party "For Britain" Anne Marie Waters both fail in different ways to fit into the dual roles of obedient femininity and warrior-woman expected of right-wing leaders.[33] Le Pen fails by dint of her status as a divorced single mother in the context of a socially Conservative and Catholic Party; Waters by dint of her lesbianism and feminism while leading an extremely macho, nationalist group. I describe the illegibility of female leaders who do not conform to the rules placed on them as examples of what I call "identity category violation," a concept I borrow from linguistics. A category violation in the linguistics sense is exemplified by Noam Chomsky's sentence: "Colorless green ideas sleep furiously." While this sentence obeys the rules of grammar and syntax, it is nonsense in terms of meaning, because the adjectives chosen contradict each other and the adverb is not appropriate to the verb it describes. Our sense of understanding is thus confounded.

However, I argue, when we transpose this concept from syntax and grammar to the codification of identity politics and identificatory labels, it demonstrates how our contemporary way of understanding of identity is *itself* faulty and unstable: "our notion that we can both understand and predict reliably the categorisation of political identity as it is imbricated with the other identity categories of sex, gender, sexuality, nationality, etc., is deeply flawed."[34] In other words, we collectively formulate expectations for certain roles (here that of "female leader" – already something of a categorical challenge for reasons explained above) and we experience dissonance when a given individual exceeds or transgresses them. Margaret Thatcher, perhaps more than any other female leader, was often able to strike the balance between the unlikely and contradictory archetypes expected of her and to blend them into a successful combination or personal brand. Indeed, even Marxist feminist Ros Brunt writes with grudging admiration of Thatcher's uncanny ability to embody "ordinary housewife, refined lady, and warrior queen"[35] in one person.

Media representations of Thatcher, both discursive and visual, at the time of her premiership, consistently focused on and exaggerated precisely this dualistic quality of Thatcher's gendered performance. In this cartoon (Figure 3.1), for example, Thatcher's power to swipe Soviet influence off the globe is tempered or balanced by the fact that she is shown to have done so using only a feather duster, recalling woman's domestic role, and while clutching the black handbag that would become her iconic accessory. Nationalistic pride at Britain's influence on the world stage is tempered by the feminine accoutrements of the destroyer. I would argue that misogyny mixes with grudging admiration in such representations, and that the shock of identity category violation potentiated by a selfish, violent, individualistic woman is reined in by references to the familiar feminine and the domestic everyday.

This ever-bubbling undercurrent of misogyny surrounding Thatcher was visible throughout political and media discourses about her. During the 1979 General Election campaign, Dennis Canavan urged voters: "Don't let that witch hang up her curtains in Downing Street."[36] In an article in *The Guardian*, ten

FIGURE 3.1 Thatcher swipes Soviet influence off the globe using her feather duster. Reproduced with permission of CagleCartoons.com.

years later, Marion Bowman reported on a sexist backlash in Parliament designed
to undermine the right-wing leader by referencing her femininity:

> Tory MP Emma Nicholson is convinced that a bitter, anti-woman un-
> dercurrent is flaring up in Parliament and not just on the Labour benches.
> "They will use anything to attack the Prime Minister and I think they
> are sacrificing their acceptance of women as equals to get at her." Inside
> and outside Westminster, there's talk of political challengers being "hand-
> bagged," of curtains being bought for the retirement home in Dulwich, of
> baby-minding the new grandson.[37]

And in *Marxism Today*, Brunt expressed how, whereas the misogyny of the Tories
with regard to their leader could be hidden behind their cultivated manners and
stiff courtesy, many leftist men were outspoken and explicit in their sexism, with
their use of the slogan "Ditch the Bitch" and their recriminations to socialist
feminists that Thatcher was somehow the logical outcome and thin end of the
wedge of feminist politics with exhortations: "See what you've done now! Look
where all this can lead."[38]

At other times, however, Thatcher is figured more explicitly as "an honorary
man," in ways that might remind us of Rand's being dubbed by Ludwig von
Mises "the bravest man in America." In this cartoon (Figure 3.2), she is depicted
waltzing with Ronald Reagan. The caption – borrowed from the words, not of
Reagan, but of German Chancellor Helmut Schmidt – tells us that she is "still

FIGURE 3.2   Thatcher waltzes with Ronald Reagan: "Still the best man in Europe."
Reproduced with permission of CagleCartoons.com.

the best man in Europe." The romantic overtones of the image of the dancing power couple has ambiguous shades of political homosociality with the figuring of Thatcher "as a man," smooching with her equal, Reagan.[39]

Moreover, Thatcher's handling of the Falklands conflict in 1982 and her election campaign the following year provided plentiful opportunity for her and her team to draw on this image of Thatcher as better than any man. Thatcher's campaign song voiced the idea of the female leader as "a fighter" with "not a man around to match her":

> Who do we want, who do we need?
> It is a leader who is bound to succeed:
> Maggie Thatcher – just Maggie for me.
> These British Isles have found a fighter
> With the coolest of styles,
> No other politician comes within miles,
> Two, three, four, Thatcher, Thatcher, Thatcher,
> Not a man around to match her.[40]

What we see in these images and discourses is the suggestion that sometimes the fact of a woman wielding power is seen to feminize the exercise of power and the field of politics, while at other times, in order to be wielding such power in the first place, Thatcher must in some way *really be a man* and, when she succeeded, *the best man*.

Rand's objection to the principle of a female President is in many ways prescient, as the notion that to govern would involve a betrayal or renunciation, or yet a grotesque deformation, of what is culturally understood as femininity was amply played out in coverage of Thatcher. In exploring the case of Rand, we have seen that she was confronted by an uneasy contradiction with regard to her desire to live, act, and write as an individual, while holding regressive ideas about womanhood that poisoned and undermined her vaunted self-regard. Thatcher trod a similar path, played out much more visibly on the surface of her very person as a public figure. To achieve election on a Tory ticket in the 1970s, Thatcher could not have appeared to be anything other than an ultra-gender-conforming C/conservative woman – fitting that classist and sexist category: "a lady."

Indeed, she was extensively coached and advised on her appearance and style by two men, former television producer Gordon Reece and advertising guru Lord Bell, who recommended a softer and more elegant feminine hairstyle and wardrobe, in tandem with vocal lessons to lower – and thereby masculinize – her voice.[41] Hence, Thatcher perfected her exaggeratedly bouffed helmet of golden hair, flawless make-up, and the fussy pussy-cat-bow blouses that were so easy to caricature in cartoons and in the Thatcher puppet created for the satirical television programme, *Spitting Image*. Called upon to police conservative ideas of traditional womanhood and family values, on the one hand, all the while being "the only real man in the cabinet" and "the best man in Europe" for the purposes of bellicose national interest, on the other, Thatcher embodied Rand's claim that a woman taking on such a role would be placed in a position of constant schizoid tension and self-contradiction. Yet, Rand's devastating error lay in believing that this was because the essential nature of woman is at odds with the desire to rule as Primary, rather than because of the rigidity of the patriarchal edict regarding what women may properly be.

In an attempt to account for the line Thatcher trod between virility and hyper-femininity, Heather Nunn's psychoanalytic reading of Thatcher's gendered performance draws on Joan Rivière's concept of the "masquerade."[42] Rivière's landmark article argued that the professional woman, easily as capable as a man in the field of professional life, experiences anxiety at the unconscious threat she perceives her competence to pose to the (symbolic) father, and therefore compensates by performing excessive or compliant femininity to offset or undermine her "masculine" achievements. In some ways this dual and contradictory behaviour certainly seems to describe Thatcher (and the archetypical female leader of cultural fantasy). Nunn reads passages from the second volume of Thatcher's autobiography, *The Path to Power* (1995), that deals with her early years, to analyze the ambivalence and anxiety that she deems to lie behind the "mask" of Thatcher. She makes links between the theory of female rivalry of the father (that is both desired and disavowed) and Thatcher's oft-discussed admiration for, and emulation of, her own literal father, the grocer and alderman Alfred. For example, she writes: "When recalling her father's influence upon the formation of her character one phrase sprang to Thatcher's lips: 'That which thy father bequeathed thee, earn it anew, if thou wouldst possess it'."[43] Nunn interprets this statement as an example of Thatcher's imitation and rivalry of the/her father, to whose legacy she is desperate to live up. Yet it could just as easily be a reflection on Thatcher's work ethic, her belief in individual striving that would hold that each person must be responsible for their own life's achievements, rather than falling back on family influence. (Such an attitude, incidentally, chimes neatly with Ayn Rand's view of literal monetary inheritance which she places in the voice of her character Francisco d'Anconia in *Atlas Shrugged*: "Only the man who does not need it, is fit to inherit wealth – the man who would make his own fortune no matter where he started."[44])

Thatcher has been open about some of the self-stylizations she chose to make. She described the voice training she underwent to lower her voice as an attempt to match the "curious deep braying" of the male Members of the House of Commons, while avoiding the "grating shrieking" associated with women.[45] Mary Beard has remarked perceptively on the kind of language used in media commentary to describe women's tone and utterances, picking up on the terms "whine" and "whinge." She asks, rhetorically:

> Do those words matter? Of course they do, because they underpin an idiom that acts to remove the authority, the force, even the humour from what women have to say. It is an idiom that effectively repositions women back into the domestic sphere (people "whinge" over things like the washing up); it trivialises their words, or it "re-privatises" them. Contrast

the "deep-voiced" man with all the connotations of profundity that the simple word "deep" brings. It is still the case that when listeners hear a female voice, they do not hear a voice that connotes authority; or rather they have not learned how to hear authority in it.[46]

Beard's words suggest a plausible – and pragmatic – explanation for Margaret Thatcher's conscious decision to deepen her voice here. Rather than an adoption of masculine traits in an unconscious attempt to rival the father, as suggested by Nunn, or owing to Thatcher's own deep-seated belief in the inherent superiority of masculinity, à la Rand, the female politician adapted to the environment that would contain her in order best to serve her own interests and further her own politics.

And on her feminine performance, Thatcher makes clear that the choices she made were consciously arrived at. After the Red Army propaganda vehicle *Red Star* named her the "Iron Lady," Thatcher delivered the following speech:

> Ladies and gentleman, I stand before you tonight, in my Red Star chiffon evening gown, my face softly made-up and my fair hair gently waved – the Iron Lady of the western world, a cold war Warrior, an Amazon Philistine, even a Peking plotter. Well, am I any of these things...? Yes, I am an Iron Lady – after all it wasn't a bad thing to be an Iron Duke. Yes, if that's how you wish to/interpret my defense of values and freedoms fundamental to our way of life.[47]

Nunn concedes here that Thatcher's words are a playful – and conscious – game, engaging with the terms in which she is being interpellated ("Iron" = warlike, masculine, tough; "Lady" = a label of class-bound femininity). Unlike Rivière's neurotic career woman, Nunn concedes, Thatcher does not defer to men's opinion of her feminine appearance; rather she uses it as an extension of her artillery. Yet, Nunn insists that alongside a possible interpretation of playful parody (that, we might note, resembles somewhat Judith Butler's idea of all exaggerated performances of gender as a form of conscious drag[48]), Thatcher's self-referential reflection on excessive femininity in the speech betrays "anxiety about being placed in the limelight as an aberrant aggressive woman."[49] Yet, speaking about the labels that were attributed to her, Thatcher was clear in her autobiography that they had not necessarily been to her disadvantage and that they enabled her to gain the upper hand:

> I was "the Iron Lady," "Battling Maggie," "Attila the Hen" [...] These generally gave opponents the impression I was a hard nut to crack, I was glad to be so portrayed even though no real person could be so single-mindedly tough.[50]

Discussing Thatcher's self-perception in *The Path to Power*, Nunn comments on the Prime Minister's refusal to admit to having experienced discomfort or "anxiety" at the roles expected and expertly delivered. She writes that "forms of femininity are presented and then denied in favour of the most phallic of images. There is no failure in this constructed identity, no gap is allowed between word and deed."[51] She notes, moreover, that her edition of the biography's cover blurb corroborates this sense of seamless coherence: "In our uncertain and increasingly rudderless world, here is a woman who knows what she thinks and why she thinks it."[52] Nunn's seeming need to problematize this rarity is the object of my scrutiny here. On the whole, while persuasively argued, I find Nunn's attempt to locate anxiety and uncertainty as the underlying motivation of a selfish women's behaviour on psychoanalytic grounds to be itself a symptom of the broader cultural phenomenon that I am exploring in this book: a reluctance to accept unpalatable women on their own terms. It is as if behaviour and beliefs such as Thatcher's can only be understood as a neurosis of femininity rather than as a rationally chosen strategy. To analyses of Thatcher as a neurotic woman I would deliberately, strategically, and provocatively – for the sake of the thought experiment it forces, if nothing else – juxtapose a rational, selfish woman, weighing up which performances and gestures are in her own self-interest, (mis)apprehended by a neurotic culture.

What is clear is that for feminist critics, as well as for the media and public, Thatcher must be read as a masquerading figure, an "honorary man," a Prime Minister in drag. There is no place in cultural discourse for her to simply have been *what she said she was* – no doubt out of exasperation at being asked constantly to reflect upon her gender: "I don't notice I'm a woman. I regard myself as the Prime Minister."[53] There is simply *no narrative* that allows simply for "Margaret Thatcher, Prime Minister," a rather ruthless individual, whose policies were seen as cruel and unusual by many, yet whose sex and gender should be irrelevant to her public role, in the way that an equivalent male prime minister's would be.[54] This is because, first, maleness is unmarked and, second, masculinity is understood as *properly* dominant and will-to-power-led – to the degree that it is apprehended at all.

Monstrous woman/monstrous mother

Thatcher, it is fair to say, was a figure who provoked intense emotion in the country she governed and in the wider world. She was hated and loved with equal vehemence. Yet, public hatred of Thatcher was freighted with so much more than hatred of her politics alone. Thatcher's famous speech that is metonymically referred to by its key soundbite, "The lady's not for turning," voiced, despite the dogmatic intransigence of the literal message of the speech (a refusal to re-consider regulation of the economy), a chilling echo of an age-old misogyny. Thatcher figures herself in the third person as "the lady," a female cipher. The "turning" draws attention to the silenced rhyme word "burning" that it puts under erasure, reminding us of the punishment meted out to those deviant women who threatened to encroach on male authority, and were scapegoated as witches in the burning times. And the brutal misogyny of witch-burning returns in the commonly seen and heard response to the death of the former Prime Minister in 2013 in the repetition of the slogan and song: "Ding Dong the Wicked Witch is Dead," from *The Wizard of Oz*. That a *woman's* death was sadistically celebrated here in specifically misogynistic terms, rather than simply the death of a controversial and ruthless former Tory leader, is an issue that it is ethically incumbent upon us not to overlook, regardless of our view of Thatcher's policies.

Nunn has stated that "Fear or indeed reluctant admiration of Thatcher stemmed from concerns about the chaotic or emotional dangers of femininity."[55] The monstering of Margaret Thatcher owing to her "dangerous" gender presentation is analyzed in an essay from 1988, in which Jacqueline Rose reads together cultural understandings of Thatcher, a pro-death-penalty female Prime Minister, and of Ruth Ellis, the last woman to be hanged in the UK, a murderer who insisted in her trial on her rational decision to kill her lover. Rose understands these two women as examples of culturally inappropriate femininity because they can be seen as simultaneously violent and rational. She makes a psychoanalytic argument for these women's location at the far limits of psychic fantasy, and as embodiments of "the social at its most perverse."[56] Using Julia Kristeva's essay "Women's Time," she discusses women's uneasy – indeed impossible in Kristevan terms – relationship with the socio-symbolic contract, "a contract to which they are subjected, from which they are also excluded, and which they can also embody in the worst of its effects."[57]

Rose writes: "the woman supporter of capital punishment is as grotesque for the dominant stereotypes of femininity as for a feminist critique of the state as the embodiment of phallic power."[58] Rose understands Thatcher's "perversity" or monstrousness via the psychoanalytic concept of the (unconsciously organized) symbolic order and the way in which phantasy plays around it. This same idea, however, is equally capable of being apprehended without a psychoanalytic framework and via my (consciously and rationally intelligible) concept of "identity category violation." In this case, it can be argued that Thatcher violates a particular identity category rule: the expectation that "woman," "reason," and "violence" belong in different categorical boxes. What is interesting is that it is both mainstream patriarchal culture and (as Rose implies) feminist ethical imperatives that expect – nay demand – this.

Rose's essay contains a secondary strand of argumentation – a critique of the arbitrarily drawn line between sanctioned and unsanctioned forms of violence (the wish to legalize state killing as a penalty for crime, or the decision to order fire on a retreating battleship being understood very differently than the intimate crime of murder). Rose writes of Thatcher: "It is a grotesque scenario – one which mimics that of Ruth Ellis in reverse – where a woman who stands for super-rationality writes violence into the law (or would do so), instead of being executed for it."[59] The similarity between the figures, however, lies in the fact that their proximity to both violence and rationality reads differently in cultural terms owing to their sex than if it were a man calling for the restoration of the death penalty or killing a lover out of revenge.

In an analysis of the effects of Thatcher's premiership on popular music and pop culture of the 1980s, Nabeel Zuberi comments on Rose's article, pointing out that both female figures discussed by Rose represent something "illegitimate" and "out-of-control" for the cultural imaginary, namely "individual female violence."[60] Zuberi further compares Thatcher to that other unnatural, monstrous British woman I have written of elsewhere: child murderer Myra Hindley.[61] As well as behaving in ways that transgress what is understandable within acceptable modes of femininity, both figures attracted extraordinary amounts of attention for their appearance and self-stylization (what Rose calls in the case of Thatcher an "ambiguous sexual self-fashioning"[62]). Zuberi writes: "aspects of Thatcher's own star image in the 1980s bear a resemblance to Hindley's 'look'."[63] That murderers and politicians are, in modernity, celebrities is a pertinent point,[64] and that female celebrities are scrutinized for their appearance in ways that their male counterparts are not is undeniable. Moreover, both Thatcher's and Hindley's appearance led to comparisons with monstrous or mythic figures: Myra Hindley was described at her trial as resembling Clytemnestra and Medusa,[65] while reggae pop band UB40's track "Madame Medusa" (1980) described a "Lady with the marble smile" based on Thatcher, who is denoted by the eponymous moniker.[66]

It is telling that two of the principal scholarly works that consider the meanings of Thatcher's gender in tandem with the particularity of her politics are written from psychoanalytic perspectives: Jacqueline Rose's article and Heather Nunn's book. A key difference between them is that Rose analyzes responses on the part of the "collective imaginary of British culture"[67] to the exceptional selfish woman that is Thatcher (i.e. she psychoanalyzes cultural response), while Nunn undertakes to psychoanalyze Margaret Thatcher herself, drawing on Thatcher's autobiographical writings about her early life. What this tendency towards psychoanalytic excavation suggests in both cases, however, is the difficulty of accepting female selfishness and female exceptionality *at face value*, as something that *just is*. It is so aberrant, so othered, that culture and, in some cases, critics need to find a hidden meaning, a hidden desire, a hidden justification behind the figure of the selfish woman. My choice to eschew psychoanalytic explanations and to examine instead ways of reading and making conscious sense of the figure of Thatcher, using the concept of identity category violation, is made in part on the basis that foregrounding the conscious and the rational may be understood as a kind of counter-discursive feminist move when discussing selfish women who propound discourses of rationality such as Thatcher and Rand. If, as Rose illustrates, Thatcher has been monstered as a result of her inappropriate, unfeminine rationality, then it is precisely a gesture of rationality that she deserves in analyses of her actions and selfhood.

The monstrousness discussed above that accrued to Thatcher as a "violent woman" was also linked to her relationship with the role and figure of mother (since "woman" is seldom thought without its association with "mother"). Thatcher is figured in discourse alternately as an overzealous or punishing matriarch and as a neglectful or unnatural mother. Many commentators have drawn attention to the way in which Thatcher offered a figure of fear and titillation for the single-sex, public school-educated men in her cabinet and Party. Nunn comments that "Thatcher's anomalous position as female Prime Minister [...] added a frisson of sexuality to [members'] memories of her premiership."[68] And Marina Warner has argued that Thatcher's oft-commented-upon association with the figures of "the nanny" or "the governess" recalls "an enormous source of female power: the right of prohibition."[69] Further, one moniker Thatcher would pick up that suggested an uncaring and neglectful – and therefore unnatural – attitude to children was that of "Mrs Thatcher, Milk Snatcher," when she made the decision in December 1970 to abolish free milk for 8 to 12-year-old schoolchildren as part of her welfare cut measures. *The Guardian* called the decision "a vindictive measure which should never have been laid before Parliament."[70] And Heather Nunn has written "for a woman to deprive children of milk implied an aberrant femininity, and Thatcher was represented as a woman divorced from the caring instincts of motherhood."[71] What all of these examples suggest is that the female leader cannot escape the role of "matriarch" – traditionally the only authoritative female role that is culturally allowed for.

British comedian and Hollywood actor (turned would-be left-wing radical intellectual) Russell Brand wrote an ambivalent piece on the occasion of Thatcher's death in 2013 that focused precisely on her qualities as a *mother* as well as/rather than as a *leader* (since the one places the other under erasure to some degree). His provocatively titled opinion piece in *The Guardian*, "I Always Felt Sorry for Her Children,"[72] says much about cultural responses to the source of social disturbance that is the woman who leads. Brand's anecdotal piece commences with a lyrical description of a stroll he took with a friend in the gardens of Temple, London, whereupon they espied the frail figure of an elderly woman watering the rose garden, who turned out to be Margaret Thatcher. He writes: "I stared like an amateur astronomer unable to describe my awe at this distant phenomenon." Yet, recollecting his reaction to Thatcher when he was a child and she was the Prime Minister, Brand recalls the stereotypical and expected images of "the headmistress of our country," "her coiffured virility," "the barren baroness." This last alliterative coining is telling. Thatcher was not "barren;" she was, of course, a literal mother to two children as well as the symbolic mother of the nation. That she was also wilful, arrogant, and powerful – in other words an individual – suggests, according to cultural norms, that she *ought not to have been a mother*, hence symbolically she is barren. This is because mother and individual(ist) in one person (as I will explore further in the next chapter) constitutes a contradiction – or an identity category violation. Brand goes on, extending the metaphor of Thatcher as headmistress, and referencing the phenomenon that many female teachers will attest to: "You could never call Margaret 'Mother' by mistake. For a national matriarch she is oddly unmaternal."

Other statements in Brand's piece repeat and reinforce the oft-commented-upon assertion that Thatcher's individualistic rise to power in a male-dominated sphere was an achievement of exceptionality, not a gain for feminism:

> It always struck me as peculiar, too, when the Spice Girls briefly championed Thatcher as an early example of girl power. I don't see that. She is an anomaly; a product of the freakonomy of her time. Barack Obama, interestingly, said in his statement that she had "broken the glass ceiling for other women." Only in the sense that all the women beneath her were blinded by falling shards. She is an icon of individualism, not of feminism.

And he confesses that he "always felt a bit sorry for [...] Mark and Carol, wondering from whom they would get their cuddles. 'Thatcher as mother' seemed, to my tiddly mind, anathema. How could anyone who was so resolutely Margaret Thatcher be anything else?" This notion of a woman as "resolutely herself" is a cultural contradiction precisely because we have not been acculturated to think of women as selves.

Yet, overall, Brand focuses in this gentle piece on the humanity of the elderly Thatcher glimpsed watering the roses that day. "None present eyed her meanly or spoke with vitriol," he writes,

> and it wasn't until an hour later that I dreamt up an Ealing comedy-style caper in which two inept crooks kidnap Thatcher from the garden but are unable to cope with the demands of dealing with her, and finally give her back.

Author Hilary Mantel, would, in fact, go on to write a more sadistic, yet still tongue-in-cheek version of Brand's fantasized scenario in the form of her short story "The Assassination of Margaret Thatcher: August 6th 1983" in 2014.[73] The story is told from the perspective of a woman who owns a house near to the hospital from which Thatcher is about to be discharged following an eye operation. An Irish sniper, posing initially as a plumber, chooses the attic of her house as his vantage point from which to shoot Thatcher. While waiting for her to appear he muses: "Three million unemployed [...] Most of them live around our way. It wouldn't be a problem here would it?",[74] suggesting an appropriately class-based political motivation for the assassination. Later he says the assassination is "about Ireland. Only Ireland, right?"[75] Yet Mantel has the female narrator put her finger on the actual source of unease and dislike that many felt for Thatcher: "It's the fake femininity I can't stand, and the counterfeit voice."[76] She later comments: "Look at my hair. She despises my hair [...] the way it just hangs there [...] instead of being in corrugations."[77] While nominally horrified at the assassination about to take place, when the sniper offers to tie her up and blindfold her prior to the killing so that she will not be implicated in it, the female narrator expresses a desire not to miss the action: "I want to see. I'm not missing this."[78] Mantel's short story perfectly emphasizes the shared, if tacit, cultural fantasy of violence, across class, nationalistic affiliation, and sex that Thatcher's inappropriate selfish femininity provoked.

Fantasies of assassinating Thatcher are, in fact, astonishingly commonly found in cultural production and in symbolic action. The closing track of Morrissey's first solo album, *Viva Hate* (1988), is titled "Margaret on the Guillotine." Its lyrics describe how "The kind people/Have a wonderful dream/Margaret on the guillotine."[79] Those who would oppose Thatcher's welfare cuts as cruel, and her pro-death penalty position and bellicose stance against Argentina as barbaric, permit themselves fantasies of a woman's death while considering themselves "kind," just as the gentle middle-class female narrator of Mantel's story does. Similarly, UB40's "Madame Medusa," referred to above, contains the lyrics "She gone off her head/We've got to shoot her dead/She gone off her head/We've got to shoot her dead," evoking the doubly misogynistic idea that perception of Thatcher as a "mad woman" justifies the fantasy of gynocide.[80] And symbolic vengeance over the country's matriarch is visible in the fact that the statue of Thatcher by sculptor Neil Simmons, on display in the Guildhall Art Gallery in the City of London, was decapitated by a protestor in 2002.[81] What is perhaps crucial here is that the extreme (auto- and allo-) mythologization of Thatcher has the result of rendering her *not quite human* which means that, depending upon the sympathies of the producer of a given discourse, sometimes she is figured as superhuman, sometimes as subhuman or dehumanized. The more violent excesses of hatred expressed for Thatcher suggest the dehumanization necessary to justify violence for the perpetrator. Pertinently, in an article covering the "milk snatcher" furore, *The Sun*'s headline ran "Is Mrs Thatcher Human?"[82] That Thatcher was so good at making of herself an "icon of individualism," as Brand puts it, results in an alibi for a violent cultural misogyny that is often breathtaking in its vehemence.[83]

Conclusion

I contend that the exceptional vitriol provoked by the figure of Margaret Thatcher and voiced by women as often as by men has just as much to do with the perception of Thatcher as an improper woman as it has to do with the assessment of Thatcher as a ruthless right-wing politician. And, in particular, it has to do with the violation of expectations of what a woman may be when that woman occupies a political position. While the socially conservative or religious right-wing woman – her husband's helpmeet and angel of the house – is a familiar and comprehensible political figure, the individualistic, selfish, bellicose, alternately libertarian and authoritarian, right-wing woman is not. Thatcher's embodiment of all of these positions at once does violence to our understanding of the categories that are used to make sense of political and gender identities. While managing to hold together the feminine lady/warrior roles expected of a female national leader, as discussed above, Thatcher failed to embody the attributes of "a woman" expected both by society and by feminists.

While it is unsurprising that those on the left would object to Thatcher's political beliefs and the policies her government introduced, it seems to be the case that many women on the left felt Thatcher additionally to be a traitor to her sex in espousing conservative and free-market ideas while female. In a long, damning, and controversial speech made in Parliament after Thatcher's death, during a day of tributes to her, Labour MP Glenda Jackson spoke the words: "The first Prime Minister of female gender, OK. But a woman? Not on my terms."[84] Thatcher is perceived here to be a traitor to the definition of woman that Jackson holds (based on an ideal of care and altruistic collectivity) to the point that Thatcher becomes *not* a woman. As Jacqueline Rose has put it: "for a feminism which has argued for the perversity and even deadliness of the social, and then called it male, Thatcher presents a particular difficulty and anxiety which has perhaps been operating in the form of a taboo."[85] One thing that the case of Thatcher reveals, then, is a trend within feminism that is disapproving of female individualism and, particularly, exceptionality, to a rather extreme degree. Thatcher's female selfishness is the real otherness that her figure represents and that causes such consternation. As Bowman put it, in her *Guardian* article, "It's almost as if, as a woman, Margaret Thatcher represents no one but herself, whoever that is."[86] And for a woman to act in her own self-interest, to be *for herself*, is, as we have seen, among the greatest of taboos.

Notes

1 Mary Beard, *Women and Power: A Manifesto* (London: Profile Books, 2017), loc. 67.
2 Anna Coote and Polly Pattullo, *Power and Prejudice: Women and Politics* (London: Weidenfeld and Nicolson, 1990), p. 265.
3 Rand, "About a Woman President" [1968] cited in Susan Love Brown, "Ayn Rand: The Woman Who Would Not Be President," in Gladstein and Sciabarra (eds), *Feminist Interpretations of Ayn Rand*, 275–298, p. 275.
4 The biographical information in this chapter is not based on original research but on the wealth of existing published sources about and by Thatcher, especially Heather Nunn, *Thatcher, Politics and Fantasy: The Political Culture of Gender and Nation* (2002); Nicholas Wapshott and George Brock, *Thatcher* (1983); Hugo Young, *One of Us* (1989), and Thatcher's autobiographies published as *The Downing Street Years* (1990) and *The Path to Power* (1995).
5 Cited in Melanie McFayden and Margaret Renn, *Thatcher's Reign: A Bad Case of the Blues* (London: Chatto and Windus, 1984), p. 31.
6 See Heather Nunn, *Thatcher, Politics and Fantasy: The Political Culture of Gender and Nation* (London: Lawrence and Wishart, 2002), pp. 33, 44.
7 Cited in Andrew S. Crines, Timothy Heppell, and Peter Dorey, *The Political Rhetoric and Oratory of Margaret Thatcher* (Basingstoke: Palgrave MacMillan, 2016), p. 164.
8 Nicholas Wapshott and George Brock, *Thatcher* (London: Macdonald and Co., 1983), p. 59. Nunn also adds: "[Thatcher] acknowledged that financial restraint alone had halted her consideration of a career in politics until the 1946 rise in politician's pay from £600 to £1,000 [...] She recalled: 'I couldn't have done a proper job as an MP on £9 a week ... I had no private income or trade union to back me. I just didn't think of being a member of parliament." Nunn, *Thatcher, Politics and Fantasy*, p. 27.

9 Margaret Thatcher, "Let the Children Grow Tall" [1975] in Alistair B. Cooke (ed.), *Margaret Thatcher: The Revival of Britain Speeches on Home and European Affairs 1975–1988* (London: Aurum Press, 1989), p. 3.

10 Thatcher, *The Downing Street Years* (London: Harper Collins 1993), p. 855.

11 Thatcher cited in *The Times*, 21 February 1975.

12 See Michael Foley, *The Rise of the British Presidency* (Manchester: Manchester University Press, 1993), p. 66.

13 Ros Brunt, "Thatcher Uses her Woman's Touch," *Marxism Today*, June 1987, 22–24, p. 23.

14 Thatcher, Interview with *The News of the World*, September, 1981.

15 Pauline Peters, "The Tidy Mind of Margaret Thatcher," *The Sunday Times Magazine*, 20 August 1978, 1, 8–14, p. 10.

16 Jessica Prestidge, *Margaret Thatcher's Politics: The Cultural and Ideological Forces of Domestic Femininity*, unpublished doctoral thesis, University of Durham, 2017, p. 1. See http://etheses.dur.ac.uk/12192/.

17 Jacqueline Rose, "Margaret Thatcher and Ruth Ellis," *New Formations*, 6, 1988, 3–29, p. 19.

18 Scholars have pointed out that, in fact, while a *rhetoric* of Keynesianism operated in the UK at this time, this did not necessarily translate into policy implementation. See, for example, Ben Pimlott, "The Myth of Consensus" in Lesley M. Smith (ed.), *The Making of Britain: Echoes of Greatness* (Basingstoke: MacMillan, 1988), 129–143.

19 See William Keegan, *Mrs Thatcher's Economic Experiment* (London: Allen Lane, 1984) and Robert Skidelsky (ed.), *Thatcherism* (London: Chatto and Windus, 1988).

20 Thatcher, "What's Wrong With Politics?," in Wapshott and Brock (eds), *Thatcher*, p. 281.

21 Thatcher, "The Renewal of Britain" [1979], in Cooke (ed.), *Margaret Thatcher: The Revival of Britain Speeches*, pp. 86–87.

22 Thatcher in Kenneth Harris, *Thatcher* (London: Weidenfeld and Nicolson, 1988), p. 109.

23 Thatcher in McFayden and Renn, *Thatcher's Reign*, p. 102.

24 Hugo Young, *One of Us* [1989] (London: Pan Books, 1990), pp. 547–548.

25 Thatcher, Interview, *The Daily Telegraph*, 6 May, 1966.

26 Thatcher in Tessa Ten Tusscher, "Patriarchy, Capitalism and the New Right," in Judith Evans et al., (eds), *Feminism and Political Theory* (London: Sage, 1986), 66–80, p. 77.

27 Brunt, "Thatcher Uses her Woman's Touch," p. 23.

28 Cited in Nunn, *Thatcher, Politics and Fantasy*, p. 42.

29 Nunn, *Thatcher, Politics and Fantasy*, p. 9.

30 Marion Bowman, "The Iron Lady Made Flesh and Blood," *The Guardian*, 30 November 1989, www.theguardian.com/world/1989/nov/30/gender.uk

31 Anne Simpson, "Thatcher: A Workaholic Warrior But No Feminist," *The Herald*, 9 April 2013, www.heraldscotland.com/news/13099500.Thatcher__A_workaholic_warrior_but_no_feminist/

32 See, for example: Paola Bacchetta and Margaret Power (eds), *Right-Wing Women: From Conservatives to Extremists around the World* (New York: Routledge, 2002); Joyce Mushaben, *Becoming Madame Chancellor: Angela Merkel and the Berlin Republic* (Cambridge: Cambridge University Press, 2017); Francesca Scrinzi, "Gender and Women in the Front National Discourse and Policy: From 'Mothers of the Nation' to 'Working Mothers'?," *New Formations*, 91, 2017, 87–101.

33 See Downing, "The Body Politic."

34 Downing, "The Body Politic," p. 9.

35 Brunt, "Thatcher Uses her Woman's Touch," p. 22.

36 Cited in Simpson, "Thatcher."

37 Bowman, "The Iron Lady Made Flesh and Blood."

38 Brunt, "Thatcher Uses her Woman's Touch," p. 24.

39 There is a bitterly ironic undertone to this association, of course, given the homophobic policies of Thatcher's government, particularly the introduction of Section 28 in 1988. This piece of legislation prevented "the promotion of homosexuality" in public institutions. It would not be repealed until 2000 in Scotland and 2003 in the rest of Britain.

40 Cited in Nunn, p. 136. Nunn further points out: "It was the first time that a British political Party had produced a specially written campaign song and revealed the broader innovative approach to electioneering in which the Director of Marketing, Christopher Lawson, drew upon American presidential techniques", p. 139.

41 See Patrick Sawyer, "How Maggie Thatcher was Remade," *The Daily Telegraph*, 8 January 2012, www.telegraph.co.uk/news/politics/margaret-thatcher/8999746/How-Maggie-Thatcher-was-remade.html

42 Joan Rivière, "Womanliness as Masquerade," *International Journal of Psychoanalysis*, 10, 1929, 303–313.

43 Nunn, *Thatcher, Politics and Fantasy*, p. 87.

44 Rand, *Atlas Shrugged*, p. 412.

45 Thatcher, *The Path to Power* (London: Harper Collins, 1995), pp. 285, 295.

46 Beard, *Women and Power*, loc. 209.

47 Cited in Nunn, *Thatcher, Politics and Fantasy*, pp. 70–71.

48 I am thinking in particular of *Gender Trouble: Feminism and the Subversion of Identity* [1990] (London and New York: Routledge, 1999), in which Butler writes of gender as both "*a stylized repetition of acts*" (her emphasis, p. 179) and "as a strategy of survival within compulsory systems" (p. 178).

49 Nunn, *Thatcher, Politics and Fantasy*, p. 71.

50 Thatcher, *The Path to Power*, 470.

51 Nunn, *Thatcher, Politics and Fantasy*, p. 92.

52 Nunn, *Thatcher, Politics and Fantasy*, p. 92.

53 Thatcher, *The Daily Mirror*, 1 March 1980, cited in Nunn, p. 40.

54 It is, however, noteworthy that this is a frustration that other female politicians of Thatcher's era reported, regardless of Party allegiance. Prestidge points out in her doctoral thesis that Labour Party Politician Barbara Castle "is quoted [...] as claiming to think of herself 'as an MP, not as a female MP'." See Prestidge, *Margaret Thatcher's Politics*, p. 86.

55 Nunn, *Thatcher, Politics and Fantasy*, p. 64.

56 Rose, "Margaret Thatcher and Ruth Ellis," p. 4.

57 Rose, "Margaret Thatcher and Ruth Ellis," p. 4.

58 Rose, "Margaret Thatcher and Ruth Ellis," p. 9.

59 Rose, "Margaret Thatcher and Ruth Ellis," p. 15.

60 Nabeel Zuberi, *Sounds English: Transnational Popular Music* (Chicago: University of Illinois Press, 2001), p. 45.

61 Downing, *The Subject of Murder*.

62 Rose, "Margaret Thatcher and Ruth Ellis," p. 19.

63 Zuberi, *Sounds English*, p. 46.

64 See: David Schmid, *Natural Born Celebrities: Serial Killers in American Culture* (Chicago: University of Chicago Press, 2005) on murderers and their place in celebrity culture, and John Street, "Celebrity Politicians: Popular Culture and Political Representation," *British Journal of Politics and International Relations*, 6, 2004, 435–452 on politicians as celebrities.

65 Pamela Hansford Johnson, who attended the trial of the Moors Murderers, described "the Medusa face of Hindley, under the melon puff-ball of hair." Johnson, *On Iniquity: Some Personal Reflections Arising out of the Moors Murders Trial* (London: Macmillan, 1967), p. 89. See also Downing, *The Subject of Murder*, pp. 99–125.

66 Anti-Tory band UB40 was named after the form issued to people seeking unemployment benefit in the 1980s. (It stood for Unemployment Benefit form 40.)

67 Rose, "Margaret Thatcher and Ruth Ellis," p. 4.
68 Nunn, *Thatcher, Politics and Fantasy*, p. 15.
69 Marina Warner, *Monuments and Maidens: The Allegory of the Female Form* (London: Weidenfeld and Nicolson, 1985), p. 52.
70 Cited in Thatcher, *The Path to Power*, p. 181.
71 Nunn, *Thatcher, Politics and Fantasy*, p. 97.
72 Russell Brand, "Russell Brand on Margaret Thatcher: 'I Always Felt Sorry for her Children'," *The Guardian*, 9 April 2013, https://www.theguardian.com/politics/2013/apr/09/russell-brand-margaret-thatcher
73 Hilary Mantel, "The Assassination of Margaret Thatcher: August 6th 1983," in *The Assassination of Margaret Thatcher and Other Stories* (London: Fourth Estate, 2014), loc. 1703–1979.
74 Mantel, "The Assassination of Margaret Thatcher," loc. 1797.
75 Mantel, "The Assassination of Margaret Thatcher," loc. 1881.
76 Mantel, "The Assassination of Margaret Thatcher," loc. 1881.
77 Mantel, "The Assassination of Margaret Thatcher," loc. 1876.
78 Mantel, "The Assassination of Margaret Thatcher," loc. 1939.
79 See Melissa McEwan's blog post "RIP Margaret Thatcher," 8 April 2003, on the feminist website Shakesville. This is an excellent analysis of the violent misogyny visible in commentary on Thatcher's life and death, which names Thatcher as "the ultimate Exceptional Woman." www.shakesville.com/2013/04/rip-margaret-thatcher.html.
80 Significantly, these are not the only songs on a theme. See also, as a non-exhaustive exemplary selection: "The Day That Margaret Thatcher Dies" by Peter Wylie, Elvis Costello's "Tramp the Dirt Down," and Hefner's "The Day that Thatcher Dies."
81 Michael White, "Thatcher Statue Decapitated," *The Guardian*, 4 July 2002, www.theguardian.com/uk/2002/jul/04/artsnews.redbox
82 Cited in Thatcher, *The Path to Power*, p. 181.
83 Fantasies of visceral violent retribution towards female politicians and public figures far outweigh what male politicians face. Thatcher pre-dates the age of Twitter, but contemporary female politicians, including outspoken Labour MP Jess Phillips and Rebel anti-Brexit former-Tory MP Anna Soubry, report facing an onslaught of violent and sexualized threats of the kind that few men would recognize. This rage against the powerful female speaks to the very phantasy of which Rose writes. See, for example, James Rodger, "Jess Phillips says Labour has problem with women in leadership," *Birmingham Mail*, 7 December 2017, https://www.birminghammail.co.uk/news/midlands-news/jess-phillips-says-labour-problem-14009290
84 See Andy McSmith, "Glenda Jackson on the Death of Margaret Thatcher: 'I had to speak out to stop history being rewritten'," *The Independent*, 11 April 2013, www.independent.co.uk/news/uk/politics/glenda-jackson-on-the-death-of-margaret-thatcher-i-had-to-speak-out-to-stop-history-being-re-written-8569392.html
85 Rose, "Margaret Thatcher and Ruth Ellis," p. 23.
86 Bowman, "The Iron Lady Made Flesh and Blood."

4

PERSONAL AND PROFESSIONAL PRACTICES OF SELFISHNESS

On babies, boardrooms, and ballot boxes

You cannot keep your small domestic peace
Your little pool of undeveloped love,
While the neglected, starved, unmothered world
Struggles and fights for lack of mother's care,
And its tempestuous, bitter, broken life
Beats in upon you in your selfish homes.

(Charlotte Perkins Gilman, "To The Indifferent Women," 1904)

The woman who is deviant because she has no children [...] is often aware of how tenuous her existence is: it is a courtesy extended to her – letting her go on – despite the fact she is not earning her womanly keep in the womanly way. She knows how little the world at large needs her or values her for anything else she does *even when she is exceptional*; and if she understands how systematic and relentless the valuation of her kind is, she also knows that at the heart of the male system there is a profound contempt for anything in women that is individual, that is independent of class definition or function, that cannot finally be perceived and justified as incidental to motherhood.

(Andrea Dworkin, *Right Wing Women*, 1983. My italics)

What both of these epigraphs evoke in, respectively, chiding and radically oppositional terms, is the social expectation placed on women to be, first and foremost, carers; that is "to mother," metaphorically, the whole world. In her poem, Charlotte Perkins Gilman calls upon the woman stuck in the domestic sphere and occupied with the trappings of maternal femininity – roles into which she has been socialized – to look beyond, towards a larger, public world. But this is not in the service of any kind of self-transformation (by, for example, seeing herself as an agentic individual citizen); rather it is in order to carry on the role of the caretaking helpmeet and mother – and to expand it to protect and nurture those beyond her own family. And the concept of heterosexual complementarity – that humanity is comprised of "man and woman," with their "equal but different" qualities that put nature in balance – is suggested in the closing lines of her poem: "When women's life in its rich power of love/is joined with man's to care for all the world." Woman's "power" here is defined as "love," and specifically the love that issues from maternal feeling. But as Jacqueline Rose writes in her book-length essay on Mothers:

> Whenever love is expected or demanded of anybody, we can be pretty sure that love is the last thing being talked about. Like the injunction to be spontaneous, a state that can only arise unbidden, the demand to love crushes its object and obliterates itself.[1]

And, as Rose insists: "Mothers do not have a monopoly of love in the world, nor should it be asked of them."[2] Moreover, the very notion that woman's capacity to love is seen as *her nature*, rather than the effect of her socialization, and is demanded from her, is as oppressive as is the implication that traditional housewives are somehow morally failing if they take any pleasure at all in the limited control they *can* exercise over the small sphere actually allocated to them, their "selfish homes" (where "selfish," as in so many examples examined in this book, is doubly negatively connoted when it is an accusation levelled at a woman).

Dworkin, by contrast with Gilman, points out in stark terms what purpose the insistence that women should be mothers first and foremost serves: It gives women a generic role that – in modern Western culture – is structurally other to that of "individual," and especially to that of "exceptional individual." And, in the devastating way that her prose has, Dworkin points out the logic according to which the equation of "woman" with "mother" is used to render female distinction invisible, since the one who, if male, would be perceived as an individual genius, may be perceived instead, if female, primarily as a failure since she is not a mother. If she *is* a mother, then her exceptionality will likely be cancelled out anyway, since the purpose of woman is only to be what she is told that her nature is. This neatly illustrates why I take exception to the term "exceptional woman" being used in a derogatory way by some feminists. If even a class-analysis-driven radical feminist such as Andrea Dworkin can see that to exempt woman from the category of "exceptional individual" is an act of symbolic patriarchal violence, then it behoves us to cast a critical eye over collectivist discourses that pursue the de-individualizing tendency to see women always as members of a group.

The double-bind described by Dworkin here is totalizing and overwhelming: The childless or childfree woman is othered as abnormal while the obediently reproductive woman, whose role is to provide infinite love, will be endlessly monitored, critiqued, and policed. It would perhaps be easy to claim that Dworkin's description may apply in the 1970s and 1980s, but that surely it does not obtain today. However, that Rose's essay which argues that society makes mothers "the objects of licensed cruelty" and asks "what are we doing *to* mothers [...] when we expect them to carry the burden of everything that is hardest to contemplate about our society and ourselves?"[3] was published in 2018 says much about the enduring power of the expectation that women should *be for others*. It appears, then, that the demand made of women by Gilman's poem and Dworkin's critique of this kind of demand are as depressingly pertinent to our current times as they were to the decade in which Dworkin was writing. To further test this thesis, I shall examine in what follows a number of discourses about women as carers and women in careers from the time of second-wave feminism to the present day that are prevalent and that shape our understanding of the female self-other relation.

Gilligan's ethics of care

In the early 1970s, psychologist Carol Gilligan began the research that would lead to the book *In a Different Voice*. This book was an attempt to counter the commonly encountered assumption that women's faculty for morality is inferior to men's. This is a discourse that is prevalent in much philosophical writing, expressed perhaps most offensively by Schopenhauer:

> Women are suited to being nurses and teachers of our earliest childhood precisely because they themselves are childish, silly and limited, in short, big children, their whole lives long: a kind of intermediate stage between the child and the man, who is the actual human being, "man."[4]

We may note in Schopenhauer's hateful screed the evocation of a natural and unbreakable linkage between women and children, which second-wave feminist Shulamith Firestone identified as a cornerstone of oppression when she wrote: "women and children are always mentioned in the same breath [...] The special tie women have with children is recognized by everyone. I submit, however, that the nature of this bond is no more than shared oppression."[5]

In Gilligan's field, psychology, discourses regarding women's moral inferiority are at least as old as the writings of Freud, who claims "for women the level of what is ethically normal is different from what it is for men. Their superego is never so impersonal, so inexorable, so independent of its emotional origin as we require it to be for men."[6] And Gilligan cites Freud's infamous assertion along similar lines that women "show less sense of justice than men, that they are less ready to submit to the great exigencies of life, that they are more often influenced in their judgments by feelings of affection or hostility."[7] But, alarmingly, this set of assumptions in psychology did not disappear with Freud's turn-of-the-century moment. Gilligan found a contemporaneous version of these beliefs in the work of her colleague, Lawrence Kohlberg, for whom she was a research assistant. Kohlberg had argued that girls, on average, both developed moral sense more slowly than boys and reached a lower level of moral development overall in adulthood. Gilligan examined Kohlberg's findings and interpreted them to show that Kohlberg's preconceptions about what moral sense *means* needed more examination. Gilligan noted that while men appeared more likely to rationalize problems on an individual basis and according to a code of "rights," women seemed to be more often driven by "responsibility" and typically to seek a relational solution to ethical dilemmas – that is, they considered who would be affected or hurt by a particular moral decision. This is exemplified by the comparison: "To Jake's ideal of perfection, against which he measures the worth of himself, Amy counterposes an ideal of care, against which she measures the worth of her activity."[8] Girls' and women's answers to questions about moral dilemmas are interpreted in standard testing as less sophisticated forms of moral reasoning as they apparently get stuck at the level of "interpersonality," rather than reaching the assumed more sophisticated level of "universal applicability." But Gilligan argues that this simply reflects an entirely different way of doing ethics.

Gilligan states that the aim of her book is to "offer [women] a representation of the thought that enables them to see better its integrity and validity...".[9] That is, rather than question in any detail precisely what type of social conditioning might lead girls to this tendency for selflessness and a moral reasoning that is relational, Gilligan sought rather to promote it as a valid ethical model for both men and women. Her discourse is perhaps not as essentialist as some of her critics have claimed.[10] Gilligan is clear that, statistically, more girls and women tend to reason in this way than boys and men, but that these what she calls "modes of thought" are not determined biologically; rather "these differences arise in a social context where factors of social status and power combine with reproductive biology."[11] We may note that women who rationalize using the "masculine" paradigm – including Ayn Rand and Margaret Thatcher – commonly appear as *unnatural women*, rather than simply as women who incline for whatever reason to one of two (though, of course, there may be more) available models of moral reasoning.

Yet it is undeniable that Gilligan is firm on the point that it *is* predominantly women who operate ethically in the relational, care-based mode. At least, she gives no example in her study of a male participant who uses this mode of ethical reasoning. Of course, this may be blamed on the author's selection bias or on the small participant sample. However, the degree to which Gilligan fails to problematize her evidence that the people doing the relational ethics are also the ones socialized to be giving and caring is a weakness. Gilligan highlights numerous women's reported fears of pursuing self-interest rather than altruism, e.g. "that it would be 'selfish' to bring her voice into relationships, that perhaps she did not know what she really wanted, or that her experience was not a reliable guide in thinking about what to do."[12] Reading *In a Different Voice* through a critical perspective that does not automatically assume that selfishness is a bad thing, but perhaps a strategically necessary attitude and a value for women, it is quite alarming to read the implicit approbation the author accords to an ethical mode that appears to harm the self-regard of those who voice it.

However, in her "Letter to Readers" that forms the new preface to the 1993 edition (so written just over ten years after the book's first edition), Gilligan seems to suggest something slightly different than her stated aims and position in the original version of the book: namely, that she recognizes that the style of ethics that women tend to prefer may work *against* them, that relational ethics may in fact be a self-sacrificial ethics without concern for self-interest or for self-respect. Gilligan writes: "Women's discovery of *the problems that ensue from rendering oneself selfless* in order to have 'relationships' was momentous in releasing women's voices and making it possible to hear what women know"[13] and "How do women come to speak of themselves *as though they were selfless, as if they did not have a voice or experience desire?*".[14] Indeed, in this 1993 preface, Gilligan herself seems to take a slightly different stance on the matter and to counsel some degree of "selfishness" (or self-fulness) in the interests of female psychological health. She writes:

> If it is good to be responsive to people, to act in connection with others and to be careful rather than careless about people's feelings and thoughts, empathic and attentive to their lives, then why is it 'selfish' to respond to yourself?[15]

What is noteworthy here, however, is how the word "selfish" continues to resonate as something negative, even while Gilligan suggests that self-interest or concern for self *is an ethical and psychological necessity*. By constructing a sentence that begins "if it is good to *y*," the expectation is that the second half of that sentence will read "then why is it *bad* to *x*?" (since "good" and "bad" form a conventional moral binary pair). By making "selfish" stand in place of "bad" in this formulation, the two terms have the weight of synonyms in the rhetorical equation. It is in the interests of countering ingrained thinking such as this that I would argue that we might adopt the term "self-ful" to describe an ethically aware strategy of self-regard.

Thus, Gilligan is a proponent of the ethics of care who nevertheless later acknowledges the compromises and dangers involved in pursuing this ethical mode for the women who are most likely to operate within it. As soon as the question of *what is in women's interests* or *for women's good* is directly evoked, any project, including a feminist project, that would seek to insist upon the female self as inherently more gentle, nurturing, altruistic, connected, and caring than the male version of the self must lay itself open to charges of stating as *proper to* and *good for* women what may, in fact, be nothing more than the effects *on women* of living under patriarchy.

To mother or not to mother? That is the question

In Meghan Daum's *Selfish, Shallow and Self-Absorbed*, she writes: "People who want children are all alike. People who don't want children don't want them in their own ways."[16] The glib paraphrase/parody from Tolstoy's *Anna Karenina* above is at once not true and yet reveals a grain of perceptiveness. If centring one's entire self-perception around the principle of caring is detrimental to the self, as is (perhaps grudgingly) acknowledged by Gilligan's later preface to her classic book, and if, as Rose has argued, mothers are expected to exist only to give love, we might wonder why more women who are in the privileged position to make the choice for themselves (realistically, this would probably mainly be Western women with access to reproductive technology) do not choose to remain free of children. The fact is that a whole series of statistics *do* reveal that increased financial independence for women leads to reduced birth rates. Kreyenfeld and Konietzka's collection of research papers on childlessness in Europe (2017) reports that 9% of English and Welsh women born in 1946 had no children, while for the cohort born in 1970 the proportion is 17%. In Germany, this is even more marked as 22% of women now reach their early 40s without children."[17] And in 2013 a UNESCO report on education for women reveals that two repeatedly seen effects of educating girls across the globe are to raise the age at which they have children and to lower the number of children they have.[18] Yet the decision not to reproduce is still so discursively freighted for women, even in the "free" West (in a way that it simply is not for men) that the very notion of "choice" (or "not wanting in one's own way," as Daum, parodying Tolstoy, would have it) becomes complex and overdetermined in this context.

As we have seen, the allegedly "natural" association between women and the loving, caring work of motherhood means that to refuse this role places the individual woman in a position of being aberrant with regard to social expectations, and, in some discourses, viewed as a failed woman. Becoming a mother is also dressed – very deliberately, I would argue – as *not a rational choice*. Discourses of hormones and emotional hungriness accrue to the language around the desire to become a mother, leading French liberal feminist Élisabeth Badinter to write *Mother Love*, published in 1981, a tract that constitutes a critique of the language of maternal "instinct" which, Badinter argues, has condemned women to the prison of reproductive identity. It argues that the notion of "mother love" was a creation of the enlightenment. Badinter writes that the imprecations of male intellectuals such as Jean-Jacques Rousseau turned "the apathetic mother of the eighteenth century [...] into the mother hen of the nineteenth and twentieth centuries."[19]

Whether "the biological clock" and "the mothering instinct" exist independently of the discourses that articulate and insist upon them is not something we can *prove*, but the sheer effort and amount of policing work that goes into shoring up the narrative of their strength and power suggests that this is something of which we should be, at the very least, suspicious. Things that simply occur in and are mandated by nature do not tend to require cultural policing to ensure their continuation. Yet, conversely, as well as being dressed as a natural, biological, animal "urge," mothering – i.e. the state of ultimate physical and psychological commitment to care – is simultaneously dressed as morally righteous; as "the right thing" for women to do, as we have seen. Many feminists have worked to refute such assumptions. In her classic text, *Of Woman Born: Mother-hood as Experience and Institution* (1976), Adrienne Rich writes "I do not see the mother with her child as either more morally credible or more morally capable than any other woman."[20]

Yet, women who choose not to have children often discuss the degree to which this decision is problematized and treated as if it is of inherent public interest. So powerfully close is the association of "woman" to "mother" that the act of rejecting this link for oneself is not allowed to be a neutral or casual personal decision. The title of the recent edited book by Daum on this topic reveals much about what is implicit, culturally, in reactions to a woman taking this path: *Selfish, Shallow and Self-Absorbed: Sixteen Writers on the Decision Not to Have Kids*. In her essay in this volume, the controversial journalist and novelist, Lionel Shriver, responds to the oft-bandied-about discourse that, given the diminishing birth rate in the West, women bear some sort of species-level responsibility to have children. Shriver writes with her characteristic tone of defiance:

> When a London *Sunday Times* reporter (who clearly thought me a chilly, typically arrogant American bitch) asked if I didn't think that declining to reproduce wasn't essentially "nihilistic," I said readily, "Of course." Or a journalist would ask tentatively on a phoner: Wasn't refusing parenthood a little … selfish? I'd cry boisterously into the receiver, "Absolutely!"[21]

Shriver goes on less glibly to conjecture that, aside from contributing factors such as the increased availability of contraception and the wholesale entry of women into the workplace, the falling Western birth rate can be explained by a more fundamental factor: a transformation in "our collective consensus on what life is for."[22] Shriver contends that "baby boomers and their offspring have shifted emphasis from the communal to the individual,"[23] echoing the discourses of the "Me Decade" or the age of "Affluenza" discussed in Chapter 1. But, this being Shriver, a thinker-against-the-grain par excellence, she refuses to issue unreservedly the typical, absolutist moral critique of this shift. "For the role of humble server, helpmate, and facilitator no longer to constitute the sole model of womanhood surely represents progress for which I am personally grateful,"[24] Shriver declares.

Moreover, she argues that the freedom to remain childless leads the subject to "the final frontier: the self, whose borders are as narrow or as infinite as we make them."[25] Shriver states with a characteristic mixture of humour and profundity:

> I could have afforded children financially. I just didn't want them. They are untidy; they would have messed up my apartment. In the main, they are ungrateful. They would have siphoned too much time away from the writing of my precious books.[26]

And Shriver goes on to quote several of her contemporary, childfree female friends, one of whom, "Gabriella," states in words that uncannily echo Rachilde's character Mary Barbe's wilful and future-negating refusal of reproduction, discussed in Chapter 1:

> I'm an atheist. I'm a solipsist. As far as I'm concerned, while I know intellectually that the world and its inhabitants will continue after my death, it has no real meaning for me. I am terrified of and obsessed with my own extinction, and what happens next is of little interest to me. I certainly don't feel I owe the future anything, and that includes my genes and my offspring. I feel absolutely no sense of responsibility for the propagation of the human race. I am happy to leave that task to someone else.[27]

Shriver's defiant essay and her citations of the words of self-focused women who refuse to accept the responsibility to reproduce proclaim the right of women, historically denied to them for thousands of years, to – as Shriver puts it – "care about my own life in the present."[28] Thinking back to Gilman's poem which opened this chapter, we hear the voices of women issuing a stark "no" to the poetic I's demand they should accept responsibility for the plight of the world and its future. In so doing, the selfish woman reveals the defining characteristic of her aberration – she says "no" to what the patriarchy tells her she is for.

The selfish woman and the (wilfully) childfree woman thus inevitably occupy the same cultural imaginary terrain. The term "childfree" is itself, however, a subject of contention. In her audaciously titled and rather aggressively gung-ho book *Childfree and Loving It!*, Nicki Defago writes:

> Outside the United States, the word childfree is relatively new, but it's gaining popularity because it suggests something positive as opposed to child*less*. It's important to acknowledge the difference between those people who choose not to have children and those who are unable.[29]

And Daum writes in her introduction to *Selfish, Shallow and Self-Absorbed* that the term, which

> was coined as a way of distinguishing the deliberately childless from those who unwillingly or unintentionally find themselves in such circumstances, rubs some people the wrong way – after all, why should children fall into the same category as cigarette smoke or gluten?[30]

Daum's joke sidesteps the fact that a second, and weightier, meaning and association accrues to the suffix "free" in the word "childfree." The debate over the language of "childless" or "childfree" in fact reveals much about the binary of boon or burden that are the terms in which being "with child" suggest. We may remember Simone de Beauvoir's view of motherhood as the most detrimental course a woman could take to alienate her from her potential for freedom, since it places the most enormous obstacle in the way of existential self-definition. For Beauvoir, a mother is "alienated in her body and her social dignity."[31] Further, she states, a child can "bring joy only to the woman capable of disinterestedly wanting the happiness of another."[32] As Rose puts it, reflecting on the existentialist's condemnation of the state of motherhood: "if your vision of being in the world is one of untrammelled self-realisation, motherhood is a bit of a shock, to say the least."[33]

The existentialist set of associations that "childfree" conjures up may, in fact, resonate most strongly when read in the context of a very rare cultural narrative: that of the woman who becomes a mother but regrets it and resents the changes her sense of self undergoes. Being "free" of the parasitic demands of a child and being "free" to self-define as an individual are the dual lost possibilities that haunt such rare narratives.[34] (The term "care-free" similarly takes on overtones when applied to women that it may not properly bear for men. To be care-free is to free oneself of the burden of care/to refuse woman's lot.) The UK-based parenting website Mumsnet, renowned for being populated by opinionated and outspoken women (a "nest of vipers"[35]), relatively frequently sees threads that discuss regretting the decision to become a parent or hating the everyday reality of motherhood. One such thread, described as "brave" by many of the posters contributing to it, has been archived to the "classics" board, where it will be preserved for posterity, rather than disappear after a number of weeks or months as Mumsnet threads posted on certain boards do. The title of the post is "I hate having kids" and the poster, "Throughautomaticdoors," writes:

> I love them but I hate being a parent. It's dull, it's relentless, it's worrying, it's thankless, it's demanding, it's monotonous, it's exhausting.
>
> I'd throw myself under a bus for them but being a parent has made me totally and utterly miserable. [...]
>
> I can't wait for them to grow up.[36]

In a later post, she adds "if I could have seen a snapshot of how it would be before I had them I wouldn't have done it. It's absolute shit." The responses she receives are generally supportive, with many posters concurring. A poster calling herself "imnotbeingfunnyright" posts:

> That's a brave thing to say/post. I've said it out loud to friends and other mum's [sic] at groups etc. and felt like a leper. I do love my children but God, I love it more when I'm home alone.

While "wheresthewine36" writes,

> I love them. I do everything they need me to do and always put them 1st in everything ... but for fucks sake, this isn't my life! [...] if I could have somehow known I would feel like this about motherhood ... I would have got a cat.

The sense of living a life that is not authentically the poster's, but rather the life she was *supposed* to want to live as the generic woman-mother figure expressed here by "wheresthewine36" is echoed in many posts on the thread.

Significantly, a poster calling herself "poisonwitch," who does not yet have children, articulates the social pressure she feels to become a mother even though this goes against her own desires and perception of herself:

> Thanks for being so honest. This honestly terrifies me as I think I'm the sort of person who will martyr myself as I have been heavily socialised to be nice and accommodating but am secretly quite selfish. I worry I will resent the loss of my freedom, time and money. I have a good life and love being able to go away on a whim or lie in till midday on a Sunday.

What is striking in this Mumsnet thread is that the women who report hating motherhood or resenting the expectations it places upon them are able to articulate very clearly that becoming a mother is an externally imposed expectation that they have been culturally conditioned to internalize. Seemingly, however, full awareness of what becoming a "good" female subject entails does not preclude the individual from capitulating to it, or lessen the impact of the negative effects when they happen. There is something rather in the order of tragedy about "poisonwitch's" lack of desire for a child coupled with what she presents as almost the *inevitability against her will* of having one. Also striking is that "being selfish" while female is discussed here as a dirty secret and/or something that is to be overcome by the duty of childbearing and rearing – equated with "growing up," pace Freud in "Of Narcissism" (expressed in Mumsnet lexicon in terms of sacrificing oneself for female duty, rather than enjoying the selfish Sunday lie-in).

In *A Life's Work* (2001), author Rachel Cusk documents in tortured detail her experience of becoming a mother as one of self-loss and "psychic loneliness"[37] of the most painful kind imaginable, as "it erodes your self-esteem and your membership of the adult world."[38] Using the metaphor of alien possession from science fiction film, *The Invasion of the Body Snatchers*, Cusk writes of birth:

> Somehow, during those tortured hours, some fundamental component of oneself is removed, so that afterwards, although one looks and sounds more or less exactly as one did before, one is in fact, a simulacrum, a brainwashed being programmed not to bear witness to the truth.[39]

The notion that the reality about birth, motherhood, and life after them is a secret that those who become mothers hold on to and refuse to share with those contemplating having children colours much of Cusk's book with a pungent bitterness.

Cusk writes that while some women spend many years of their early life contemplating motherhood:

> I arrived at the fact of motherhood shocked and unprepared, ignorant of what the consequences of this arrival would be, and with the unfounded but distinct impression that my journey there had been at once so random and so determined by forces greater than myself that I could hardly be said to have had any choice in the matter at all.[40]

Cusk's statement that motherhood was a matter in which she had "hardly any choice," echoing Mumsnet poster "poisonwitch's" sense that although she doesn't really want children, she will probably have them anyway, is at once both disingenuous and apposite. On the one hand, women in the West undeniably have the real privilege of making precisely this decision based on their own desires and ambitions and, one might argue, therefore have a *responsibility* to both self and other to do so carefully. On the other, female socialization does inculcate into girls and women the idea that having children is simply *what women do*, such that it is plausible that one could "fall" into it as simply the "next life stage" if one is not exceptionally self-aware. The devastatingly irrevocable nature of what becoming a mother can mean for a woman is articulated by Cusk when she writes: "my appetite for the world was insatiable, omnivorous, an expression of longing for some lost, prematernal self, and for the freedom that that self had perhaps enjoyed, perhaps squandered."[41] Cusk describes the state of motherhood into which she "fell" as a loss of self and of freedom, acknowledging the "squandering" of said freedom in the existentialist sense I alluded to above.

Cusk reflects on the problem that:

> After a child is born the lives of its mother and father diverge [...] the father's day would gradually gather to it the armour of the outside world, of money and authority and importance, while the mother's remit would extend to cover the entire domestic sphere.

This is the case, Cusk points out, even when both parents work outside of the home. Mothers do not *completely* belong to the world of work and action. They are expected to sacrifice a portion of the attention they would give to the world, the energy they would expend on it, by shouldering the burden of "wifework," as Susan Maushart terms it in her classic study.[42] It is undeniable that this unequal narrative is widely discussed – in opinion pieces in news outlets (especially on "women's pages") and on online parenting fora. Yet Cusk describes feeling that its inevitability still took her by surprise when it happened to her. At stake in motherhood, as currently constituted, is a necessary, even if partial, abnegation of self that fathers simply do not experience. Cusk puts it powerfully, thus:

> Birth is not merely that which divides women from men: it also divides women from themselves, so that a woman's understanding of what it is to exist is profoundly changed. Another person has existed in her, and after their birth they live within the jurisdiction of her consciousness. When she is with them she is not herself; when she is without them she is not herself; and so it is as difficult to leave your children as it is to stay with them.[43]

This is striking for the consideration of female self and female selfishness we are undertaking. A crucial point that Cusk makes here is that motherhood extends selfhood into the realm of the other, or perhaps better incorporates other within self, forever changing and deforming that self. This "related" mode of being, discussed at various points in this book, is encouraged – or forced – for women by the bearing of progeny. While welcome for some, for others such as Cusk and the posters on the Mumsnet thread discussed above, it is experienced as a monstrous and unreasonable imposition.

Perhaps the most cautionary tale, albeit a fictional one, about regretting motherhood is found in another text by Lionel Shriver. In Orange Prize-winning novel, *We Need to Talk About Kevin* (2005), Shriver evokes, via her protagonist Eva, the figure of the ambivalent mother who has agreed to have child to please her husband, Franklin. Eva gives birth to Kevin, a child she does not really want, with whom she does not bond, and who will go on to become a high-school mass-killer. Maternal regret is therefore – for the most justifiable of reasons – a key theme of the novel. Eva muses: "Although the infertile are entitled to sour grapes, it's against the rules, isn't it, to actually have a baby and spend any time at all on the banished parallel life in which you didn't."[44] The book provoked a huge amount of debate on publication about whether the narrative fell back on the trope of "blaming the mother" for all of a child's failings, and was therefore misogynistic and anti-mother, or whether it, in fact, offered a more nuanced view of its unreliable narrator Eva Khatchadourian and her motivations. Shriver has Eva herself tarry with this question, when she places the (self)accusation in her protagonist's mouth: "'I expect it's my fault,' I said defiantly. 'I wasn't a very good mother – cold, judgmental, selfish. Though you can't say that I haven't paid the price'."[45] Nicki Defago devotes part of a chapter of *Childfree and Loving It!* to an interview with Shriver about *Kevin*, in which Shriver describes the writing of the book as a way of working through her own "doubts and fears about motherhood" via fiction.[46] Eva's reflection on looking back on the decision to bring a baby into her relationship could strike fear in the heart of any ambivalent potential mother: "What possessed us? We were so happy! Why then did we take the stake of all we had and place it on this outrageous gamble of having a child?"[47]

The book's reception by users of Mumsnet is particularly striking, as it evidences a stark division between, on the one hand, posters expressing a vicious, almost visceral, hatred of the book and condemnation of Shriver, and, on the other, those professing admiration for the book's refreshing and shockingly honest portrayal of (the more common than is readily acknowledged phenomenon of) maternal ambivalence and regret. Some posters in particular berate Shriver for her arrogance in stating that "writing in the character of Eva was like writing about my own child. I came through knowing it wasn't for me."[48] One poster, "Curmudgeonlett," opines that she "can't help feeling that it would have been a far rounder book if the author had the experience of raising a child,"[49] and "Twiglett" writes that it was "patently written by someone who had never experienced parenthood."[50] Resorting to ad hominems, "expatinscotland" writes: "it wasn't about Kevin, it was about Lionel and all her twisted problems."[51] Yet, the fact that Cusk's memoir echoes the very sense of self-loss described by Eva in Shriver's fictional text corroborates the validity of *Kevin* and speaks to the import of voicing unpopular resistance to the too-common idea that motherhood is always welcome and positive.

Babies and ballot boxes

As discussed above, whatever else women may do, the question of whether or not they (also) fulfil the role of mother has long been, and continues to be, a discourse that shapes the expectations placed on women – and colours or taints the stories of women's lives. While women's representation in parliaments has increased fourfold in the past half-century, researchers express concern that the percentage of successful female politicians who are childfree is disproportionate compared to the number of childfree women in the population as a whole.[52]

Interest on the part of the mainstream media – not confined to the "gutter press" – in the reproductive status of powerful and professional women has been exemplified in recent years by several stories in the UK news. The 17–23 July 2015 issue of the left-wing, highbrow publication the *New Statesman* featured drawn cover art showing four female politicians who do not have children: First Minister of Scotland Nicola Sturgeon, the German Chancellor Angela Merkel, the UK's then Home Secretary, now Prime Minister Theresa May, and UK Labour MP – at the time a party leadership contender – Liz Kendall (Figure 4.1).[53] These women were pictured standing over a crib containing a ballot box where usually there would be a baby, and the image was accompanied by the headline "The Motherhood Trap: Why Are so Many Successful Women Childless?". This was also the title of the article by deputy editor Helen Lewis that featured in the magazine. Nicola Sturgeon objected strongly to the image on Twitter stating "Jeezo! We appear to have woken up in 1965 this morning!,"[54] which then prompted debate about whether the cover was indeed sexist or, in fact, whether it was deliberately chosen to emphasize the double-bind that professional and political women face when deciding whether or not to have children.[55]

Lewis's article focuses on how women "are vilified as 'selfish' when they decide not to become mothers, yet face barriers to career progression once they are on the 'mummy track'."[56] Lewis highlights the question of the gendered character of the labour of care as being at the heart of the problem for women who do choose to have children and pursue a political or professional career:

> The "motherhood trap" exposes one of capitalism's most uncomfortable secrets – the way it relies on so much unpaid labour, often from women, to sustain itself. This labour comes at the expense of career opportunities, and their lifetime earning power: the pay gap between men and women in their twenties is all but eradicated, but a "maternity gap" still exists, and women's wages never recover from the time devoted to childbearing.[57]

FIGURE 4.1   Cover of the *New Statesman*, 17–23 July 2015. Photograph by Lisa Downing.

Lewis reports that many of the female politicians she interviewed in the course of doing research for her article spoke of the difficulty of fitting caring duties around a parliamentary career, while also expressing the awareness that "selectors, voters and the media often expect a politician to have a family as a way of signalling that they are 'normal'."[58] This is not so much a double-bind as a multiple bind: to be "normal" and relatable, a woman, so much more than a man, must be a parent. Yet the labour entailed in parenthood is still disproportionately heavier for mothers than for fathers. While practical change regarding the distribution of caring duties among the sexes is doubtless needed, a change that also needs to occur at the level of the cultural imaginary is in the direction of seeing childfree women – women who identify as individuals – as valid (while also, possibly, as exceptional – and there is nothing wrong with that either).

Almost a year to the day after the *New Statesman* cover furore, in July 2016, the Conservative Party leadership contest saw two women vying for the top role following the resignation of David Cameron after the EU referendum result: Theresa May and Andrea Leadsom. In an interview with political journalist Rachel Sylvester for *The Times*, in response to the question: "Do you feel like a mum in politics?", Leadsom made the following statement which was widely broadcast, and just as widely condemned:

> Yes. So really carefully because I don't know Theresa really well, but I'm sure she will be really sad that she doesn't have children so I don't want this to be "Andrea's got children, Theresa hasn't" – do you know what I mean? Because I think that would be really horrible. But genuinely I feel being a mum means you have a very real stake in the future of our country. A tangible stake. She possibly has nieces, nephews, lots of people. But I have children who are going to have children who will directly be a part of what happens next. So it really keeps you focused on what are you really saying because what it means is you don't want a downturn – but then "never mind let's look to the ten years hence it will all be fine." But my children will be starting their lives in that next ten years so I have a real stake in the next year.[59]

That Leadsom's comments were roundly criticized, to the point that she subsequently apologized and stood down from the contest, ensuring May's victory, does not completely negate the longevity and power of the assumptions contained in Leadsom's statements. Nor does it detract from the larger point that a contender for leader of a political Party was drawn to comment on whether her status as a parent would affect her ability to lead the country, a question that we can never imagine being asked of a man. Indeed, Leadsom later commented for an article in *The Times*: "I was pressed to say how my children had formed my views. I didn't want it to be used as an issue."[60] This suggests to some degree that, despite the apparent spite of Leadsom's initial statement, both women contenders were affected negatively by assumptions about the importance of their reproductive status and what is permissible for a woman and a female leader (relatedness and being "relatable" – rather than stark individualism).

To return to the problematic sentiment in Leadsom's words, however – that those women who are not mothers have less investment in the future – while it was roundly censured as hurtful and inappropriate, I wonder about its truth value. In her essay on being childfree, Lionel Shriver suggests that this attitude applies to her when she writes, on the one hand, that "I think I should be, but – doubtless because I don't have children – I'm honestly not very fussed about what happens after I die"[61] and, on the other, that this attitude – which she shares with her other, successful, ambitious, creative, career-focused childfree female friends – constitutes "an economic, cultural, and moral disaster"[62] (from the rather contentious viewpoint that it would be desirable for elite genes to be propagated). It may be that what a selfish woman (suggested by the woman without a child) conjures up for us is the spectacle of the woman who refuses to attend to the future. The assumptions about what makes a mother are problematically closely aligned, if not identical with, the stereotypes and characteristics of what makes a woman.

On female ambition

The ambitious woman is a troubling figure for culture. In her recent study of representations of how "aggressive women" are represented onscreen, Maud Levin writes of how sportswomen in particular fascinate us "with their connotations of both traditionally attractive femininity [...] and traditionally masculine behaviour."[63] Lionel Shriver's novel *Double Fault*, set in the world of professional tennis, offers a fascinating and painful portrayal of aggressive female ambition. Having been published originally in the USA in 1997 to critical and commercial indifference, the novel was reissued in both the USA and the UK in 2006 following the runaway, prize-winning success of *We Need to Talk About Kevin* a year earlier. The novel describes the marriage between two aspiring professional tennis players, Willy Novinsky and Eric Oberdorf. While Willy has single-mindedly devoted her life to the pursuit of her sport from the age of 4, and is on the brink of stardom in women's tennis when the novel opens, Eric, a middle-class Princeton graduate, has come late to the sport at 18 and is still building his reputation. Both partners are competitive and ambitious – indeed, Willy's attraction to Eric is based in large part on the fact that he is the first person she has met whose drive equals her own. The novel explores the effects on the relationship and on Willy's self-regard when, following an injury, her career begins to take a downturn at the very same time as Eric's begins to take off.

The psychologically pivotal episode of the novel is the chapter, located halfway through the book, in which, on their anniversary, Willy and Eric play their traditional yearly match against each other and, for the first time, Eric beats Willy. Exhausted, Willy perceives the failure as a violent, existential vanquishing: "If Eric wanted her soul he could have it, though it grieved her that more than anything that's what he craved: her dignity like a lamb on an altar."[64] And, when Eric comments glibly "Sweetheart, you've been pasting me for over a year. And somebody has to win, don't they?",[65] Shriver reveals to us Willy's own sense of the inevitability of the vanquishing: "in her own mind, Willy has not been 'pasting' him; she'd won nothing but delay."[66]

Reviews of the novel on its reissue, even positive ones, almost without exception focus on how "unlikeable" Willy is, and the word "selfish" recurs a significant number of times in accounts of her: "Like Eva in *We Need to Talk About Kevin*, Willy is not a likeable character. She is intensely selfish and self-pitying," Soumya Bhattacharya opines for *The Independent*.[67] Writing in *The Guardian*, Viv Groskop describes Willy as "the novel's anti-heroine" and also adds that "she is from the same mould as Eva Khatchadourian (Kevin's mother): honest, intense, fiercely intelligent."[68] Bhattacharya claims that "Willy, who has always defined herself by tennis, begins to lose her sense of self-respect – and her sense of self (Shriver labours the point: the one quibble about this riveting, disquieting book)."[69] I fundamentally disagree that this point is laboured by Shriver. On the contrary, Willy's self-fulness as a female character is so unusual that the exposition of it may strike the reader as "overdone" simply by dint of its rarity. And, for a female reader invested in female self-fulness, following the journey of Willy's devastating loss of self is truly harrowing. More than anything, I suspect, Willy's tale is disquieting because it is the story of a woman who values her own professional life project above both her husband's professional success (refusing the role of helpmeet, the "great woman behind the great man") and, indeed, above her own marriage (the life project in which women are supposed to invest most of their emotional energy). In seeing Eric's very existence as rival to, and enemy of, her own success, Willy disobeys all of the rules of heterosexual femininity.

And yet, this perception of Eric – of what Eric *stands for* – reveals an uncomfortable truth about how ambition is sexed and gendered. The structural social factors that militate against ambitious women, in combination with the material reality of Willy's biology that ensured that one day the taller, stronger player – her husband – would beat her at tennis, account for her bitterness as her own star falters and fails at the very moment that her husband's is in the ascendency. The novel devastatingly shows how Willy's socioeconomic and sexed realities do not permit her the same possibility of a relaxed graciousness in the face of both triumph and disaster as Eric. The stakes of female ambition and female success are so much higher – and the chances of them so much more fragile that they are freighted with judgment and precarity. One anonymously authored review of the novel that appeared in *Publishers' Weekly* reveals a startling lack of awareness of the gendered dynamics of ambition and individuality in describing Willy as filled with "mean-spirited insecurities," while Eric is described as both "more individualized" and "nicer," without any thought given to why *both* of these qualities are easier and more available to Eric.[70] *Double Fault* offers a near-perfect, albeit fictional, portrayal of how ambition as a quality is experienced and judged when the ambitious individual is female.

As I was drafting an earlier version of this chapter, reflecting on ambitious female tennis players, a news item broke concerning Serena Williams's outburst at the US Open against an umpire, Carlos Ramos, who accused her of violating the rules by receiving an instruction from her coach. In response to the incident and the fine she received, Williams asserted that a male player would not have been sanctioned in the same way. She claimed that in speaking out, she was making a stand for "women's rights and for women's equality."[71] Indeed, the African-American female champion, who has won 21 Grand Slam singles titles in her career, is an exemplary case of an exceptional, driven, and ambitious woman whose sex, in combination with her race, has led to media and public speculation and criticism about her body, her professionalism, and her persona that are vastly disproportionate to the negative attention received by (white) male tennis stars – including violently argumentative ones, such as John McEnroe.

In an article for *The New York Times* titled "The Meaning of Serena Williams: On Tennis and Black Excellence,"[72] Claudia Rankine discusses the "belief among some African-Americans that to defeat racism, they have to work harder, be smarter, be *better*."[73] Moreover, they have to be gracious in the face of racism: "for black people, there is an unspoken script that demands the humble absorption of racist assaults."[74] The demand on exceptional black winners to be humble is compounded in the case of women of colour, who must contend with the racist and misogynistic stereotype of "aggressive black woman," that has so often been attributed to Serena. As Rankine points out, knowing that as a black female winner in the public realm, she cannot *win*, Williams has chosen to be very much her*self*: "Somehow, along the way, she made a decision to be excellent while still being Serena."[75] Williams's frequent asides to the audience, her opponent, or the umpire and her exuberant expressions of rage and of joy demonstrate, in Rankine's words, "the whole range of what it is to be human, and yet there are those who can't bear it, who can't tolerate the humanity of an ordinary extraordinary person."[76]

Serena Williams's persona represents a challenge to several sex and race-based double-binds. As a black woman, Williams is fully *expected* to be aggressive, assertive, and competent. In fact, these are the qualities of black femininity that place pressure on women of colour to hide or repress feelings of weakness or depression. In an article for *Ebony* magazine, Josie Pickens has written of the pressure to deliver the "strong Black woman speech to ourselves and everyone else," which can mean that "we lose our ability to connect to our humanness, and thus our frailty."[77] Pickens articulates the tension that women, and especially black women, face when called upon to be self-possessed and strong for the other. This is a kind of imposed self-possession that is little to do with self-fulness, it is an expectation instead to be full of self *for the other* – to be the mother figure who indefatigably cares and *does not let the other down*. Yet, as a female public figure and sports star, while being expected to be strong according to this "Black Superwoman" stereotype, Serena is also expected to be *likeable*. She is expected to temper her ambitious self-ful joy, rage, and competitiveness with a modesty and femininity that she refuses. As Rankine writes: "There is nothing wrong with Serena but surely there is something wrong with the expectation that she be 'good' while she is achieving greatness."[78] At the close of her article, Rankine movingly discusses how travelling to New York to see Serena Williams play, following her own battle with cancer and a year in which she had faced multiple exhausting examples of "everyday racism," was meaningful to her as "I had just passed through a year when so much was out of my control, and Serena epitomized not so much winning as *the pure drive to win*."[79] Williams inspires as a woman who embodies ambition and self-fulness, and who refuses to compromise her humanity to do so. And for that, she is punished relentlessly, not only by the umpire in the 2018 match, but by a scathing public.

A question forced by these reflections on female ambition and on how – thinking of Serena Williams – *even winners so often lose* – is the following: If female success is so hard-won, how should we approach the potentially self-defeating project of women and ambition? Two – ideologically opposing – attempts to answer this question are found in the recent work of Angela McRobbie and Sheryl Sandberg.

Writing on the competitive nature of the profession, not of tennis but of academia, Angela McRobbie has explored in a blog post for the London School of Economics how workload distribution between the sexes works in the academy in ways that are structurally unequal, albeit hard to measure. She muses on the home lives of left-wing French intellectuals Thomas Piketty and Jacques Derrida, both of whom reported needing to spend most of every day alone, engaged in reading and writing, in order to have a successful academic authoring career.[80] The implication is that this lifestyle evidently relies on behind-the-scenes "wife-work." McRobbie muses on how distant this prospect is from the lived reality of a female academic who has – or wants to have – children. She suggests that the very notion of scholarly achievement, as we understand it, is shaped by, and embodied in the figure of, the individualistic young man (the genius):

> The ideal career track in the academy especially one which carried all the laurels of prizes, awards, fellowships and a high volume of grants seemed to have been tailored around the image of the brilliant young man untrammelled by any of the fine details of domestic life. And if the young woman was to follow this pathway and plan the right time to have a child, then when would this right time be?

McRobbie insists: "Female academics ought to be able to demonstrate to enthusiastic young women that it is possible to succeed and to have children. Otherwise feminism has failed." Her point here is well-made, with the caveat that the logic she follows risks shoring up the notion of women as understandable in rather homogeneous group terms (family-oriented; wanting to be mothers). The figure of the exceptional, individualistic female genius is concomitantly made invisible and implicitly derided. (The exceptional woman, with or without children, who manages to succeed in career terms, is perceived as a traitor to her class and a problem for – or barrier to – the project of structural change that is wished for.) Additionally, McRobbie's argument needs to be understood in the larger context of what we might call "excellence culture" in academia. "Excellence" has, for some, become a tainted term recalling the measuring of outputs and productivity in, for example, the UK's Research Excellence Framework (REF) exercise. In such a (neoliberal) context, it can be argued, genuine excellence that cannot easily be measured has receded from view.

McRobbie pushes her argument further in this direction when she writes:

> If [...] the modern work regime has a corrosive effect on the individual, then for women embracing the idea of ordinariness may be good for the soul, while letting go of the drive to succeed, or to get the perfect "balance"

in life and work, could mean inventing new ways of thinking about work which replaces the logic of the talent led economy with the more commonplace idea of a "good job well done."

The suggestion, then, is for a compromise. Much as Donald Winnicott attempted to respond to psychoanalysis's impossible demands for perfection from the mother with the figure of the "good-enough mother," McRobbie here seems to be suggesting the emergence of a "good-enough" professional intellectual woman and to express the hope that broader expectations of all academics will concomitantly shift in tandem. Yet, I cannot help but think that the advice that women should embrace mediocrity and strategically eschew excellence in the hope that the wider profession will begin to expect less – or different – from all of its employees is as defeatist as it is unlikely to work. In this proposal, men will continue to seek excellence in the terms of the current (corporatized) university, while women will continue to fall into the roles that fail to lead both to academic promotion and to personal and professional satisfaction. While I fully recognize the problem that the "traditional" idea of the genius is constructed in the image of a young man, I do not agree that women's best strategy with regard to professional competition with young men is to aspire instead to being average. The suggestion on the part of some feminists (consciously or unconsciously made) that the association between women and the collective reveals either a transcendental truth or an unproblematic and desirable artificial state is one of the currents against which I am arguing most strongly in this book.

Turning from academia to the corporate world, in 2013, Sheryl Sandberg, COO of Facebook, published *Lean In: Women, Work and the Will to Lead*. This book is an exhortation to women to persevere in their career ambitions and insist ever harder on their right to a slice of the economic pie. Contrary to McRobbie's suggestion that female academics *do less*, Sandberg encourages "girls and women who want to sit at the table, [to] seek challenges, and *lean in* to their careers."[81] The women Sandberg writes for are implicitly affluent, white, straight, and partnered. Unsurprisingly, several critiques of Sandberg's book from a left-wing, anti-capitalist perspective have been produced.[82] While there is much that is valuable in these critiques, the bald argument that, by focusing on corporate language, culture, and norms, the book is not sufficiently "inclusive" seems an unreasonable one, since this is a title aimed precisely at women working in large corporations, written by a woman from such a background. Indeed, I confess to finding myself agreeing with certain points Sandberg makes. For example, she argues that women should "advocate for their own interests,"[83] and points out the unfairness of women leaders being perceived as "unlikeable,"[84] while "men are continually applauded for being ambitious and powerful."[85] However, I also have significant reservations about the book. In particular, one of the most depressing facets of Sandberg's text is its unrelenting hetero- and repro-normativity, its lack of imagination about what the life and worldview of an individualistic woman might look like. Telling the story of a female peer who was single, and therefore felt that she picked up a lot of slack at work for coupled and parent co-workers, Sandberg quotes – approvingly – the following:

> My coworkers should understand that I need to go to a party tonight – and this is just as legitimate as their kids' soccer game – because going to a party is the only way I might actually meet someone and start a family so I can have a soccer game to go to one day![86]

The implication that the only reason a single woman might want some time to herself is to find a partner in order to live a socially approved, "real," "mature" life that involves career *and* family is impossible to miss. For a self-confessed individualist, advocating for women recognizing their self-interest, Sandberg is stultifyingly conventional and unoriginal in her imagination of women's lives. She excludes from her book's remit any woman who is in any way eccentric and who might want to succeed in the corporate world.

This said, even Sandberg's attitude to parents in the most conventional of nuclear family set-ups seems a little unrealistic. She argues, exactly as McRobbie has done, that the care-giving burden falls disproportionately on working mothers. Yet, the solution she offers to this problem is that women should simply *insist* that their male partners (who are assumed to be willing in every case) do more childcare. She offers as incentive the (homophobic, anti-single-mother) argument – passed off as statistical fact – that:

> In comparison to children with less-involved fathers, children with involved and loving fathers have higher levels of psychological well-being and better cognitive abilities. When fathers provide even just routine child care, children have higher levels of educational and economic achievement and lower delinquency rates. Their children even tend to be more empathetic and socially competent.[87]

That genius and leadership are conventionally *gendered male*, as pointed out by both McRobbie and Sandberg, is undeniable. But throwing the aspiration for female excellence out altogether, as McRobbie advocates, is surely not the best way of tackling the *impasse* we are considering. Such an approach involves a *collective* lowering of expectations. Sandberg's approach, by contrast, involves a form of very peripheral tweaking of the normative gender roles of identikit heterosexual reproductive subjects, rather than any major resignification of "woman" and "individual." The fact is that neither of these responses is adequate – and both, to some extent, accept the received narrative that individuality is male/masculine while collaboration is female/feminine. (Sandberg, after all, literally advises women simply to act more like men at work – and to get men to act a tiny bit more like traditional women at home.) I dare to imagine a third model, though it is not a programmatic agenda that can be followed step-by-step as McRobbie's and Sandberg's prescriptions can. The shape of it is vague and elusive. It concerns resistance, a counter-discourse, a tenacious celebration, à la Rankine's connection to and investment in Serena Williams, of *the pure — female — drive to win*. We may also think back to Dworkin's point, with which this chapter opened, that an "exceptional" woman is *illegible* to patriarchy. *Making her legible* has to be a valid feminist project. This would be a *collective* female valuing of *individual*, selfish, female exceptionality; it would involve holding up and valuing exceptional women (rather than very ordinary men) as a source of inspiration.

Julia Kristeva may have come closest of any female writer of recent times to articulating this making-legible and holding up of the inspirational exceptional woman. In writing her "triptych" of books devoted to female geniuses – Hannah Arendt, Melanie Klein, and Colette – Kristeva attempted to write "a response to the kind of feminism that I call 'massifying'."[88] Her term "massifying" is a way of articulating and lambasting the assumption of feminism as inevitably collectivist, to which I have alluded throughout this book. The association of feminism with the collective is so powerful that Kristeva is forced to reason that, insofar as she dares to "ask [her]self questions about singularity," she may be "not really 'feminist'."[89] Yet, I would argue, against the author herself, that there is something eminently feminist in Kristeva's assertion that genius involves self-definition – and that, for women, this involves imagining a self-redefinition that exceeds and deforms the patriarchal, in ways that are directly oppositional to what Sandberg calls for:

> It seems to me that each subject invents, for himself, his own particular sex: this is where his genius, which is his creativity, lies [...] Women, traditionally relegated to reproductive tasks but having acceded to subjective excellence in every domain, highlight the special meaning I give to the idea of genius.[90]

Recognizing and celebrating the singular female genius as offering a blueprint for reimagining *the potentiality of women as a group* is, I contend, a properly feminist project.

Conclusion

In her study *Women and Power*, Beard discusses the reasons why it is assumed that getting more women into political positions would be a good thing. She notes that one reason often given is that more equal representation has been shown to increase the number of times "women's issues" (which she summarizes as "childcare and the rest") are raised in Parliament.[91] But then she makes the following excellent point about why this is *not* the point on which we should focus:

> It is flagrantly unjust to keep women out, by whatever unconscious means we do so; and *we simply cannot afford to do without women's expertise*, whether it is in technology, the economy or social care.[92]

Beard is pointing out that some of the preeminent experts in any field will be women, and that their expertise *must* be heard. Individual women should not have to represent, every time they speak, the multiple and sometimes contradictory concerns of "class woman." For no man would ever be expected to do this on behalf of his whole sex. But Beard then undermines her very valid point about the importance of viewing women as individuals with individual abilities, as well as members of a class with shared experiences of oppression, in the following terms:

> You cannot easily fit women into a structure that is already coded as male; *you have to change the structure.* That means thinking about power differently. It means decoupling it from public prestige. It means thinking collaboratively, about the power of followers not just of leaders.[93]

It is hard to interpret this as Beard doing anything other than shoring up a belief that the nature of women is collective and, moreover, that it is fine for women to aim for ordinariness, for mediocrity – for being "followers," as per Angela McRobbie's argument with regard to expectations of women in academia. Men, on the other hand, are, of course, at liberty to continue to essay individual distinction. It also assumes that men are, *by nature, and not because this is what patriarchy has taught us* – individuals. Beard argues here that men should become more like what we are told women are, and that power should be "feminized" (if we *believe* what we are told femininity is like).

This perpetuates a very commonplace narrative and, in some ways, repeats the very problem that I am arguing in this book we should work to overcome: *Some women wish to be "I," not "we."* And this is not regressive, perverse, or bad. Moreover, I would insist that women who experience and express such a self-perception (Thatcher being, perhaps, the limit case of this) are only understood as "being like a man" because we have been taught since birth that individual distinction is *properly* man's. We must not allow "woman" to be a synonym for "altruist" or "socialist" or "follower." What we need is not a mediocratization of culture, politics, or power, in order that women may gain a (small) piece of the (diminished) pie; but rather (in combination, it goes without saying, with fair and reasonable working practices), a way of understanding "woman as I," woman as self-ful outside of the interpretative paradigm presented to us by the patriarchy that suggests that this figure is either "like a man" or "trying to be a man." We need to lose the perception that concerted and proud individuality is *by definition* masculine.

A parallel to the problem raised in my reading of Beard's analysis of women in politics and McRobbie's analysis of the lot of female academics can be raised with regard to Rose's critique of expectations of motherhood. Her concluding gesture in *Mothers* is to celebrate motherhood, not because it shores up externally imposed notions about women being caring and loving, but precisely because of the "joy" it offers the woman who experiences it. Rose defines this "joy" as the shattering of "the carapace of selfhood."[94] Rose argues that through motherhood – whether via adoption, surrogacy, or the physical act of birth – women connect intimately with the whole world. In making a psychoanalytic point (that ego-shattering is good for us, since the ego is seen as illusory in the Lacanian tradition), Rose hints that Beauvoir's view of motherhood is faulty because the overall existentialist commitment to self-creation is faulty. She writes: "in the hands of Beauvoir [...] motherhood became the place where a philosophy in thrall to self-mastery reached its limits and started to disintegrate."[95] To the intolerable burden placed on mothers that her book has so beautifully set out: the demand to love without limit, to sacrifice and self-deny, to be responsible for the future in the figure of the other, Rose – disappointingly, and predictably, perhaps – counters with a renunciation of selfhood. She repeats the psychoanalytic logic that it is in the (erotic/loving/joyous) ecstasy of self-shattering that *true* transcendence – or freedom – may lie, not in the individualistic self-realization that the existentialist celebrates. Rose argues this as a riposte to the claim she makes that: "[one] of the most unrealistic demands made of mothers is that they should be so inhumanly confident and sure of themselves."[96] It is no doubt true that expecting so much of mothers while offering them so little in the way of social support and resources is the worst of all worlds. Yet, I would argue that the expectations placed on women as other are *almost always impossible*. So, why, then should women not pursue an arguably more desirable impossibility – *self* – than the self-shattering that is linked, in the psychoanalytic tradition, to a masochistic feminine *jouissance*? In place of a revalorized repackaging of what we have been told is the feminine lot, why should women *not* plunder men's territory and essay instead transcendence via reasoned self-interest à la Beauvoir, à la Kristeva's female geniuses (and, indeed, à la Rand)?

Moreover, having used the tale of her own adoption journey, and transgender activist Susan Stryker's account of her participation in her partner's giving birth, as examples of how the self-shattering of mothering connects one to the whole world, Rose writes: "in an ideal world, everyone, whatever the impulses driving them hard and fast in the opposite direction, would be capable of thinking of themselves as mothers."[97] This is a rather parallel logic to Gilligan's. The ethics of care mode of reasoning is usually women's moral lot, but the world may be better if men were to use it too. However, until they do adopt it en masse (we are still waiting), the first, urgent, and pragmatic step is surely to counsel girls and women to stop doing the extra emotional labour of being for the other and to occupy themselves with the interests of the self. Rose's point here also parallels Beard's and McRobbie's. Rather than women being recognized and respected *as individuals* within politics or academia, politics and academia should transform to look more like the stereotypical view of collective, collaborative femininity.

Needless to say, perhaps, I find all such gestures unhelpful. Rather than calling for women not to be associated with the characteristics expected of mothers – hell, for *mothers* not to be reduced to those stereotypes – and leaving her argument there, Rose argues instead that *everyone* should undergo the experience of psychical connectedness that she suggests is found in mothering – or at least be willing to imagine doing so. I would counter this with the assertion that women, so routinely encouraged *from their own birth* to imagine themselves one day as mothers – that is, as intimately connected to and responsible for the other, might do better to essay instead the far more challenging thought experiment of thinking of themselves primarily, and without apology, first only as *selves*.

Notes

1 Jacqueline Rose, *Mothers: An Essay on Love and Cruelty* (London: Faber and Faber, 2018), loc. 1026.
2 Rose, *Mothers*, loc. 1101.
3 Rose, *Mothers*, loc. 40.
4 Arthur Schopenhauer, "On Women," *Studies in Pessimism*, translated by T. Bailey Saunders (New York: Cosimo Classics, 2007), 62–75, p. 62.
5 Firestone, *The Dialectic of Sex*, p. 73.
6 Freud, "Some Psychical Consequences of the Anatomical Distinction Between the Sexes," [1925], translated by James Strachey, in *On Sexuality: Three Essays on the Theory of Sexuality and Other Works* (Harmondsworth: Penguin, 1991), 323–343, p. 342.
7 Freud, "Some Psychical Consequences," p. 342.
8 Carol Gilligan, *In a Different Voice: Psychological Theory and Women's Development*, new edition [1982] (Cambridge: Harvard University Press, 1993), p. 35.
9 Gilligan, *In a Different Voice*, p. 3.
10 For a critique of Gilligan's project, on feminist rather than methodological grounds, and arguing for the misplaced essentialism of Gilligan and a number of other "psychologists of women," see especially the work of Naomi Weisstein, e.g. "Power, Resistance and Science: A Call for a Revitalized Feminist Psychology," *Feminism and Psychology*, 3:2, 1993, 239–245, p. 145.
11 Gilligan, *In a Different Voice*, p. 2.
12 Gilligan, *In a Different Voice*, p. 39.
13 Gilligan, *In a Different Voice*, p. x. My emphasis.
14 Gilligan, *In a Different Voice*, p. xiii. My emphasis.
15 Gilligan, *In a Different Voice*, p. xiii.
16 Daum, *Selfish, Shallow and Self-Absorbed*, epigraph n.p.
17 Michaela Kreyenfeld and Dirk Konietzka (eds), *Childlessness in Europe: Contexts, Causes and Consequences* (Dordrecht: Springer Open, 2017).
18 See https://en.unesco.org/gem-report/sites/gem-report/files/girls-factsheet-en.pdf.
19 Badinter, *Mother Love: Myth and Reality: Motherhood in Modern History* (New York: Macmillan, 1981), p. xx.
20 Adrienne Rich, *Of Woman Born: Motherhood as Experience and Institution* (New York: Norton, 1976), p. xxiv.
21 Lionel Shriver, "Be Here Now Means Be Gone Later," in Daum (ed.), *Selfish, Shallow, and Self-Absorbed*, 77–96, p. 78.
22 Shriver, "Be Here Now Means Be Gone Later," p. 80.
23 Shriver, "Be Here Now Means Be Gone Later," p. 82.
24 Shriver, "Be Here Now Means Be Gone Later," p. 83.
25 Shriver, "Be Here Now Means Be Gone Later," pp. 83–84.
26 Shriver, "Be Here Now Means Be Gone Later," p. 78.
27 Cited in Shriver, "Be Here Now Means Be Gone Later," p. 88.
28 Shriver, "Be Here Now Means Be Gone Later," p. 93.
29 Nicki Defago, *Childfree and Loving It!* (London: Fusion Press, 2005), loc. 146.
30 Daum, Introduction, in *Selfish, Shallow and Self-Absorbed*, p. 4.
31 Beauvoir, *The Second Sex*, loc. 11285.

32 Beauvoir, *The Second Sex*, loc. 11826.

33 Rose, *Mothers*, loc. 1731.

34 Rose points out that so strong a taboo is disliking being a parent or regretting having children, that when Estela Welldon published *Mother, Madonna, Whore: The Idealization and Degradation of Motherhood* in 1988, a book which demonstrated the inherent ambivalence many women feel towards the child they both love and resent, her book was not sold in many feminist bookshops, banned for apparently contributing to the trend of "blaming mothers for any damage to their children" (see Rose, *Mothers*, loc. 1656).

35 See Nick Duerden, "Why Has Mumsnet Developed Such an Awkward Reputation," *The Independent*, 12 May 2013, www.independent.co.uk/life-style/gadgets-and-tech/features/why-has-mumsnet-developed-such-an-awkward-reputation-8607914.html

36 www.mumsnet.com/Talk/mumsnet_classics/2731884-I-hate-having-kids.

37 Rachel Cusk, *A Life's Work: On Becoming a Mother* (London: Faber and Faber, 1997), p. 5.

38 Cusk, *A Life's Work*, p. 13.

39 Cusk, *A Life's Work*, p. 13.

40 Cusk, *A Life's Work*, p. 7.

41 Cusk, *A Life's Work*, p. 8.

42 Susan Maushart, *Wifework: What Marriage Really Means for Women* (New York: Bloomsbury, 2001).

43 Cusk, *A Life's Work*, p. 12.

44 Shriver, *We Need to Talk About Kevin* (London: Serpent's Tail, 2005), p. 12.

45 Shriver, *We Need to Talk About Kevin*, p. 165.

46 Shriver, quoted in Defago, *Childfree and Loving It!*, loc. 3170.

47 Shriver, *We Need to Talk About Kevin*, p. 12.

48 Shriver, quoted in Defago, *Childfree and Loving It!*, loc. 3255.

49 www.mumsnet.com/Talk/what_were_reading/125980-i-need-to-talk-about-we-need-to-talk-about?pg=2.

50 www.mumsnet.com/Talk/what_were_reading/266735-we-need-to-talk-about-kevin. In a Mumsnet Q&A with Shriver, the author comments: "I think it was not having kids that made it possible for me to write that book." www.mumsnet.com/qanda/lionel-shriver

51 www.mumsnet.com/Talk/what_were_reading/125980-i-need-to-talk-about-we-need-to-talk-about?pg=1.

52 For numbers, see www.onlinewomeninpolitics.org, 2007 (referenced in Sjoberg and Gentry, *Mothers, Monsters, Whores*, loc. 267.) My personal view regarding this phenomenon is a bit ambivalent: I find it quite likely that those women with political ambition may be the same women who have no interest in having children, and I do not think that this should be a matter of concern to anyone. However, if mothers who are inclined to enter politics are discouraged or prevented from doing so *because of their status as a mother*, this suggests the continuing existence of an unacceptable barrier to access and equity. So, while forcing equality of outcome would be undesirable, to my mind, equality of opportunity is of paramount importance.

53 The cover image credit inside the magazine is given as David Young.

54 See https://twitter.com/nicolasturgeon/status/621621589038235648.

55 See Heather Saul, "Nicola Sturgeon Blasts 'Crass' *New Statesman* Cover of Female MPs around a Crib with Headline 'Why Are So Many Successful Women Childless?'," *The Independent*, Thursday 16 July 2015, www.independent.co.uk/news/people/nicola-sturgeon-blasts-crass-news-statesman-cover-of-female-mps-around-a-crib-with-headline-why-are-10393439.html

56 Helen Lewis, "The Motherhood Trap: Why Are So Many Senior Politicians Childless?," *New Statesman*, 16 July 2015, www.newstatesman.com/politics/2015/07/motherhood-trap

57 Lewis, "The Motherhood Trap."

58 Lewis, "The Motherhood Trap."

59 Transcript taken from May Bulman, "Andrea Leadsom on Theresa May and Motherhood," *The Independent*, 9 July 2016, www.independent.co.uk/news/uk/politics/andrea leadsom-interview-theresa-may-mother-tory-leadership-campaign-a7128331.html

60 See Anon, "Andrea Leadsom Apologises to Theresa May over Motherhood Remark," BBC News, 11 July 2016, www.bbc.co.uk/news/uk-politics-36760986

61 Shriver, "Be Here Now Means Be Gone Later," p. 78.

62 Shriver, "Be Here Now Means Be Gone Later," p. 95.

63 Maud Lavin, *Push Comes to Shove: New Images of Aggressive Women* (Cambridge: MIT Press, 2010), p.13.

64 Shriver, *Double Fault* [1997] (London: Serpent's Tale, 2006), p. 145.

65 Shriver, *Double Fault*, p. 145.

66 Shriver, *Double Fault*, p. 145.

67 Soumya Bhattacharya, "*Double Fault* by Lionel Shriver: Game, Set and a Mistimed Match", *The Independent*, 19 May 2006, www.independent.co.uk/arts-entertainment/books/reviews/double-fault-by-lionel-shriver-478729.html

68 Viv Groskop, "Advantage Miss Shriver," *The Guardian*, 7 May 2006 https://www.theguardian.com/books/2006/may/07/fiction.features1

69 Bhattacharya, "*Double Fault*."

70 Anon, "*Double Fault*," *Publisher's Weekly*, n.d., www.publishersweekly.com/978-0-385-48830-3

71 See www.independent.co.uk/sport/tennis/serena-williams-umpire-us-open-final-video-naomi-osaka-carlos-ramos-a8533736.html.

72 Claudia Rankine, "The Meaning of Serena Williams: On Tennis and Black Excellence," *The New York Times*, 25 August 2018, www.nytimes.com/2015/08/30/magazine/the-meaning-of-serena-williams.html

73 Rankine, "The Meaning of Serena Williams."

74 Rankine, "The Meaning of Serena Williams."

75 Rankine, "The Meaning of Serena Williams."

76 Rankine, "The Meaning of Serena Williams."

77 Josie Pickens, "Depression and the Black Superwoman Syndrome," *Ebony*, 13 November 2017, www.ebony.com/wellness-empowerment/depression-black-superwoman-syndrome-real

78 Rankine, "The Meaning of Serena Williams."

79 Rankine, "The Meaning of Serena Williams." My emphasis.

80 McRobbie, "Women's Working Lives in the Managerial University and the Pernicious Effects of the 'Normal' Academic Career." http://blogs.lse.ac.uk/impactofsocial sciences/2015/09/03/womens-working-lives-in-the-managerialuniversity/

81 Sheryl Sandberg, *Lean In: Women, Work and the Will to Lead* (New York: WH Allen, 2013), loc. 2373.

82 See Dawn Foster (ed.), *Lean Out* (New York: Repeater Books, 2015). In her Forward to the book, Nina Power writes of the need to criticize "'individualist' feminism, 'choice' feminism, 'corporate' feminism, 'imperialist' feminism and all the other right-wing hellspawn positions that proliferate today under its banner," 7–8, p. 7. And, in a race-and-class-aware critique of the Sandberg phenomenon, bell hooks argues: "Sandberg's definition of feminism begins and ends with the notion that it's all about gender equality within the existing social system. From this perspective, the structures of imperialist white supremacist capitalist patriarchy need not be challenged." "Dig Deep: Beyond Lean-In," *The Feminist Wire*, 28 October 2013, www.thefeministwire.com/2013/10/17973/

83 Sandberg, *Lean In*, loc. 679.

84 Sandberg, *Lean In*, loc. 2400.

85 Sandberg, *Lean In*, loc. 253.

86 Sandberg, *Lean In*, loc. 1979.

87 Sandberg, *Lean In*, loc. 1673.

88 Kristeva, *This Incredible Need to Believe*, p. 38.
89 Kristeva, *This Incredible Need to Believe*, p. 39.
90 Kristeva, *This Incredible Need to Believe*, p. 40.
91 Beard writes: "A report from the Fawcett Society recently suggested a link between the 50/50 balance between women and men in the Welsh Assembly and the number of times 'women's issues' were raised there." *Women and Power*, loc. 501.
92 Beard, *Women and Power*, loc. 505. My emphasis.
93 Beard, *Women and Power*, loc. 512. My emphasis.
94 Rose, *Mothers*, loc. 2600.
95 Rose, *Mothers*, loc. 2615.
96 Rose, *Mothers*, loc. 2580.
97 Rose, *Mothers*, loc. 2650.

5

A FEMINIST ETHICS OF SELFISHNESS?

Beyond individualism and collectivism

It [feminism] proposes, in the words of Elizabeth Cady Stanton, "the individuality of each human soul... in discussing the rights of woman, we are to consider first what belongs to her as an individual, in a world of her own, the arbiter of her own destiny..." This is simply a recognition of the human condition in which women are included. [...] It is the imposition of the sex-class definition of women on women – by any means necessary – that devastates the human capacities of women, making them men's subordinates, making them "women." Feminists have a vision of women, even women, *as individual human beings*; and this vision annihilates the system of gender polarity in which men are superior and powerful. This is not a bourgeois notion of individuality; it is not a self-indulgent notion of individuality; it is the recognition that every human being lives a separate life in a separate body and dies alone. In proposing "the individuality of each human soul," feminists propose that women are not their sex; nor their sex plus some other little thing – a liberal additive of personality, for instance; but that each life – including each woman's life – must be a person's own, not predetermined before her birth by totalitarian ideas about her nature and her function, not subject to guardianship by some more powerful class, not determined in the aggregate but worked out by herself, for herself.

(Andrea Dworkin, *Right Wing Women*, 1983. My italics)

Individualism regards man – every man – as an independent, sovereign entity who possesses an inalienable right to his own life.

(Ayn Rand, "Racism," 1963)

Do not make the mistake of the ignorant who think that an individualist is a man who says: "I'll do as I please at everybody else's expense." An individualist is a man who recognizes the inalienable individual rights of man – his own and those of others.

(Ayn Rand, "Textbook of Americanism," 1946)

In the first quotation of this epigraph, Andrea Dworkin draws on the words of American suffragist Elizabeth Cady Stanton (1815–1902) to explain what feminism might offer to women. This offering is nothing less than autonomy and self-determination as individual human beings: "what belongs to her as an individual, in a world of her own, the arbiter of her own destiny." It is irresistible to note that in certain, very striking, ways, both Stanton's and Dworkin's words and sentiments here, in summarizing the promise of feminism, echo those of Ayn Rand summarizing the values of individualism. While the necessity of individuality for dignity and self-esteem is acknowledged by Stanton, Dworkin, and Rand equally, Rand of course thinks that each wo/man (though she annoyingly always uses the universal masculine pronoun and the term "man") can attain the freedom and dignity of which Stanton and Dworkin speak through *rational volition* alone. This is because she does not believe in the power of structural or class-based inequality as a barrier to freedom, or in the existence of the patriarchy as a system that might contribute to the socialization of girls and women as less assertive, as *self-less*. About feminism, in fact, as we have noted previously, Rand writes that of all the rights movements it is the least convincing in its claims. I read Stanton, Dworkin, and Rand together here, then, not to argue for Rand's feminism, but rather to argue for a legitimate feminist interest in individuality – though not necessarily a feminist commitment to full-blown individualism.

As discussed in the Introduction, and in Chapter 4 with regard to Angela McRobbie, Sheryl Sandberg, and the problem of women and work, many critiques of individual-focused projects from a feminist (and especially a leftist) perspective are driven by the perception that they are per se identical with the subject of (the ill-defined, catch-all term) "neoliberalism." In this chapter, I shall work to identify strategies and understandings of individuality that can be productive for feminists and that cannot be dismissed by immediate recourse to equivalence with "neoliberalism." I shall propose that a feminism that promotes female individuality is a valid and valuable contribution to contemporary politics and theory. In the quotation above, Dworkin hints at the possibility of this kind of individual freedom, when she writes: "This is not a bourgeois notion of individuality; it is not a self-indulgent notion of individuality; it is the recognition that every human being lives a separate life in a separate body and dies alone." That Dworkin's dream, in the 1970s and 1980s, of a feminism that would deliver the possibility of a self-ful existence to women has not been achieved at the time of publication in 2019, is to be regretted. It also suggests that neither the divisive individualistic techniques described in the former chapter, associated with names such as Sheryl Sandberg, nor the collective project essayed by Dworkin has ultimately succeeded.

As well as essaying the counter-intuitive and unpopular project of proposing a feminism that renews its interest in the individual, I shall also no doubt upset many by suggesting that the way in which we might best achieve such a feminist vision is by revisiting the second-wave radical feminism of Dworkin and her contemporaries and mining it for what is valuable in its dreaming about the relationship between collectivity and the individual. My gesture of opening this chapter and the previous one with epigraphs taken from Dworkin and my reading here of Dworkin with and through Rand indicate my conviction that the best insights for a feminist concept of the individual fit for the present and the future were produced in the past, and this serves as a model for the perhaps unlikely intellectual and political marriage I intend to deploy here.

In what follows I shall explore how discourses of and about feminism from the 1990s to the present moment deal with the question of women's self-interest inadequately. These are both the forms of cultural practice and politics known as "postfeminism," and the third- and fourth-wave branch of feminism that is built on an ethic of "inclusion" and "intersectionality," known as "intersectional feminism." Both movements define themselves against the "second wave," the former by claiming that the second wave's work has already been achieved, and the latter by arguing that in its white and middle-class-centrism, as well as in its focus on analysis of "class woman," 1970s and 1980s feminism ethically failed by not "centring" previously othered individuals – whether on the basis of race, socio-economic class, dis/ability, trans status, sexuality, or fat/thin privilege/lack of privilege. It is my contention that, ironically, these recent modes of feminism or responses to feminism that nominally elevate, in different ways and for different ethical reasons, forms of identity over class-based analysis, may be uniquely bad at promoting properly *self-ful* models.

In a final section, I shall look to the past and revisit the maligned second wave. Via an analysis of the strategies suggested by a range of voices of the 1970s and 1980s, I will attempt to articulate a version of feminism that makes room for individuality (self-fulness) while recognizing the problems still facing women as a group – or, to give credit to the intersectional ethos – as a *number* of groups. To do this, I will articulate how resistant strategies may be borrowed from the misunderstood second-wave tradition of radical feminism, which, understood as an experiment in collectivism with the aim of producing a different form of individuality, may help us to imagine a feminism for the future that we might term "self-ful feminism."

Postfeminism

"Postfeminism" became a term with cultural currency in the 1990s. It is a contentious term, and one with more than one meaning. To some, it is "post-" in the sense of being the feminism that "comes next," building on something already firmly embedded in the cultural imaginary. It attempts to bring up to date the feminist project of the first and second waves for a younger generation and for late-twentieth and twenty-first-century concerns, including consumerism and so-called "sex positivism." In *Manifesta: Young Women, Feminism, and the Future* (2000) Jennifer Baumgardner and Amy Richards aim to differentiate younger women's feminism from that of "the suffragettes and bluestockings of the late nineteenth century and from our serious sisters of the sixties and seventies,"[1] since they claim that the success of historical feminism means that the feminist movement now "has such a firm and organic toehold in women's lives"[2] that it is simply an unspoken part of women's being in the world. The authors go on:

> Whether it's volunteering at a women's shelter, attending an all-women's college or a speak-out for Take Back the Night, or dancing at a strip club [...] whenever women are gathered together there is great potential for individual women, and even the location itself, to become radicalized.[3]

Whatever the merits of these individual activities, placing them all together under the umbrella term "feminism" effectively ensures that that term has ceased to mean anything very specific at all and has become a catch-all for "things that women do" (implicitly "while exercising 'choice'").

In another – and perhaps the dominant – meaning of "postfeminism," the "post" signals a reaction *against* feminism, proceeding from the position that all necessary women's rights have already been won, and that feminism per se (often dismissed as prescriptive, sex-negative, and fun-negative), is therefore no longer relevant. Deborah Siegal explains postfeminism as:

> a movement when women's movements are [...] no longer moving, no longer vital, no longer relevant; the term suggests that the gains forged by previous generations of women have so completely pervaded all tiers of our social existence that those still "harping" about women's victim status are embarrassingly out of touch.[4]

And Jane Gerhard comments that, in the 1990s, "the question was no longer 'are you a cultural or radical feminist,' but 'is feminism dead or alive?'."[5] Though, as Joan Smith has pointed out, obituaries for feminism, or articles proclaiming "false feminist death syndrome" are so common as to constitute a genre of their own:

> We vividly recall *Newsweek* declaring "the failure of feminism" in 1990; *The New York Times* assuring its readers that "the radical days of feminism are gone" in 1980; and *Harpers* magazine publishing a "requiem for the women's movement" as early as 1976.[6]

(One might almost think that these headlines are symptoms of broader cultural wishful thinking!)

Some postfeminist discourses go further than merely proclaiming that feminism is over, suggesting instead that some of the changes wrought on society by feminism may, in fact, have been *against* women's own best interests (using a stereotypical, heteronormative idea of what women's best interests might be). In her Pulitzer Prize-winning book, *Backlash: The Undeclared War Against American Women* (1991), Susan Faludi argues that the mainstream media has engaged in a campaign of propaganda aimed at undermining the gains of second-wave feminism and delivering the message that feminism had made women unhappy. According to Faludi, anti-feminism insidiously announced itself in stories about professional women suffering "burnout," women increasingly experiencing infertility, and lonely, ageing women bemoaning a "man shortage" – all at the same time as some women were declaring themselves no longer in need of feminist analysis and politics.[7] Dressing issues of continuing structural inequality as the *fault of feminism* (the opening section of Faludi's first chapter is called "Blame It on Feminism") is a sleight of hand that was designed to alienate women from any residual allegiance to the term and movement. This constitutes a cultural act of gaslighting with the aim of causing women to misrecognize both self-interest and the source of their discontent. Indeed, in 1990 just 14% of women of all ages polled in the USA identified as "feminist."[8]

The ambivalence about feminism created for women by this "backlash" in the 1990s is beautifully exemplified by the popular legal comedy-drama *Ally McBeal* (1997–2002, created by David E. Kelley).[9] The eponymous character is presented as a hopelessly romantic and whimsical, endlessly vain yet good-hearted, as well as professionally talented, 30-something lawyer, played by Calista Flockhart. Ally McBeal's unhappiness, explored at length in the series, is attributed to her contradictory desires: for somebody she "can be totally weak with. Somebody who will hold me and make me feel held," on the one hand, and for professional and personal independence, on the other. The show was the object of postfeminist commentary and it also engaged self-reflexively with contemporaneous debates in feminism and postfeminism.

On 29 June 1998 *Time* magazine ran a cover which depicted Flockhart's character alongside three pioneering first- and second-wave feminists, Susan B. Anthony, Betty Friedan, and Gloria Steinem, with the legend: "Is Feminism Dead?" (See Figure 5.1.) The eponymous question echoed and referenced the iconic *Time* cover of 8 April 1966 which asked "Is God Dead?" The replacement of "God" with "feminism" suggests that the latter is also both a tyrant and a source of comfort, a to-be-obeyed authority from which courageous rebels might liberate themselves by declaring unbelief. This neatly and subtly reinforces Faludi's message that backlash media seeks to recast feminism as the cause of women's apparent suffering, something of which they might do well to divest themselves, something to stop believing in. Second, by placing a fictional character (the words "Ally McBeal" not "Calista Flockhart" appear above her photograph) alongside three real, historically distinguished, feminist women, the image suggests irresistibly that "real" or "authentic" feminism is dead and that what is in its place is a simulacrum, a weakened facsimile. In a direct reference and response to the publication of the *Time* cover, in "Love Unlimited," episode 12 of the second season of the show, Ally has a dream that she has won the title of "Professional Woman of the Year" and that *Time* magazine has put her on their cover. In her dream, a pushy, power-suit-wearing journalist, Lara Dipson (played by Caroline Aaron), approaches her to be featured in *Pleasure Magazine* as a role model, telling

FIGURE 5.1 Cover of *Time*, 29 June 1998. Photograph by Rachel Mesch.

her: "we are going to have to make a few adjustments in the way you dress. And I'd really like to fatten you up a bit. We don't want young girls glamorizing that 'thin' thing." In response, dream-Ally bites off her nose. Later, in a scene at the law firm, Ally tells her co-worker John Cage (Peter MacNicoll): "You know, I had a dream that they put my face on the cover of *Time* magazine as 'the face of feminism'." This is a prospect that Ally evidently apprehends with horror.

In an essay entitled "(Un)fashionable Feminists: The Media and Ally McBeal," Kristyn Gordon describes the relationship of unease that the 1990s woman, represented by Ally McBeal, is thought to experience with regard to feminism:

Ally McBeal is characterised as a woman who wants the power to make choices in her life, but does not want to have to fight for them herself – or for them to impinge on her personal expression. That is, she wants the benefits of feminism without running the risk of being associated with the criticisms of feminism. Ally McBeal has come to represent a woman who has achieved some of the goals of second-wave feminism, in that she is financially independent, successful in her career, and unafraid to demand sexual satisfaction. Yet [...] she is in emotional turmoil over her status as a single woman.[10]

Two equally unsatisfactory notions of "individuality" are at war in the figure that Ally McBeal represents. The archetype of the career woman, on the one hand, confronts – and is defeated by – the spectre of the unhappy, heterosexual single woman (or "singleton," a figure immortalized around the same time in the UK by Helen Fielding's creation of Bridget Jones), on the other.[11] Critical understandings of *Ally McBeal* hold it to demonstrate that individual professional achievement will always be secondary to marriage and family in women's hierarchy of wants, despite any flimsy protests to the contrary – and the implication is that feminism, which promised satisfaction in the former, has sold women a pup. Yet, as Gordon points out, this version of 1990s woman is a media construct that may be used both to shore up and obscure the anti-feminist leanings of the mainstream press, as described in Faludi's *Backlash*. The *Time* cover implies that the death of feminism is spelled by regressively sentimental, superficial, and apolitical women like Ally. By juxtaposing the blonde, pouting, made-up (in both senses of the term) Ally McBeal with the "serious" black-and-white portraits of Anthony, Friedan, and Steinem, we are irresistibly drawn to understand that the previous generation of feminism has failed to produce the strong women it promised. Or, as Gordon puts it: "The *Time* cover suggests a linear progression which implies that feminism has moved from a 'we' solidarity of the 1960s and 1970s to a 'me' based feminism in the twenty-first century."[12]

A historical understanding of the cultural apprehension of feminism, as provided by Imogen Tyler, however, shows that "selfish" (or "me-based") is, in fact, an accusation that has been levelled at feminism since its earliest days. She writes that "in the 1970s the figure of the selfish feminist became a predominant caricature of the women's movement and the focus of claims that the nation had spiralled into a state of apolitical narcissistic malaise."[13] Postfeminist-era criticisms of Ally McBeal are simply later versions of these same critiques adapted to the cultural moment. The difference between the two decades lies in how the second-wave feminist project is perceived, and what the function of feminism is seen to be. In the 1970s, feminism was the ravenous id, enabling the woman's (selfish) ambitions to the detriment of the husband's pipe and slippers. In the 1990s, it had instead taken on the role of superego, so that when Ally McBeal describes simultaneously wanting "to be independent" and "to be *held*," and worrying that "that makes me a failure as a woman," it is the imagined second-wave feminist in her dream whom she disappoints, not the patriarch/y. As Gordon writes, "there is confusion over what it is to be a feminist as well as what it means to be a successful woman."[14] At the heart of this confusion is an expectation that women owe fidelity to something beyond themselves, be it family life and the role of "perfect wife and mother," or the demand to sacrifice the same in adherence to demands to be a "perfect feminist" (understood as the caricatural figure of Lara Dipson's power-suit-wearing, ball-breaking, fun-hating professional woman). What is most instructive for us to take from *Ally McBeal* is that it is in the interests of patriarchy, rather than in the interests of women, for women to live this guilt-ridden tension.

If *Ally McBeal* dramatizes some of the effects of the backlash of which Faludi wrote on an individual woman (attempting – and failing – to live up to one myth of "ideal feminism" put about by anti-feminist forces), Ariel Levy's *Female Chauvinist Pigs* (2005) identifies a trend in 1990s and 2000s popular culture that, she argues, further undermines the feminist project while pretending that it is doing feminism's work. Levy's book explores women's negotiation of what she terms "raunch culture."[15] She uses this term to describe a growing trend in the late-1990s and early 2000s for sexually explicit or suggestive fashions, publications, and attitudes, inspired by aesthetics emerging from pornography and sex work, that were presumed to be enthusiastically enjoyed by both men and women. Raunch culture is perhaps best exemplified by the rise of the "lads' mag," a genre of magazine with names such as *Maxim* and *FHM* that featured tongue-in-cheek, humorous text, while reproducing the visual stuff of *Playboy* – images of "greased celebrities in little scraps of fabric humping the floor."[16] The implication was that the magazine and its readers were too sophisticated for old-fashioned, unironic sexism, but that female objectification repackaged as sexy, postmodern fun was harmless and crucially apolitical. As Rosalind Gill puts it, such sexism "is articulated in an ironic and knowing register in which feminism is simultaneously taken for granted and repudiated."[17] Following the emergence of the "lad," the figure of the "ladette" emerged, a female persona that aspired to the *FHM* aesthetic, sexually permissive attitude, and consumerist ethos, all the while proclaiming her "feminism." According to Levy, the "look" of the ladette, whom she renames the "Female Chauvinist Pig," was exemplified by "miniature tops that showed off breast implants and pierced navels alike. Sometimes, in case the overall message was too subtle, the shirts would be emblazoned with the Playboy bunny or say PORN STAR across the chest."[18] Levy reports how many women in her circle enthusiastically participated in this culture, favouring pole-dancing as a form of effective work-out with the bonus side-effect of "turning on their man," attending strip clubs as audience members (while heterosexual), and professing a taste for pornography. Just as irony exculpates the readers of lads' mags of sexism, so humour is used to justify the participation of women in the same raunch culture. Levy writes: "We decided long ago that the Male Chauvinist Pig was an unenlightened rube, but the Female Chauvinist Pig (FCP) has risen to a kind of exalted state. She is post-feminist. She is funny. She *gets it*."[19]

The logic of raunch culture, as described by Levy, echoes that of the backlash variety of postfeminism discussed above. It is assumed that, since feminism's work is roundly agreed (By whom? According to what measure?) to be "done," *any* activity carried out in the postfeminist culture would be sufficiently imbued with the character of historical feminism as to be unassailable and unproblematic. Accordingly:

> This new raunch culture didn't mark the death of feminism, they told me; it was evidence that the feminist project had already been achieved. [...] Women had come so far, I learned, we no longer needed to worry about objectification or misogyny. Instead, it was time for us to join the frat party of pop culture, where men had been enjoying themselves all along. If Male Chauvinist Pigs were men who regarded women as pieces of meat, we would outdo them and be Female Chauvinist Pigs: women who make sex objects out of other women and of ourselves.[20]

When she asked what her friends and the women she interviewed got out of their engagement in raunch culture, Levy reports having heard the word "empowerment" multiple times. "Empowerment," especially in the context of sexual expression, is often used as a byword for feminist liberation by so-called "sex-positive" feminists, for whom women's ability to participate without guilt in a sexualized culture is the marker of feminism's success. This discourse is a legacy of the feminist "sex-wars" of the 1980s, which saw pro-sex work, pro-BDSM, and pro-pornography feminists, such as Ellen Willis and Candida Royalle, at ideological war with women such as Andrea Dworkin and Catharine MacKinnon who saw pornography as hate speech and prostitution as inherently coercive.[21] In the context of the 2000s, however, such "empowerment" via sex positivism is inevitably tainted, as Levy notes, with a distinct (internalized) misogyny.

Levy describes how a group of young women she interviews, who fit the pro-raunch culture, FCP type, express simultaneous disdain and envy for those women they perceive as sexually attractive and "high value" in their culture, the so-called "girly-girls": "Girly-girls are people who 'starve themselves and paint their nails every fucking second,' as Anyssa put it; people who have nothing better to think about than the way they look."[22] Yet, Levy comments, "while the FCP shuns girly-girls from her social life, she is fixated on them for her entertainment."[23] The dynamic described – a heterosexual woman objectifying another woman for pleasure and entertainment, while despising her as a person – is very obviously at odds with the aims of the feminism with which FCP-ism is supposed to be in keeping. Levy writes:

> Anyssa is not different from most FCPs: they want to be like men and profess to disdain women who are overly focused on the appearance of femininity. But men seem to like those women, those girly-girls, or like to look at them, at least. So to *really* be like men, FCPs have to enjoy looking at those women too. At the same time, they wouldn't mind being looked at a little bit themselves.[24]

Levy argues that what raunch culture offers is a way for women to be like men: "It is a way both to flaunt your coolness and to mark yourself as different, tougher, looser, funnier – a new sort of loophole woman who is 'not like other women', who is instead 'like a man'."[25] This "wanting to be like men" while also wanting men's attention as heterosexual women is a particularly striking dynamic. In a culture in which women's exchangeable object-value is not even in question – indeed, it is celebrated – any woman who sees herself as a *person* can presumably have no choice but to identify with those *for whom* women are consumable items – men. This offers us a version of the "exceptional woman" narrative that might go some way to explaining why many feminists find the notion to be a political problem. Levy writes: "If you are the exception that proves the rule, and the rule is that women are inferior, you haven't made any progress."[26] The FCP *is* a position of individualism, insofar as women in this system compete with each other to be the "coolest," that is to be the most accommodating of the particular version of misogyny that shapes their cultural norms. However, it is a particularly *self-less* version of individualism insofar as it involves aping a form of toxic masculine attitude that deprives woman of being and divides them against other women and against themselves.

Levy comments pertinently that this desire to "be like a man" is not new: "some of the most glamorous and intriguing women in our history have been compared to men, either by admirers or detractors."[27] And "There is a certain kind of woman – talented, powerful, unrepentant – whom we've always found difficult to describe without some version of the phrase 'like a man'."[28] Here we think irresistibly of the discourses about Rand and Thatcher that figure them, respectively, as the "bravest man in America" or "best man in Europe." In each case – the FCP, Rand, and Thatcher – the desire to be like a man has to do with the desire to be recognized as a worthwhile subject, a worthwhile *self* in a culture in which only men are seen in this way. In the cases of Rand and Thatcher, however, the characteristics presumed to be "of a man," for which they seek recognition are the characteristics of being, respectively, an original thinker and strong political leader. In the case of the FCP, the characteristics of "being like a man" concern enjoying the sexual subjugation of women. While a certain misogyny no doubt underpins both Rand's and Thatcher's enjoyment of the "like a man" rhetoric, since both openly prized men above women, the FCP's aspiration to "be like a man" involves nothing more – no character strength or ability – than *being complicit with misogyny*. So, while it may be worth an attempt to recuperate values such as intelligence, originality, and strength – even ruthlessness – from their association with masculinity and place them squarely back in the category of personality traits that may belong to any person, the same cannot be said of the FCP values that are entirely predicated on misogyny.

On the basis of this, Levy concludes that "FCPs have relinquished any sense of themselves as a collective group with a linked fate."[29] We might note here that the sense of being a member of a group does not have to issue from a commitment to altruism or a desire to work always for the good of the collective. It requires only the sober willingness to see that the amount of dignity and respect *as an individual person* one is accorded by others – by society at large – is linked to one's membership of a sex class. Women are members of the sex class that has historically been, and continues to be, disadvantaged and oppressed by the other sex class. In the light of such a recognition, it becomes inescapable that one's own search for legitimation of self is necessarily linked in some intrinsic way to that of others in the same class. Ensuring the possibility of female dignity – the potential coming-into-being of female self-fulness – does not have to issue from a position of love for others. It can be an exercise of pure self-interest *that also benefits others as a by-product.* This is Rand's point about individualism as an ethic, with which I opened the chapter, applied to feminism. So, we might rewrite her words: "An individualist is a ~~man~~ woman who recognizes the inalienable individual rights of ~~man~~ woman – ~~his~~ her own and those of others." While objectifying other women as silly "girly-girls" (and secretly hoping to be objectified in the same way oneself – with that toxic mixture of acquisitive desire and contempt), one cannot properly achieve self-fulness. Levy goes on, pertinently:

> Even if you are a woman who achieves the ultimate and becomes like a man, you will always still be like a woman. And as long as womanhood is still thought of as something to escape from, something less than manhood, you will be thought less of too.[30]

Levy closes her book with words that exemplify my claim that individuality is a proper, feminist aim for women:

> If we believed that we were sexy and funny and competent and smart, we would not need to be like strippers or like men or like anyone other than our own specific, individual selves. More importantly, the rewards would be the very things Female Chauvinist Pigs want so desperately, the things women deserve: freedom and power.[31]

Intersectional feminism and "centring the other"

The "intersectional feminism" of the so-called third and fourth waves has arisen as a response to various perceived failings of earlier forms of feminism. These include the white-centric, trans-exclusive bias of the second wave, and the middle-class, able-bodied, capitalistic subject assumed by recent forms of liberal feminism or postfeminism, such as those described above. Instead of focusing on a "sex class," intersectional feminism seeks instead to attend to the multiple disadvantages – including race, economic class, (dis)ability, sexuality, body type, and gender identity – that individuals may face from a system of oppression often referred to as "kyriarchy" (the rule of the oppressors) in preference to "patriarchy" (the rule of the fathers).

The theory of "intersectionality" was first introduced in 1989, in Kimberlé Crenshaw's article "Demarginalizing the Intersection of Race and Sex: A Black

Feminist Critique of Antidiscrimination Doctrine." Here Crenshaw demon-strated how viewing the position of black women with regard to discrimination law can avoid thinking of oppression erroneously as "disadvantage occurring along a single categorical axis."[32] Crenshaw explains how discrimination claims brought against employers by women of colour were dismissed on the basis that neither discrimination on the grounds of sex nor on the grounds of race could be proved. (General Motors hired both white women in customer-facing roles and black men on the factory floor.) Crenshaw demonstrates how the discrimi-nation experienced by these women was located precisely at the "crossroads" of their sex and their race – a place that is neither occupied nor often seen by white feminists. While the ideas contained in Crenshaw's article offered a valuable and much-needed corrective to the blinkered, white-centric perspective of the law, and would influence feminism and critical race studies inside the academy in much-needed ways, the politics that it would go on to inspire in the twenty-first century have expanded considerably from Crenshaw's aims.

In the decade of the 2010s, with much feminist and social justice activism being played out online, "intersectionality" has become a ubiquitous ideology in feminism to the point that the slogan "my feminism will be intersectional or it will be bullshit!," coined by Flavia Dzodan as the title of an article for *Tiger Beatdown* in 2011,[33] has been turned into an Internet meme. It is, however, in-structive to note that this meme has since been marketized in order to profit others than Dzodan – in fact this feminist of colour has not seen a penny from the commodification of her words.[34] Moreover, these words are often accorded the status of a moral truism, questioned at the price of shaming or of feminist ex-communication, with many – often white and "privileged"– feminists policing each other's intersectional credentials.

In an article written by a second-wave socialist feminist evaluating the effects of third- and fourth-wave feminism, Linda Gordon writes that intersectionality "can signal a kind of pluralism, in which identities are represented as equivalents on a field of competing interest groups."[35]She goes on:

> [T]he focus on representing various categories of people presupposes in-nate homogeneity within each category [...]. Thus efforts to bring repre-sentatives of different races or sex/gender identities may assume that each person represents her or his entire race, sexual preference, for example.[36]

Twenty-first-century intersectionality, then, promotes a particular version of in-dividuality, so that each person needs to think of themselves in terms of the par-ticular multiple oppressions to which they are subject and the particular privileges from which they benefit – that then become the sum of their situated political identity. This both sidelines class-based analysis or strategic consensus-building, such as that on which much second-wave feminism rested, *and* silences the possi-bility of eccentric individual dissent. A glance at the prominent website *Everyday Feminism*, which subtitles itself "Intersectional Feminism for your Everyday Life," illustrates this at once atomizing and reifying tendency nicely, as its posts are organized according to categories ranged in the toolbar, including "race," "disability," "class," "religion," "trans and GNC" (gender non-conforming).[37]

A key concern of intersectional feminism is the question of whom it "centres." A feminist engaging with this discourse is exhorted to "check her privilege" in every situation and to ensure that she is not putting her own self-interest above that of a person or group who might be less privileged. "Centring the other" as a discourse appears all over the feminist and social justice Internet, including and especially *Everyday Feminism*. Examples of articles that instruct readers how to do this include: "4 Ways to Center Trans Women in Reproductive Justice"[38] and "Here's How We Can Center Queer and Trans Survivors in the #MeToo Movement."[39] In a whole article on why one's feminism should centre the *principle* of intersectionality, the authors, Jarune Uwujaren and Jamie Utt write: "Decenter your privilege [...] make an effort to avoid centering feminism around yourself."[40] These articles make some very valid points about the place of those with different or non-hegemonic experiences with regard to medical, social, and disciplinary institutions and political movements, but the insistent demand to "centre," "decentre," and "check" lends something thoroughgoingly scolding to the tone of such titles and articles, despite Uwujaren and Utt's insistence that "when people call each other out in social justice work," it is "an act of love."[41]

A real problem lies in the way in which respect and justice seem to be positioned as scarce resources to be "competed for." Any meaningful call to "centre" another more vulnerable individual or group relies on it being possible to decide which individual or group is the more oppressed. This is a necessarily subjective and inexact project. As a result, this form of politics often finds itself mired in in-fighting and unhelpful pile-ons. A telling example is the case of the Nigerian writer Chimamanda Ngozi Adichie. In an interview broadcast on Channel 4 on 10 March 2017, the writer, who has worked for LGBTQ rights in her home country and globally, expressed her view that trans women will have different experiences while growing up than those brought up as girls. She claimed:

> I think the whole problem of gender in the world is about our experiences. It's not about how we wear our hair or whether we have a vagina or a penis. It's about the way the world treats us, and I think if you've lived in the world as a man with the privileges that the world accords to men and then sort of change gender, it's difficult for me to accept that then we can equate your experience with the experience of a woman who has lived from the beginning as a woman and who has not been accorded those privileges that men are.[42]

This is in keeping with Adichie's broader feminist agenda, as she has written elsewhere about the ways in which girls are socialized in very specific ways – and of the disadvantages this socialization brings: "We teach girls to shrink themselves, to make themselves smaller. We say to girls, you can have ambition, but not

too much. You should aim to be successful, but not too successful."[43] In response
to Adichie's words about the different experiences of socialization, she faced a
glut of criticism on Twitter and in the LGBTQ media, including accusations
of being a "TERF" (trans exclusionary radical feminist) – a slur often equated
with "fascist"– and of "speaking over" trans people. In a public comment on
her Facebook page, Adichie clarified her position, but refrained from issuing
the apology demanded of her. She wrote that the furore illustrates a prevalent
"language orthodoxy" operating within feminism and social justice politics that
is coercive: "You're supposed to participate in [it], and when you don't there's
a kind of backlash that gets very personal and very hostile and very closed to
debate."[44] Adichie further points out that this "language orthodoxy" means that
the words one uses are often treated as if they are more important than one's
long-standing beliefs and history of activism.

The way in which intersectional feminism is currently practised – especially
in the heated echo chambers of online fora – thus pits the members of one mar-
ginalized "identity group" against another. In this case, a woman of colour activist was pitted against trans women in a competition over which had the greater
claim to oppression. Rather than allowing for and respecting difference, intersectionality, in its current iteration, divides. It is, in fact, much more like the
"neoliberal model of competition" that the left purports to despise than either
straightforward individualism or straightforward collectivism. On this point,
Naomi Zack has called for a less divisive "inclusive feminism" than intersectionality has led to. She argues that intersectionality encourages "a fragmentation
of women that precludes common goals as well as basic empathy."[45] The point
about empathy is especially valid. If one "centres" – i.e. places before oneself –
the interests of another, then that is not a matter of practising that long-standing
virtue of feminism: solidarity or *standing alongside*; rather it is a practice of self-
effacement. The risk, then, is that *both* self-interest *and* the making of strategic
common cause are effectively prevented. Yet, when second-wave feminism is
evoked by third- and fourth-wavers, it is commonly – and predictably – seen to
fail the stringent morality tests of intersectional feminism. Susan Archer Mann
and Douglas Huffman write:

> The second wave of American feminism was often blind to the ways its
> theories and political praxis failed to adequately address the everyday con-
> cerns of women of color and ethnicity [...]. It was also blind to how it
> appeared to many in the younger generation as an austere and disciplinary
> feminism. [...] By contrast, the new discourse of the third wave embraced
> a more diverse and polyvocal feminism that appealed to those who felt
> marginalized or restricted within the second wave.[46]

The third wave is presented here as the ethical corrective to earlier feminism –
and as a superior mode. This is, in itself, a problem. First, the imposition of the
political values of one age onto those of an earlier one is an anachronism which

promotes a simplistic narrative of progress whereby each generation is assumed to be more "enlightened" than the previous one. Second, it risks resulting in a kind of historical purge and a programmatic silencing of earlier voices. And third, the naming of second-wave radical feminism as "authoritarian" is ironic, given that the trend for calling out, no-platforming, and purity-testing carried out in the name of twenty-first-century social justice politics, as exemplified by the Adichie row, is at least as well suited to such a descriptor.

Liberal writer Helen Pluckrose has issued the following critique of contemporary forms of intersectionality from a pro-individualism stance: "Intersectionality, by undervaluing shared human experience and rights – universality – and personal autonomy and distinctiveness – individuality – and focusing intensely on group identity and intersectional ideology, places individuals in a very restricted 'collectivist' position previously only found in very conservative cultures."[47] She goes on to lament that intersectionality so often manifests "exclusionary tactics," "hostility," and "tribalism," and finishes by stating that this is "regrettable because liberalism could be benefitted by specialist attention to the ways in which specific groups within society are advantaged or disadvantaged." She closes with the strong objection that "until intersectionality respects diversity of ideas as well as of identity and supports every individual's right to hold any of them regardless of their group identity, it cannot be said to represent anything except its own ideology." Some liberal critiques of identity politics issuing from libertarian and pro-individualist writing tend to ignore structural oppression entirely, leading to a watered-down analysis that is often genuinely negligent of issues such as racism and sexism. However, Pluckrose's words here – especially the final sentence – are on point and deeply insightful. At a discursive level, twenty-first-century intersectional feminism has become ideologically purist to the point of not only demanding that women think of the other first, but effectively silencing those who either do not comply with this requirement or who express solidarity in the "wrong" words.

Indeed, much twenty-first-century feminist writing and activism is hectoring in a way that many may find unhelpful or unapproachable. In a recent book on "callout culture," Dianne Anderson describes this style of feminism as "a toxic culture of perfectionism" that has "made the perfect the enemy of the good."[48] It weaponizes the discourse of vulnerability, casting as bad feminists – or worse – those who react poorly to being told *in whose interests they must think and act*. This is, in fact, the very opposite of a strategy of awareness-raising that would enable an individual to become aware and then perhaps – though the *demand* cannot *properly* be made – to care about and want to act on behalf of other people's issues that are different from her own and that might indeed, in some cases, constitute an experience of greater oppression.

Radical feminism – and radical self-fulness

"Radical" feminism is the branch of that political movement that seeks, as the etymology of its name would suggest, to go to the very *roots* of patriarchal oppression in order to imagine and work for fundamental change.[49] Radical feminism of the 1960s, 1970s, and 1980s is often thought of now as a movement that was concerned only with collectivity – albeit a collectivity that failed to be inclusive. Critical accounts of the second wave tell how a group of privileged white women defined "class woman" in their own image, excluding black women, trans people, and non-middle-class women, despite the significant amount of activism, writing, and innovating being done by women in those groups. Second-wave radical feminism by white women has been criticized repeatedly – and with justification – for referring to the lives and words of women of colour only tokenistically, ignoring key texts of the period written by them, such as Cherríe Moraga and Gloria Anzaldúa's edited collection of radical writings by women of colour, *This Bridge Called My Back* (1981),[50] and being ignorant of the activism that was happening independently in African American, Chicana, Native American, and other contexts.[51] In light of this, the impulses behind the recent move towards a more intersectional feminism are understandable and laudable, but its execution in our present moment, as described above, is sometimes counterproductive and inimical to free expression. In what follows, I intend to mine texts of the second wave, by white Western writers and writers of colour alike, for their reflections on the relationship between individualism and collectivity with the aim of revealing that at least *one* commonly held perception about the feminism of our forebears – that it was only a feminism of the collective – is an unhelpful misperception.

As noted previously, Imogen Tyler has demonstrated how the feminism of the 1960s, 1970s, and 1980s in the USA was criticized precisely for being *selfish*, that is for daring to imagine that women might be individuals with desires and political agency of their own, whose ambitions extended beyond family. Tyler notes how challenges to "'selfless femininity' as a social ideal"[52] were found in the writings of radical lesbians (or women identified women) such as Adrienne Rich, who wrote of the "invisible violence"[53] inflicted on heterosexual women by the expectations of wifehood and motherhood. Similarly, the "Radicalesbians" collective explicitly articulated in their manifesto the problem of women having "internalized the male culture's definition of ourselves" which consigned women to "sexual and family functions." The manifesto goes on:

> The consequence of internalizing this role is an enormous reservoir of self-hate … poisoning her existence, keeping her alienated from herself, her own needs, and rendering her a stranger to other women. [...] As the source of self-hate is rooted in our male-given identity, we must create a new sense of self.[54]

There is something invigorating about the radical feminism of the 1970s insofar as the project of returning to the root cause of inequality, attempting to eradicate the effects on women of patriarchy, and seeing what might emerge in terms of female selfhood is enormously ambitious, in a way that is quite unparalleled in contemporary feminist writing.

One can go so far as to posit that the methods inaugurated by second-wave feminism, including collective struggle and group consciousness-raising sessions, were the tools designed by the *group* to engender the emergence of the *individual*. Tyler's analysis supports such a theory, as she shows that it was precisely these group activities that attracted to feminism the label "selfish." Consciousness-raising sessions, in which between 5 and 15 women met to talk through their experiences of living as women in patriarchy, had as their aim nothing less than "the resocialization' of female psychology."[55] This activity and the politics it promoted were derided by commentators such as (self-declared "feminist") Jean Bethke Elshtain who described consciousness-raising in 1979 as "a highly personalized sexual politics that is simultaneously depoliticizing, individualistic, and potentially pernicious in its implications,"[56] as well as by stridently anti-feminist conservative, Phyllis Schlafly, who argued: "Feminism puts women at the centre of the universe. They chose the word 'liberation' because they mean liberation from home, husband, family and children."[57] This idea that group activities were both designed to bring out and slowly gave way to the emergence of individuality is also corroborated by Robin Morgan who, in an article for *Ms.* magazine in 1975, described an evolution in the radical feminist circles she was involved in from a somewhat authoritarian focus on the collective to the appreciation and valuing of the individual. She writes that: "the early excesses of collective tyranny have shifted into an understanding that there is a difference between individualism and individuality – and that the latter is admirable and to be cherished."[58] She goes on "The early ultra-egalitarianism and guilt-ridden 'downward mobility' motifs of certain radical feminist groups [...] have modulated into a realization that women deserve to have credit for what we accomplish."[59] Similarly, Mimi Gladstein has noted that Betty Friedan and Gloria Steinem often discussed the import of nourishing one's inner life and self-interest first, favouring a movement of dipping in and out of collective action.[60] Yet, it is doubtless the case that the conscious embrace of "taking credit" is largely a white Western concern.

Many of the contributors to Moraga and Anzaldúa's collection *This Bridge Called My Back* focus instead on the commitment a woman of colour often experiences to furthering the liberation of both women and the members of her community, regardless of sex. Where "belonging" and "acting collectively" for white Western radical feminists often pertains only to feminist affiliations, and indeed excludes men as a badge of emancipation, Andrea Canaan writes passionately of her role in ensuring the continued survival of children, women, and men in her community:

> The fact is I am brown and female, and my growth and development are tied to the entire community. I must nurture and develop brown self, woman, man, and child. I must address the issues of my own oppression and survival. When I separate them, isolate them, and ignore them, I separate, isolate, and ignore myself. I am a unit. A part of brownness. My health, energy, intellect, and talent are resources of my community. When

I fall ill my community is weakened. When my community is invaded by disease I am affected, even killed. I must work both as an individual and as a part of my community in order to survive in order for my community to survive.[61]

Canaan's article articulates the relationship between flourishing as an individual and ensuring the flourishing of one's community – and asserts that the former may, in some circumstances, be the prerequisite for the latter.

Parallel tensions regarding self and community are operative in writings by feminists working from a Marxist perspective. In her manifesto, *The Dialectic of Sex: The Case for Feminist Revolution* (1970), Shulamith Firestone argues that it is unacceptable to expect a given woman to sacrifice her bodily integrity in the project of procreation "for the sake of the species." Since some subjects (rich and/or white) are more incentivized to reproduce than others (poor and/or black), as in the case of the coerced sterilization of women of colour, unmarried mothers, and immigrants at various moments in twentieth-century US history, critics are right to point out Firestone's white bias here.[62] Yet Firestone recognizes that female selfhood has not yet been sufficiently articulated as a liveable possibility, such that refusing *to sacrifice* – whether for the species, or for the feminist cause – becomes in and of itself a feminist act. I return again (as I love the image so much) to Firestone's reflections on her fascination for the character of the capitalistic Uncle Scrooge McDuck, which she discusses in a section of *The Dialectic of Sex* that focuses on how women have to inhabit, uneasily, male culture. We may recall that she links the female state of being "deprived of Self" to her vicarious thrill at "the selfish extravagance of [Scrooge McDuck's] bathing in money."[63] The young Firestone explains how she drew on the figure of the duck as an antidote to the shortage of available examples of female selfishness or of female selfhood at all outside of the roles stereotypically allocated to those in the "sex class." With the only roles available to girls in the 1960s being those of wife and mother, one can understand the rebellious pleasure found in identification with an imaginary figure whose self-regard and self-indulgence know no bounds, who would sacrifice himself for nothing.

Along similar lines, French materialist feminist, Monique Wittig echoes the rebellion of refusing to sacrifice when she explains in "The Straight Mind" how members of oppressed classes do not easily find themselves *as subjects* through collectivist struggles, such as Marxist politics, which risk simply reinscribing their belonging to a class. She writes of the "real necessity for everyone to exist as an individual," while arguing simultaneously that "without class and class consciousness there are no real subjects, only alienated individuals."[64] And, in a section discussing the incarcerated Chinese feminist writer Ding Ling – "a communist, a loving, fighting woman" – Asian-American feminist Nellie Wong writes that Ling was "imprisoned for expressing her anguish, her love and compassion for China's women, for recording the conditions of their lives, [...] attacked for her feminism, *supposedly bourgeois, individualistic*, impeding the movement of communism in her native land."[65]

In these extracts, then, Firestone, Wittig, and Wong – all writers from different contexts who are sympathetic to Marxist or communist agendas – acknowledge the importance of individual action and self-realization for women that cannot be reduced simply to "bourgeois self-indulgence," to recall the words of Dworkin in the epigraph to this chapter. And Audre Lorde summarizes how the collective struggle for liberation for women (especially, here, women of colour) must not fall into the trap of eliding differences between women or eliding the potential of the individual who "stand[s] alone, unpopular and sometimes reviled":

> As women, we have been taught to either ignore our differences or to view them as causes for separation and suspicion rather than as forces for change. Without community, there is no liberation, only the most vulnerable and temporary armistice between an individual and her oppression. But community must not mean a shedding of our differences, nor the pathetic pretense that these differences do not exist. [...] It is learning how to stand alone, unpopular and sometimes reviled, and how to make common cause with those other identified as outside the structures, in order to define and seek a world in which we can all flourish.[66]

The female writers cited in this section destabilize the commonplace discourse that second-wave radical feminism places the collective over the individual, showing instead different contexts in which their interplay is crucial, and in which the health of the former can only be assured by cherishing the latter. They dismiss the notion that a selfish or self-interested female individuality perpetuates harmful and oppressive norms for the collective of women. Even when speaking of the situation of those women of colour whose struggle is not only for liberation on the grounds of sex, but for survival of a threatened ethnic community, Andrea Canaan stresses the need for the woman fighting on behalf of her community to be able first to self-define as an individual agent when she writes: "I must work both as an individual and as a part of my community in order to survive in order for my community to survive."[67] The lack of a conjunction between "in order to survive" and "in order for my community to survive" here emphasizes stylistically the essential interrelatedness of the two ideas for Canaan.

Lorde writes of the importance of enabling "the 'I' to 'be,' not in order to be used, but in order to be creative."[68] The awareness on the part of radical female writers of the 1960s, 1970s, and 1980s, issuing from multiple traditions, of the need to be able to say "I" meaningfully, stands in stark contrast to commonplace assumptions and accusations of the second wave as concerned *only* with collectivism. Also, in the same address, Lorde writes "difference must not be merely tolerated but seen as a fund of necessary polarities between which our creativity can spark like a dialectic."[69] How different is this appeal for productive genuine dialogue between subjects with different experiences of oppression from much twenty-first-century feminist discourse, in which women are constantly reminded to police other feminists and themselves to ensure that they are centring others in their activism – a process at once self-evacuating and patronizing.

Conclusion: towards a feminist ethics of self-fulness

In the first two sections of this chapter, I have examined recent feminist and postfeminist discourses that nominally focus on and valorize the individual rather than the collective model of "class woman" associated with second-wave feminism. However, the models of self that these recent discourses propose are often, in fact, forms of subjectification that encourage women to internalize, in place of self-interest or self-esteem, values of conformism to an ideal that comes from patriarchal interests, rather than from either feminist or genuinely individualist energies. When a woman is being told by the mainstream media that her unhappiness with regard to juggling a high-flying career, a partner, and a family (whether she wants any or all of those things or not) is *the fault of feminism*, or when she is being told to "check her privilege" and "centre" the interests of an identity category that excludes her before she may engage in political activity – *or even be allowed to speak* – then that woman is being interpellated in each case by a discourse of inadequacy, of guilt, and of shame. These are silencing, gaslighting, undermining strategies that repeat the age-old patriarchal instruction to women to be "nice," to be compliant, and to be *for the other*. By injecting guilt into the question of "who I am," much recent feminism of all stripes, in fact, further alienates women from selfhood. It is for this reason that this book has included and taken seriously the words of unpalatable, individualistic women, whom many today find rebarbative. In an increasingly politically polarized age, when those suspected of "wrong think" are no-platformed or simply ignored, it is important to keep returning to such women. Hence, I have repeatedly returned to Rand. Repurposed and used against the grain, Ayn Rand's message of self-interest and individualism, not at the expense of the other, but as a way of recognizing "the inalienable individual rights of ~~man~~ woman – ~~his~~ her own and those of others," is a reminder of the need to question the dichotomy of pure collectivism and apolitical individualism.

It is for all of these reasons also that I have turned back to the 1970s – to the radical feminist agenda that is now so out of fashion and maligned – for inspiration for many of the epigraphs in this book and in order to make my argument in this chapter for a version of feminist self-fulness that is not identical to the "empowerment" of postfeminism or the tortured, twitchy self-effacement of contemporary callout culture. Giving up the "self" in any way cannot be the answer to the crushing problems of the present. Feminists today, as warned by their forebears in the 1970s, should beware of giving up something that women have never properly owned, and on which our grasp is still tenuous. A disproportionate amount of *giving* has been expected historically of women, and the sacrifice of self-interest may not be one that it is proper, quite yet, to ask women to make.

Notes

1 Jennifer Baumgardner and Amy Richards, *Manifesta: Young Women, Feminism, and the Future*, [2000] 10th anniversary edition (New York: Farrar, Straus and Giroux, 2010), p. 17.
2 Baumgardner and Richards, *Manifesta*, p. 15.

3 Baumgardner and Richards, *Manifesta*, pp. 14–15.
4 Deborah L. Siegal, "Reading Between the Waves: Feminist Historiography in a 'Post-Feminist' Moment," in Leslie Heywood and Jennifer Drake (eds), *Third-Wave Agenda: Being Feminist, Doing Feminism* (Minneapolis: Minnesota University Press, 1997), 55–82, p. 75.
5 Jane Gerhard, "*Sex and the City*: Carrie Bradshaw's Queer Postfeminism," *Feminist Media Studies*, 5:1, 2005, 37–49, p. 40.
6 Joan Smith, "I'm a Feminist So I Suppose I Must be Dead," *The Independent*, 6 July 2003, cited in Tyler, "Who Put the 'Me' in Feminism?," p. 26.
7 Susan Faludi, *Backlash: The Undeclared War Against American Women* [1991] (New York: Anchor, 1992), p. ix. These three "symptoms" were reported in *Time* magazine, according to Faludi.
8 For details, see www.elle.com/culture/career-politics/news/a27864/are-we-really-ready-to-call-ourselves-feminists/
    The results of recent polls suggest that feminism has increased in popularity over the past almost 20 years. A poll carried out in 2018 by CBS News and Refinery29 in the USA in 2018 the same year returned a figure of 48% (of 2,093 women surveyed), while a comparable poll of British women conducted by UGov in the same year saw the percentage identifying as "feminist" stand at 46%.
9 Alongside Ally McBeal, there are several other candidates for "postfeminist poster girl." In the USA, another obvious candidate would be Carrie Bradshaw, the sex columnist heroine of the hit TV show *Sex and the City*, created by Darren Star and based on columns and a book of the same name by Candace Bushnell (1998–2004). This series showcased the lifestyle, adventures, and friendship of Carrie and her three wealthy, white, educated, straight friends, with sexually liberated attitudes and high-flying careers, who were nevertheless often riddled with insecurities about their desirability to the opposite sex and potential lonely futures. As Gerhard puts it, "the series [sic] postfeminist sensibility undoes some of its potentially liberating aspects. At the same time the talk focuses on the pleasures of heterosexual sex, it also centres on their search for 'the right man'" (Gerhard, "*Sex and the City*," p. 45). In the UK, a contender would be Helen Fielding's Bridget Jones, who celebrates single life and her chosen "urban family" of single women and gay men, while also bemoaning her lack of a husband and obsessing about her weight and appearance. Fielding introduced the character of Bridget Jones in a column in *The Independent* in 1995. She published *Bridget Jones's Diary* as a novel in 1996, and sequels in 1999 and 2013. Film adaptations of the three books appeared in 2001, 2004, and 2016, respectively. Contemporaneously, in music, I would draw attention to the "girl power"-promoting Spice Girls who exploded onto the formerly male-dominated "Britpop" scene as Tony Blair entered 10 Downing Street. (The trivializing language of "girls" in place of "women" to describe adults has increasingly crept into linguistic currency over the past three decades.)
10 Kristyn Gordon, "(Un) fashionable Feminists: The Media and Ally McBeal," in Stacy Gillis, Gillian Howie, and Rebecca Munford (eds), *Third Wave Feminism: A Critical Exploration. Expanded Second Edition* (Basingstoke: Palgrave MacMillan, 2007), 212–223, p. 214.
11 In 2016, Bridget Jones, along with Margaret Thatcher and Germaine Greer, was named in the BBC Radio 4 *Women's Hour* "Power List," a list of seven women who had made the greatest impact on women's lives over the past 70 years.
12 Gordon, "(Un) fashionable Feminists," p. 215.
13 Tyler, "The Selfish Feminist," p. 173.
14 Gordon, "(Un) fashionable Feminists," p. 217.
15 Ariel Levy, *Female Chauvinist Pigs: The Rise of Raunch Culture* (New York: Free Press, 2005).
16 Levy, *Female Chauvinist Pigs*, p. 2.
17 Gill, *Gender and the Media* (Cambridge: Polity, 2007), p. 271.
18 Levy, *Female Chauvinist Pigs*, p. 2.

19 Levy, *Female Chauvinist Pigs*, p. 93.
20 Levy, *Female Chauvinist Pigs*, pp. 3–4.
21 For an account of the feminist sex wars of the 1980s, see Lisa Duggan and Nan D. Hunter, *Sex Wars: Sexual Dissent and Political Culture* (New York: Routledge, 1995).
22 Levy, *Female Chauvinist Pigs*, p. 101.
23 Levy, *Female Chauvinist Pigs*, p. 101.
24 Levy, *Female Chauvinist Pigs*, p. 99.
25 Levy, *Female Chauvinist Pigs*, p. 96.
26 Levy, *Female Chauvinist Pigs*, p. 117.
27 Levy, *Female Chauvinist Pigs*, p. 95.
28 Levy, *Female Chauvinist Pigs*, p. 95.
29 Levy, *Female Chauvinist Pigs*, p. 101.
30 Levy, *Female Chauvinist Pigs*, p. 112.
31 Levy, *Female Chauvinist Pigs*, p. 200.
32 Kimberlé Crenshaw, "Demarginalizing the Intersections of Race and Sex: A Black Feminist Critique of Antidiscrimination Doctrine," *University of Chicago Legal Forum*, 1, 1989, 139–167, p. 140.
33 Flavia Dzodan, "My Feminism will be Intersectional or It Will be bullshit!," *Tiger Beatdown*, http://tigerbeatdown.com/2011/10/10/my-feminism-will-be-intersectional-or-it-will-be-bullshit/
34 See Aja Romana, "This Feminist's Most Famous Quote Has Been Sold All Over the Internet. She Hasn't Seen a Cent," *Vox*, www.vox.com/2016/8/12/12406648/flavia-dzodan-my-feminism-will-be-intersectional-merchandise
35 Linda Gordon, "'Intersectionality,' Socialist Feminism and Contemporary Activism: Musings by a Second-Wave Socialist Feminist," *Gender and History*, 28:2, 2016, 340–357, p. 347.
36 Gordon, "'Intersectionality,' Socialist Feminism and Contemporary Activism," p. 347.
37 https://everydayfeminism.com/.
38 Luna Merbruja, "4 Ways to Center Trans Women in Reproductive Justice," *Everyday Feminism*, 15 November 2015, https://everydayfeminism.com/2015/11/trans-women-reproductive-justice/
39 Neesha Powell, "Here's How We Can Center Queer and Trans Survivors in the #Metoo Movement," *Everyday Feminism*, 29 November 2017, https://everydayfeminism.com/2017/11/lets-center-queer-trans-survivors/
40 Jarune Uwujaren and Jamie Utt, "Why Our Feminism Must be Intersectional (And 3 Ways to Practice It)," *Everyday Feminism*, 11 January 2015, https://everydayfeminism.com/2015/01/why-our-feminism-must-be-intersectional/
41 Uwujaren and Utt, "Why Our Feminism Must be Intersectional."
42 Danuta Kean, "Chimamanda Ngozi Adichie Clarifies Transgender Comments as Backlash Grows," *The Guardian*, 13 March 2017, www.theguardian.com/books/2017/mar/13/chimamanda-ngozi-adichie-clarifies-transgender-comments
43 Chimamanda Ngozi Adichie, *We Should All Be Feminists* (London: Fourth Estate, 2014), p. 27.
44 She further writes: "Had I said, 'a cis woman is a cis woman, and a trans woman is a trans woman,' I don't think I would get all the crap that I'm getting, but that's actually really what I was saying. But because 'cis' is not a part of my vocabulary – it just isn't – it really becomes about language. And the reason I find that troubling is to insist that you have to speak in a certain way and use certain expressions, otherwise we cannot have a conversation, can close up debate. And if we can't have conversations, we can't have progress." www.facebook.com/chimamandaadichie/photos/a.469824145943/10154893542340944/?type=3&theater. See also David Smith, "Chimamanda Ngozi Adichie on Transgender Row: 'I Have Nothing to Apologize For'," *The Guardian*, 21 March 2017.
45 Naomi Zack, *Inclusive Feminism: A Third-Wave Theory of Women's Commonality* (Oxford: Rowman and Little, 2005), p. 7.

46 Susan Archer Mann and Douglas J. Huffman, "The Decentering of Second Wave Feminism and the Rise of the Third Wave," *Science and Society*, 69:1, 2005, 56–91, p. 87.
47 Helen Pluckrose, "The Problem with Intersectional Feminism," *Areo Magazine*, 15 February 2017, https://areomagazine.com/2017/02/15/the-problem-with-intersectional-feminism/
48 See Dianne E. Anderson, *Problematic: How Toxic Callout Culture Is Destroying Feminism* (Lincoln: University of Nebraska Press, 2018), loc. 140; loc. 130.
49 Kathie Sarachild writes of "radical" that "it is a word that is often used to suggest extremist, but actually it doesn't mean that. The dictionary says radical means root, coming from the Latin word for root. And that is what we meant by calling ourselves radicals. We were interested in getting to the roots of problems in society. You might say we wanted to pull up weeds in the garden by their roots, not just pick off the leaves at the top to make things look good momentarily." "Consciousness-raising: A radical weapon" (1978), cited in Tyler, "The Selfish Feminist," p. 174.
50 Cherríe Moraga and Gloria Anzaldúa (eds), *This Bridge Called My Back: Radical Writings by Women of Color* [1981] *fourth edition* (Albany: SUNY Press, 2015).
51 See Benita Roth, *Separate Roads to Feminism: Black, Chicana, and White Feminist Movements in America's Second Wave* (Cambridge: Cambridge University Press, 2004); Becky Thompson, "Multiracial Feminism: Recasting the Chronology of Second-Wave Feminism," *Feminist Studies*, 28:2, 2002, 336–360; and Paola Bacchetta, Jules Falquet, and Norma Alarcón (eds),"Théories féministes et queers décoloniales: interventions Chicanas et Latinas états-uniennes," *Les Cahiers du CEDREF*, 18, 2011.
52 Tyler, "The Selfish Feminist," p. 175.
53 Rich, *Of Woman Born*, p. 277.
54 From Radicalesbian collective, "The Woman Identified Woman" [c. 1970], cited in Tyler, "The Selfish Feminist," p. 175.
55 Tyler, "The Selfish Feminist," p. 176.
56 Jean Bethke Elshtain, "Feminists Against the Family," *The Nation*, 17 November 1979, 481–500, p. 500.
57 Schlafly quoted in Tyler, "The Selfish Feminist," p. 174.
58 Robin Morgan, state of the movement article in *Ms.*, no. 4, September 1975, p. 78.
59 Morgan, state of the movement article in *Ms.*, p. 78.
60 See Gladstein, "Ayn Rand and Feminism," p. 50.
61 Andrea Canaan, "Brownness," in Moraga and Anzaldúa (eds), *This Bridge Called My Back*, 232–237, p. 234.
62 See, for example, J. David Smith, *The Eugenic Assault on America: Scenes in Red, White and Black* (Fairfax: George Mason University Press, 1992).
63 Firestone, *The Dialectic of Sex*, p. 152.
64 Monique Wittig, "The Straight Mind," in Monique Wittig (ed.), *The Straight Mind and Other Essays* (Boston: Beacon, 1992), 9–20, p. 19.
65 Nellie Wong, "In Search of the Self as Hero: Confetti of Voices on New Year's Night. A Letter to Myself," in Moraga and Anzaldúa (eds), *This Bridge Called My Back*, 176–180, p. 177. My emphasis.
66 Audre Lorde, "The Master's Tools Will Never Dismantle the Master's House," in Moraga and Anzaldúa (eds), *This Bridge Called My Back*, 94–97, p. 95.
67 Andrea Canaan, "Brownness," p. 234.
68 Lorde, "The Master's Tools," p. 95.
69 Lorde, "The Master's Tools," p. 95.

CONCLUSION

> Could you have become a recluse, simply an observer of life, content to roam by the sea, thinking and dreaming and stopping to eat only when you had to? Could you have become a hobo, an alcoholic, a sleeping princess, content to live through the deeds and accomplishments of others? And what is this adventure, this hunger, that roars in you now, as a woman, a writer, an Asian American, a feminist? And why? And what is this satisfaction, this self-assuredness, of individuality, or spirit, of aloneness? And finally, what is this thrust toward community, toward interaction with women and men, this arrow toward creativity, toward freedom.
>
> (Nellie Wong "In Search of the Self as Hero")

In this beautiful passage from her essay in *This Bridge Called My Back*, Nellie Wong engages in a creative journey in search of the self. She dreams of being "a recluse," "a woman," "a feminist," who is buoyed by the spirit of "self-assuredness," of "individuality," "of aloneness." Yet she also envisions being pulled towards "interaction." It is in the meeting of these two ideas, conventionally constituted as opposite poles, that she finally espies a creative vision of "freedom."[1] Though crucially, for Wong, the capacity to imagine the self as a full and free individual comes first and is the *prerequisite* to embracing "community." The readings in this book have sought, via a range of strategies, arguments, and thought experiments, to undermine the entrenched cultural view that individuality is always negative and that collectivism is both morally superior and the "best resort" for women's interests.

Herein, I have allowed myself to explore ideas that are unpopular for the leftist feminist and academic consensus, and to tarry with the works and words of difficult, unpalatable, and *inconvenient* women. When, after publishing *The Subject of Murder*, I told colleagues that my next project, examining a different aspect of female exceptionality, would probably involve looking at Ayn Rand and Margaret Thatcher, I received expressions of horror, with one commenting that she could not imagine how I could bear to "spend time in Rand's company." It seems that an interest in Myra Hindley and Aileen Wuornos is less controversial and more culturally acceptable (in my circles at least) than an interest in selfish right-wing women. My desire to engage with "deplorables" in this book also has to do with my heightened awareness of living in a culture in which the status of debate is increasingly under suspicion and ideas proscribed. I experience dread when contemplating the spirit of authoritarianism that I perceive to be growing in our contemporary moment, issuing from both the left and the right wings. This is characterized by the policing of speech and the fashion for no-platforming in universities on the part of the former, and racial intolerance, nationalistic tendencies, and sanctions on freedom of intellectual expression on the part of the latter. It is possible to be deeply uncomfortable with the no-platforming of feminists such as Germaine Greer or Linda Bellos in the UK (whether or not one shares their views concerning the ontology of "woman") *and* to oppose the Orbán government's closure of gender studies programmes in Hungarian universities on the grounds that they are an assault on traditional morality and "family values."[2] Moreover, it is possible to see both as issuing from the same crisis of liberalism.

In this vein, when I decided to cite the words of Helen Pluckrose in Chapter 5, in the context of a discussion of the relationship between individualism and intersectionality, it was in full awareness of the fact that this *in itself* would constitute a provocation too far for many in light of the recent controversy surrounding her co-authorship of spoof articles in an attempt to show up what she perceives to be the low scholarly standards of disciplines such as gender studies or what she calls "grievance studies."[3] However, my decision was both strategic and deliberate. I consider using the words of unpalatable women – if I judge those words to be *useful* or *true* – to be a kind of anti-censorious ethical feminist citational practice. For as long as it is intellectually respectable in cultural studies and critical theory texts to cite the words of Martin Heidegger or Louis Althusser, regardless of our view of their politics or wife-killing, it needs to be acceptable to cite women with whom many disagree and whom many find rebarbative. Because, as I have been arguing, women too are human beings, and "not being nice" is a feature of being human for which women are particularly harshly punished. (And, in the case of Helen Pluckrose, unlike in the case of Althusser, it is worth noting that nobody died.)

I posit, then, that there are very sound *feminist* as well as pro-freedom-of-speech-related reasons for examining the voices of women such as Rand and Thatcher, arch-individualists dismissed as psychopaths and narcissists, who renounce feminism and refuse to make common cause with other women. One reason is that, if we ignore them, then our view of *women as people* (my favourite definition of feminism, as previously noted) remains inevitably partial and damaged. Women are not all paragons of virtue, self-sacrificial animals, or – worst of all worlds – blandly *nice*. Women are complex, multifaceted – and yes, sometimes selfish and unlikeable. And when we ignore this, we shore up patriarchy's view of women as one-dimensional. A second – and related – reason is that by excluding unlikeable, selfish women from any study of female interests and feminist concerns, we give credence to the oft-repeated, and much discussed in this book, discourse that such difficult women are not *really* women and must somehow *be (or be like) men*. To even "qualify" as women, we must not demand that individuals bear the qualities of which feminism approves (collectivity, solidarity, caring). For to do so means that we also accord approval to patriarchy's notions of what kinds of behaviours, personalities, and tastes *make* a woman. It means too that we effectively repeat the structure of the logic that Rand and Thatcher themselves indulged in, in reverse. Both – while extoling the possibility of living as individuals – failed to account fully for a properly *female* individuality (that is, for the ways in which being female in the world affected their view of self). Their own deeply entrenched anti-feminism and internalized misogyny suggest their reluctance to see "woman" fully as "self," such that Rand celebrated being dubbed "the bravest man," while Thatcher claimed she thought of herself never *as a woman* but only *as the Prime Minister.*

As much as I want us to acknowledge female selfishness as a genuine "achievement," to paraphrase Rand, I would also – and even more intensely – have wanted her to evacuate from her life-project of self-interest a persistent internalized misogyny. It is notable that it was her sometime lover and disciple, Nathaniel Branden, rather than Rand herself, who made an explicitly feminist argument for Objectivism, noting that:

> Women historically have been taught that self-sacrifice is their noblest duty. Objectivism opposes the entire notion of sacrifice, whether the sacrifice of self to others or others to self. [...] In upholding an ethics of rational or enlightened self-interest, Objectivism champions a woman's right to live as a free, independent entity.[4]

Rand's core value, as expressed throughout her body of work, is "concern with one's own interests." Yet her deep-seated view of women as inferior and her belief in a masochistic essence called "femininity" both negate the surface-level claims that Objectivism offers men and women equally the opportunity to *hold the self as one's own highest value.* Her dogmatic refusal to accept that "interests" may sometimes *have to* be defined on a class basis – such as that of class woman – as well as defined at the individual level, is in stark contradiction to her willingness to herd women together as a psychologically definable group characterized by a propensity for what she called "hero-worship." This is simply not logical. For if one can claim (erroneously in my view) that women share, as a group, something called psychological femininity, then one cannot also – logically – claim, as Rand does, that feminism is a groundless movement based on a falsely construed shared interest.

Relatedly, I believe that it is important to listen when women speak in ways that are shocking, that are eccentric, that question long-held discourses about what women *are* and are *for*. One such cultural discourse (relentlessly repeated) is that which expects women to be the guardians of the future as the bearers and carers of children – while simultaneously treating mothers with depersonalized disrespect, as *exemplars of the maternal function* rather than as *selves*, as argued persuasively by Jacqueline Rose in *Mothers*. Without wishing to disrespect those women who become mothers, I cannot deny that I experience a frisson of invigoration when I read the words of radical refusal to take responsibility for the future voiced by the (fictional and non-fictional) women discussed in this book. When Rachilde's heroine Mary Barbe says "*I am enough*, JUST BY BEING, and if I could take the world with me when I die, I would do so;"[5] when Ayn Rand paraphrases the saying: "It is not I who will die, it is the world that will end;"[6] and when Lionel Shriver reports her aggressively childfree friend's words "I'm an atheist. I'm a solipsist. [...] I certainly don't feel I owe the future anything, and that includes my genes and my offspring. I feel absolutely no sense of responsibility for the propagation of the human race,"[7] I am struck by a rare sense of witnessing something genuinely transgressive: women being asked to shoulder a heavy burden on behalf of the world and instead choosing to *shrug*.

For this reason, I always thought that Lee Edelman's polemical work of antisocial queer, *No Future: Queer Theory and the Death Drive* (2004), would have been *so much better* if it had been written by a woman. *No Future* exhorts readers to resist the imperative of reproductive futurism that involves sacrificing the self in the present for the sake of "The Child" in the future (that is the symbolic, upper-case Child of political discourse, who is the figure of "reproductive futurism,"[8] rather than any literal child). This is exactly what is at stake in my defence of selfish women too. Women are *presumed* to be incubators-in-waiting, symbolic carers, worrying about symbolic children, even if they are not current, actual mothers – and have no intention of becoming them. While gay men are indeed stigmatized as "sterile" and their sexuality equated with death in the homophobic cultural imaginary (a position Edelman urges queers to "embrace," rather than reject, by embodying the transgressive figure that he calls the *sinthomosexual*, a Lacanian pun on "homosexual," "symptom," and "saint"[9]), women who refuse to reproduce – and thereby refuse to be the guardians of the future – are even more culturally abjected by dint of their sterility. Such self-ful women (denounced by wider culture as selfish – or just unnatural) are also, or perhaps pre-eminently, the disavowed female sinthomosexuals described in Edelman's system.

What is at stake in embracing an ethic of female self-fulness is making the demand for respect on one's own terms. Martha Nussbaum, in an essay entitled simply "Objectification," talks about what it means to accord respect to a human being. Following a Kantian model of ethics, this means treating individuals as "ends in themselves," rather than as the means to achieve another's aims or interests. The ways in which personhood can be stripped away from an individual are enumerated in her "seven ways to treat a person as a thing":

1. Instrumentality: The objectifier treats the object as a tool of his or her purposes.
2. Denial of autonomy: The objectifier treats the object as lacking in autonomy and self-determination.
3. Inertness: The objectifer treats the object as lacking in agency and perhaps also in activity.
4. Fungibility: The objectifier treats the object as interchangeable (a) with other objects of the same type and/or (b) with objects of other types.
5. Violability: The objectifier treats the object as lacking in boundary-integrity.
6. Ownership: The objectifier treats the object as something that is owned by another can be bought or sold, etc.
7. Denial of subjectivity: The objectifier treats the object as something whose experience and feelings (if any) need not be taken into account.[10]

One thing of which we can be sure is that all of these strategies will have been used in gestures against, and actions done to, women somewhere in the world today – whether in ways that are horrific in their literal violence, such as the "instrumentality" of rape as a crime against the individual person or as a systematic weapon of war, or in ways that are "merely" examples of "everyday sexism," such as the misogynistic "denial of autonomy" of a husband or a boss belittling or infantilizing a wife or a female worker. It is also the case that everyday cultural discourse casually engages – rhetorically – in most of these strategies in its dismissive and reductive representations and assumptions of women's nature and functions. The figure of the self-ful woman is a woman who is an "end in herself" – not an object and not a self-sacrificial martyr whose experience and desires can legitimately be discounted by the lack of full personhood accorded her.

While valorizing female self-fulness as a legitimate end in itself, at the same time the readings in this book have suggested that any attempt to achieve a sense of radical individuality for women also needs to be tempered by some form of feminist analysis of the kind brought to us by Dworkin, by Canaan, by Firestone, and by Lorde. This is because the kind of class analysis produced by these feminists, and by others in the radical tradition, is about recognizing *how society positions and views women* and therefore what barriers and prejudices need to be understood and dismantled in the search for *self*. Equally, though, feminism needs to overcome its resistance to taking onboard a productive model of self-interest and its very deep suspicion of individuality, which it consistently confuses with the effects of the neoliberalism it deplores. Kristeva, in examining the concept of female genius, came to a parallel conclusion when she wrote of the wrongheadedness of any feminism that, "ignorant of the uniqueness of individual subjects, believes that it can encompass all womankind [...] within a set of demands that are as passionate as they are desperate."[11] It is incumbent upon feminists to work through their tendency to be contemptuous of the principle of self-interest if a way of being, such as that of which Nellie Wong dreams in the quotation with which I opened this conclusion, is to have any chance of ever coming into being. That would be a way of being in which individual female self-fulness and strategic common-cause-making can co-exist and flourish.

Notes

1 Wong, "In Search of the Self as Hero," p. 178.
2 For critical coverage of the no-platforming of Greer and Bellos, see, respectively: Zoe Williams, "Silencing Germaine Greer Will Let Prejudice against Trans People Flourish," *The Guardian*, 25 October 2015, www.theguardian.com/commentisfree/2015/oct/25/germaine-greer-prejudice-trans-people and Claire Heuchen, "If feminist Linda Bellos Is Seen as a Risk, Progressive Politics Has Lost Its Way," *The Guardian*, 6 October 2017, www.theguardian.com/commentisfree/2017/oct/06/feminist-linda-bellos-women-trans-male-violence. On the Hungarian government's banning of gender studies programmes, see, for example, Anna Zsubori's article of 9 October 2018 in *The Conversation*, http://theconversation.com/gender-studies-banned-at-university-the-hungariangovernments-latest-attack-on-equality-103150.
3 See, for example: Zach Beauchamp, "The Controversy around Hoax Studies in Critical Theory, Explained," *Vox*, 15 October 2018, www.vox.com/2018/10/15/17951492/grievance-studies-sokal-squared-hoax
4 Nathaniel Branden, "Was Ayn Rand a Feminist?," p. 225.
5 Rachilde, *La Marquise de Sade*, p. 285.
6 Barbara Branden, *The Passion of Ayn Rand*, loc. 9822.
7 Cited in Shriver, "Be Here Now Means Be Gone Later," p. 88.
8 Lee Edelman, *No Future: Queer Theory and the Death Drive* (Durham: Duke University press, 2004), p. 27.
9 Edelman, *No Future*, pp. 6, 50.
10 Martha Nussbaum, "Objectification," in Soble (ed.), *The Philosophy of Sex: Contemporary Readings*, 3rd ed. (Oxford: Rowman and Little, 1997), 283–321, pp. 289–290.
11 Kristeva, "Is There a Feminine Genius?," *Critical Enquiry*, 30, Spring 2004, 493–504, p. 495.

INDEX